FAREWELL TO GOODISON

FOR THE GOODISON GANG.

THE LIFEBLOOD OF THE OLD LADY.

1892   2025

FAREWELL TO GOODISON

100 MEMORIES OF THE GRAND OLD LADY

Reach Sport

www.reachsport.com

Reach Sport

www.reachsport.com

Written by David Prentice

Production by Christine Costello and Simon Monk

First published in Great Britain and Ireland in 2024 by Reach Sport.

www.reachsport.com
@Reach_Sport

ISBN: 9781916811294

Reach Sport is a part of Reach PLC.

Photographic acknowledgements:
With thanks to Ivor Game, Archive Picture Editor, and
Vito Inglese, Head Archivist, at Mirrorpix

Every effort has been made to trace copyright.
Any oversight will be rectified in future editions.

Printed and bound by CPI Group (UK) Ltd,
Croydon, CR0 4YY.

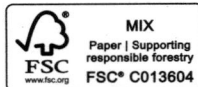

MIX
Paper | Supporting
responsible forestry
FSC
www.fsc.org
FSC® C013604

CONTENTS

FOREWORD

---×/∧\×---

JOE ROYLE

ON APRIL 11, 1981, I SCORED the 165th and final goal of my 15-year playing career.

It was at Goodison Park, for Norwich City, and it meant that Everton lost.

But I was cheered by the home fans.

Our manager, Ken Brown, said to me afterwards: "I've never heard anything like that before."

I just smiled and told him: "This place is different."

And it is. Very, very different.

It's a special place with a unique character and an atmosphere all of its own.

I was clapped off the pitch at the end of that match. Every time I got the ball I was applauded – and I'd scored against Everton!

It was a very emotional day for me. But I'm lucky enough to have had many emotional afternoons and evenings here, many of which feature in this book.

I've seen Goodison Park from so many different perspectives.

My first visit here was as an errand boy! I was a nine or 10-year-old schoolboy at Ranworth Square School in Norris Green and the headmaster, Mr McKay, who was also a selector for the Liverpool Boys team, sent me up to Goodison to collect some tickets for a reserve game.

Believe me that was a big deal at my age!

I had to wait outside the manager's office to pick up the tickets and take them back down the East Lancs Road – and while I was there I met the manager, Johnny Carey, who was a lovely man.

He sat there smoking his pipe, talking football and I could have stayed there all day.

Next time I came back was as a fan.

The fella who used to bring me was a tugboat captain called Tommy Stewart. His boys weren't really interested in football so he used to bring me on a Saturday afternoon. He was also at one stage a top amateur boxer so he could look after himself.

We were behind the goal for an FA Cup 5th round tie against Aston Villa in 1959 and we lost 4-1. I think a forward called Ron Wylie scored three. Some fans had been throwing coins onto the pitch so he picked me up and put me over the wall to go and collect some money. I think I got about half a crown for him!

I was never a small kid, but at eight or nine I used to stand in the paddock under the clock. The older fellas used to let me stand in front of the crash barriers to start with but as I grew they used to say, "hey get back here, no-one can see!"

A few years later I was out there playing. I was still very young when I made my home debut in 1967 against Chelsea. I scored. It wasn't a great goal. I think it went in off my backside, but nevertheless it was a goal. I got one near the end as well and I loved my first experience of Goodison as a player.

When you're that young and you're playing you can't really take the atmosphere and the noise in.

But I certainly did when I came back as Everton manager in 1994.

The chairman at Oldham had obviously agreed with Everton that I could come here and my uncle Norman, Chief Superintendent

Norman Dainty to give him his full title, was in one of the lounges and knew before I did that I'd got the job!

My first match was a derby and it was very emotional. Everyone knows the story now. We were bottom of the league, Liverpool were second or third and flying, but we won and won well.

I was upstairs with the board celebrating when there was a knock on the door and the steward said: "The manager of the Winslow pub over the road has asked you to come over and see the punters, because they're not going home until they've seen you!"

It's true. So I went over and had to squeeze in and it was just amazing. The atmosphere, the buzz in there – and the acceptance as well.

I've got so many special memories of this place but that night, when Duncan scored the first goal and no-one expected us to win, was just amazing.

It set us off and Goodison can do that.

We started by being hard to beat and by the end of it were playing some good stuff culminating in the cup final and beating Manchester United at Wembley.

I came back to stand on the touchline again with one of my players from that day, David Unsworth, as caretaker-bosses for the last match of the 2015/16 season.

We won that one too, which was another special memory.

So I've been an errand boy, a fan, a player, an opposition player, a manager, an opposing manager and now a guest of the club.

And I've loved every moment.

Even today, the roar of the place before the match when that air raid siren goes off really revs you up. It's a great place and it's going to be so hard to replace in the new stadium.

But it's going to be exciting as well. The new stadium will generate its own memories – but nothing will ever replace this place for me.

Some of its greatest moments are celebrated in this book – I believe I feature in a few of them! So I'm looking forward to sitting back and reliving some of those great moments in the history of a truly great place.

INTRODUCTION

THERE IS NO PLACE ON EARTH like Goodison Park. She is unique. The Grand Old Lady, as Everton Football Club's longest official residence became affectionately known, is an atmospheric sporting cathedral.

She has played a pivotal part in millions of lives.

England's first purpose built football stadium, she has staged more top flight matches than any other football ground.

She was the first club ground to host an FA Cup final, she was the first stadium to boast four sides with two-tier stands, the first to have a three tiered stand, the first to see programmes sold to spectators and the first to install both dugouts and undersoil heating.

But she's been versatile, too.

Goodison Park has hosted World Cup matches, including a semi-final, a world title boxing bill, American baseball and played host to the visit of a reigning monarch – twice.

She has starred in a Rocky movie, has played host to wedding proposals and marriages, seen 21st birthday celebrations staged there and is also a sombre shrine, the final resting place for hundreds of Evertonians.

Goodison Park means so many different things to so many different people.

Visually, she's beautiful.

From the unique St Luke's Church which has always stood in the North-west corner, to Archibald Leitch's trademark criss-cross design; from the statues dedicated to some of her favourite sons to the emerald green pitch lit up under the floodlights at night.

Sure she's aged. But throughout the decades she has remained atmospheric, inspiring – and authentic.

She means so many things to so many people – and as we prepare to say a poignant farewell to a place we've loved and cherished, we've attempted to select a century of memorable Goodison moments.

They're not exclusive. You'll all have your own individual selections.

But we think they're representative of a very, very special place which for 133 years has played a huge part in all of our lives – and will continue to play a significant role in the lives of L4 residents after we have relocated.

We hope you enjoy them.

Settle down with a cup of Bovril, pop Z-Cars on the turntable and relive some evocative moments in the life of a very, very special lady.

IN THE
BEGINNING

————⋙⁄⌃⁄⋘————

WEDNESDAY, AUGUST 24, 1892 &
THURSDAY, SEPTEMBER 1, 1892

"ONE OF THOSE GLORIOUSLY FINE DAYS that linger in our minds," wrote Thomas Keates in his Jubilee History of the Everton Football Club.

"A day which was one of the greatest in the history of the Everton Club," reported the Field Sports newspaper.

While The Cricket and Football Field prophetically printed: "The party drove in carriages to the scene of what, it is to be hoped, will some day be historic incidents in connection with international matches or cup-ties."

All three were describing the day Goodison Park opened its turnstiles for the first time.

The date was Wednesday, August 24, 1892. It wasn't a football match – but it was an occasion as grand and as ceremonial as such a significant moment should be.

It was also of its time.

Earlier in the afternoon a celebration dinner had been hosted at the Adelphi Hotel in Liverpool city centre, where the President of the FA, Lord Kinnaird, delivered a speech toasting "Success to Everton."

In the same speech he also urged Everton's officials to secure the freehold on their new stadium "for the next generation".

Everton duly acquired the ground – for £650 less than they had paid for Anfield – within three years.

The Lord's speech was a prelude to carriages heading the two-and-a-half miles from the city centre to the new stadium, where 10,000 spectators were already assembled.

On arrival, greeted by a retort of fireworks, Lord Kinnaird officially declared the ground open, then the band of the 3rd Volunteer Battalion King's Liverpool Regiment played – before an athletics display by members of the first team squad entertained the crowd.

The accent was very much on having fun, with events including a three-legged race, described by local media as "hilarious".

A century later it's difficult to imagine Seamus Coleman going head to head with Dwight McNeil in a 100m sprint challenge, or Jordan Pickford lashing his leg to James Tarkowski and attempting to beat Vitaliy Mykolenko and James Garner in in an ungainly race.

But the grand opening of Goodison Park was a typically Victorian affair.

Club officials had even arranged for their players to be properly fortified for the big day – resolving at a board meeting that the Club Secretary arrange for "eggs and sherry and coffee" to be given to the players before training every day in the build up!

The athletics display began with the 120yds handicap.

Suitably fortified, Everton's speedy forward, Fred Geary, sailed through in first place in the opening heat, "aided by a flying start", with Bob Kelso second.

Hope Robertson won the second heat, ahead of Robert Jones, while the last heat saw goalkeeper David Jardine easily beat Jack Elliott.

According to contemporary reports "The final was worth witnessing, David giving Hope a yard and beating him by four. The scratched man got off wretchedly, but sprinted smartly in for the third prize."

The three-legged race was the cause of much merriment.

Newspaper reports described how: "The lengthy Archibald Pinnell and the goalkeeper (Jardine) appeared to be in a knot from which they could not extricate themselves. The laughter was frequent and full, as this contest was run in two heats of three couples (irrespective of the final), and in each there was something of comedy.

"Eventually Alf Milward and Robert Jones divided the first prize of £4, whilst the two 'Macs', James McMillan and Duncan McLaren, were each repaid for their funny efforts by a sovereign."

Even a walking race provided rich entertainment.

"Walking races are, as a rule in athletic sports dull, stale and uninteresting," reported local media "but here was a notable and surprisingly agreeable exception.

"The prominent thrusting forward figure of Pinnell, the serious gait of McLaren, the fun-of-the-thing style of Jardine, the tenacious sticking of Gordon, and the plucky pedalling of Rogers, diversified now and then (where the officials were not) by a little mixing and crowding, put the usual monotony out of the contest.

"Rogers deserved better than third, but none can gainsay that the scratch man, Pinnell, did not deserve the premier. Gordon was second.

"In high jumping, Jardine's ability is generally acknowledged. He cleared 5ft, tying with Robertson, to whom he conceded four inches. Pinnell captured another prize here.

"The half-mile was run in semi-darkness, nought to be seen but flitting shadows, who arrived corporeally home in the persons of Ross Muir, Robertson, and George Smith. The contests on the whole reflect great credit on the handicappers messrs. Clayton and Molyneux."

A spectacular firework display concluded the evening, before the crowd dispersed from the new stadium – for eight days.

Everton's new home already had a name.

At a board meeting on June 27, 1892, the Everton directors "resolved that the Football Ground be called 'Goodison Park.' "

No explanation or rationale was recorded – after all the ground bordered Bullens Road and Gwladys Street, as well as Goodison Road – but it was a name which would quickly become famous throughout football.

After the acrimonious row which had seen Everton quit Anfield, the stadium itself had been constructed in little more than four months.

Despite the speed of construction it was described as "without doubt one of the best appointed and most commodious football enclosures in the country."

With an estimated capacity of 50,000, the board of the day had ensured that its facilities were the best in the country – not just for spectators and players, but for match officials too.

A correspondent for the Athletics News, under the pseudonym The Loiterer, wrote: "That occasionally obnoxious individual, the referee, will I am sure, appreciate the effort that has been made for his comfort.

"Before and after finishing his arduous duties he will find that he has only to mount some dozen steps and pass down the reserved portion of the stand before he is in a comfortable room, which is heated with a stove and fitted with everything to promote his comfort.

"The visiting team are next door, fitted with the most modern means of producing hot water. Then comes the home team's rooms with similar convenience."

Such luxuries were not common in the Victorian era.

Those first changing rooms were located on the Bullens Road side of the new stadium.

The first major stand to be erected at Goodison Park was also on Bullens Road. It was another decade before Goodison Road followed suit.

Loiterer added: "The grand stand is a big one, and will be a fine sight when full. Other stands, uncovered, are placed behind each goal, and the Goodison-Road side (opposite the grand stand) has been banked up with I don't know how many thousand loads of cinders, and will afford sight-seeing for a vast number of spectators."

The Sunderland Daily Echo and Shipping Gazette – Goodison's fame had already extended nationwide – estimated that the covered stand could accommodate at least 4,000 spectators.

"It is so constructed that each individual spectator can get a perfect view of the game. Extensive stands have also been erected on the northern and southern extremities of the enclosure, whilst the western side being banked up in such a way as to afford standing room for quite 20,000 people."

The Liverpool Courier was even more detailed in its description.

"The covered grand stand on the eastern side is a magnificent structure of its kind, close upon 420 feet in length, with an elevation furnishing thirteen tiers of seats," it reported.

"The uncovered stands at the rear of the goal posts stretch the full width of the playing ground, that at the north end considerably beyond, and each of these thus an elevation of eighteen tiers, the standing space being double towards the sunset.

"Beneath the grand stand there is a complete suite of rooms, including dressing apartments for the players, fitted with batons and every convenience to the comfort of both the resident and visiting teams.

"On the western side the ground has been banked up for a distance of 40 yards so that provision has been made for fully 30,000 spectators; but although this may exceed the present requirements of the club, there can be no doubt that Goodison park is destined to become an extremely popular winter resort, conveniently situated as it is to rail and tram, and within easy distance of the city."

The new grand stand was clearly an innovation for football grounds of the day and news outlets were full of comprehensive descriptions.

The Athletic News added: "Now as to the stands. The covered one opposite Goodison-Road is a very comfortable one, although a person of aldermanic proportions might find some difficulty in walking between the seats.

"The entrances are at the back and you therefore go down to your seat. Nice, warm cushions there are for the reserved people, and this portion is in the centre of the ground, for the stand runs the whole length of the touchline.

"The covered stand has 13 tiers, and the only objection is that on the top seat the unfortunate occupants will have some difficulty in following the play on a dark, dismal day.

"Going down the staircase, we find a cinder track, on which the players may do a sprint, and then we are introduced to the dressing rooms – two and a bathroom for each team – fitted up with lockers. The baths are not the ordinary iron painted affairs, but are built of substantial timber, and about half a dozen can use them at the same time.

"The next room is nicely fitted up for the referee, and this is not only an original idea, but a real good one, for the much-abused official can now retire from field and dress in solitude, without being compelled to overhear uncomplimentary remarks about some of his decisions.

"The door is fitted with a substantial lock, and, if necessary, the directors are prepared to have it coated with sheet iron. At any rate, they have done all they could to make the referee comfortable.

"They have not put down a running track, being of the opinion that the nearer you can get your spectators to the play the more your spectators will appreciate it; (Dan Meis, the architect of the Everton Stadium at Bramley-Moore Dock had exactly the same idea 130 years later) but, all the same, a good track on a popular ground would have done well.

"I might mention that the publicans in the neighbourhood are fully alive to the necessities of trade, and are making most extensive alterations for the sale of liquor, and are spending a small fortune in paint of various hues."

The Winslow Hotel had only been serving pints for six years but was about to become an iconic Everton hostelry.

In the 21st century there is standing room only on matchdays in the Winslow – and that was presumably the case on Thursday, September 1, 1892, when Goodison Park staged its first football match.

Local rivals Bolton Wanderers, who had finished third in the previous league season – two places above Everton – were the visitors for a prestige friendly.

The board had originally invited celebrated Scottish side Queens Park, and when they proved unavailable, Dumbarton, who had won the previous two Scottish championships.

They were also unable to commit so Bolton pocketed the £35 fee for agreeing to fulfil the fixture.

The attendance was estimated to be 10,000 and the teams for the historic fixture were;- Everton; Jardine, goal; Howarth and Dewar, backs; Boyle, Holt (captain) and Robertson, half-backs; Latta, Maxwell, Geary, Chadwick and Milward, forwards.

Bolton Wanderers;- Sutcliffe, goal; Somerville and Jones, backs; Paton, Gardiner, and McFetteridge, half-backs; Munro, Willock, Cassidy, Wilson, and Dickinson, forwards.

Club chairman George Mahon delivered a ceremonial kick-off "eliciting cheers" – but they were doused as Bolton's Jim Cassidy scored the first goal at Goodison Park, swiftly followed by another from Joseph Dickenson!

Perhaps appropriately it was centre-forward, Fred Geary, who scored Everton's first goal at Goodison Park "beating the Wanderers' custodian with a low shot," according to press reports of the day.

Alex Latta equalised "scoring a grand goal from a pass" before the Blues laid siege to the Wanderers' goal and scored a third before the interval through Edgar Chadwick.

Dickie Boyle scored a fourth after the break to ensure that Everton's first appearance at their new home was a winning one.

Life at Goodison Park had begun.

HUNGRY HORACE

———⋊⋌⟋⋀⟍⋊⋌———

SATURDAY, SEPTEMBER 3, 1892

HORACE PIKE HOLDS A NOTABLE PLACE in football history.

The youngest of three brothers who all played for Nottingham Forest, winger Horace scored Forest's first ever league goal on September 3, 1892.

It was also the first goal ever scored in a league match at Goodison Park.

It came after just 10 minutes.

The kudos of becoming the first Everton player to score a league goal at Goodison Park went to Fred Geary 10 minutes later.

Geary was the first in a long line of great Everton centre-forwards, but he was atypical of those who followed him.

Small and powerful, he was built more like a Bobby Collins than a Duncan Ferguson.

He stood barely 5ft 2ins and weighed 9st 6lbs. But the statistics which really mattered were 98 appearances for Everton, with the remarkable return of 86 goals.

As a youngster he had won many sprinting titles on the athletics track and relied on his pace and acceleration to get away from defenders.

The Blues board had actively targeted a goalscorer following an inaugural league season which saw them struggle in front of goal. The search took them to Grimsby where 21-year-old Geary was snapped up.

He proved an astute purchase, scoring the goals which fired Everton to their first league title in their penultimate season at Anfield.

His performances were enough to earn him a call up to the England side, but he wasn't admired everywhere.

After firing the goal which effectively clinched the club's first league title in 1891 he was set upon by a pack of Wolves fans!

The Blues had won 1-0 at Molineux and under the headline "DISGRACEFUL SCENE" a report ran: "An exciting and disgraceful scene followed the match.

"As the Everton players were leaving the ground they were surrounded by an infuriated crowd and literally mobbed.

"Geary, who had already been severely kicked on the knee, was stoned and was also badly mauled by several of the spectators. A number of Everton gentlemen who were trying to protect the players were maltreated, one Evertonian narrowly escaping serious injuries at the hands of a police inspector who was striking wildly at the crowd in order to keep them away."

Happily that was not a regular occurrence!

Stricken by injuries towards the end of his career, he signed for Liverpool in 1895 for £60. Although his pace had been eroded, he still managed 14 goals in 45 appearances before returning to Everton as a groundsman.

But that was all in the future.

On September 3, 1892 he was the toast of Goodison.

The Liverpool Football Echo described his historic strike as "a beautiful goal for the homesters."

The Cricket and Football Field was more detailed. "Geary threaded his way magnificently through his opponents, and made the game one-all amidst great cheering."

While The Liverpool Courier was even more fulsome in its description. "Geary came out in a lovely dribble in which he slipped round the half-backs and before reaching the backs took a well-judged shot, the ball going a few inches inside the post entirely out of the reach of Brown. It was a remarkably smart individual effort, and was warmly appreciated by the spectators, the applause being deafening."

Everton, wearing their new colours for that season of "blue shirts and white knickers" – but not Royal Blue, that came in 1901 – were denied a victory in their opening league fixture.

The Football Echo estimated that there were "about 14,000 spectators" present to witness the match – but with the match kicking off at 4pm the Liverpool Courier reported that after half-time "the attendance had greatly increased and there were nearly two thousand to be added to the statement previously given."

Those late arrivals saw Geary restore Everton's lead from a Maxwell pass 10 minutes from time, then "just before time, Pike scored the equalising goal with a shot which Jardine touched, but could not hold."

The Everton team on that historic afternoon was: Jardine, goal; Howarth (captain) and Dewar, backs; Boyle, Holt and Robertson, half-backs; Latta, Maxwell, Geary, Chadwick and Milward, forwards.

It would be another three weeks before Everton were back in action at Goodison Park – and the home fans could finally celebrate a first league victory at their new home.

THE NAME GAME

SATURDAY, SEPTEMBER 24, 1892

EVERTON CELEBRATED THEIR FIRST LEAGUE VICTORY at Goodison Park against foes who would become very familiar – but in 1892 boasted an unfamiliar name.

Newton Heath were the visitors to Goodison Park three weeks after the curtain raiser against Nottingham Forest, and 10 years before four Manchester businessmen invested £500 each in the struggling club and changed their name to "Manchester United".

In 1892 Newton Heath were Football League new boys, having been elected into the league that summer.

It was a gruelling introduction.

After a 4-3 defeat at Blackburn, a 1-1 draw with Burnley and a 4-1 drubbing at Burnley – they came to Goodison Park and were ruthlessly demolished.

Everton had warmed up for the fixture in confident fashion – travelling to Edinburgh in midweek to become the first team to triumph at the home of the Scottish league leaders, Heart of Midlothian, since April 1891.

That was a friendly match and after the 3-0 victory that night The Toffees fired six past the league's new boys.

The Blues made a flying start. The Athletic News reported: "Everton were not slow in showing that they meant business; in fact, it was exactly 53 and half seconds, from the kick-off when Alex Latta with a magnificent shot almost broke the netting."

Some local media, the Liverpool Football Echo and Monday morning's Daily Post, actually gave the credit for the first goal to Geary. But other reports, including those who described the goal in more detail, favoured Latta.

One thing they were all united about though was that the goal did come after 53 seconds!

And if Latta was credited with the opening goal, Fred Geary wasn't off the scoresheet for long, following up his brace on the opening day against Nottingham Forest with another after 15 minutes.

Edgar Chadwick made it three before half-time and with the visitors utterly demoralised it became a question of simply how many the Blues would score.

Chadwick scored his second from an Alex Latta shot which rebounded back off the crossbar before Allan Maxwell and Alf Milward made it six.

"On Saturday's form Everton are the Everton of their championship year," enthused the Athletic News, but a wounded Newton Heath proved a different proposition when the Blues travelled to Manchester for the return fixture just three days later.

While Everton were unchanged, Newton made two changes – and a Fred Geary goal levelled a first half deficit before the referee, Mr Fitzroy Norris, called a premature halt with 16 minutes remaining and abandoned the match because of bad light!

"The matter of course will be placed in the hands of the league, who will no doubt order the game to be replayed," reported the Liverpool Mercury.

It was – and proved a propitious abandonment for the Blues – Everton winning the rearranged match 4-3 when Alex Latta scored all four goals on Wednesday, October 19.

But Saturday, September 24, 1892 marked the historic date of Everton's first league victory at Goodison Park.

SIX SHOOTER JACK

SATURDAY, DECEMBER 30, 1893

IT REMAINS THE GREATEST INDIVIDUAL SCORING feat in the club's history.

Jack Southworth, a Victorian goal-getter dubbed 'the prince of dribblers', scored a double hat-trick the day before New Year's Eve 1893.

It was an individual goal haul unmatched in the 130 years which have elapsed since ... yet it received little fanfare at the time.

Victorian newspapers stoically preferred the values of fair play and teamwork over individual excellence.

The Goodison fans appreciated it though.

The double hat-trick came in a 7-1 defeat of West Bromwich Albion. The gate at kick-off of 12,000 was described as "enormous" by that day's Football Echo. When the second half commenced the attendance had increased to "some 18,000" and before the finish had swollen to "about 25,000."

Maybe the extra numbers had been attracted by word of Southworth's goal-getting feats spreading around the city?

"Southworth gave one of his wonderfully good displays," reported the Football Echo. "There is not the slightest doubt but that the whole of the Everton successes now are traceable to the skilful manipulation of the ball by Southworth. The rest of the team apparently recognises Southworth's grand form and unselfishly afford him every opportunity for displaying it."

Southworth ended his only full campaign at Everton as the top division's top scorer, a remarkable 27 goals in 22 appearances.

His haul in that 1893/94 campaign was boosted by a remarkable Christmas blitz of 15 goals in seven matches, a run sparked by two goals in a 3-0 win at Sheffield United, followed by another in a 4-3 defeat at his former club Blackburn Rovers, then a wonderful four goal haul in an 8-1 annihilation of Sheffield Wednesday – a week before his double hat-trick heroism against West Brom.

The incredible spree ended with goals in successive matches against Darwen, Newton Heath and Preston before Nottingham Forest finally found a way to put out the Southworth fire.

On his double hat-trick The Cricket and Football Field newspaper, a publication printed in Bolton and devoted to cricket, football, and athletics reports of the day, declared: "It would be unfair to pick out individuals on the home side, for they all played grandly, and were head and shoulders above their opponents in all round work.

"It may, however, be said that Parry and Arridge, who were tried as an experiment, answered very well indeed, and that a special word ought to be written as to Southworth's shooting and Bell's magnificent skill and judgement which gave the centre the chances."

Ah well, a 'special word' for a scoring achievement which has stood the test of time.

Southworth's career was cruelly curtailed by injury – but until that moment it carried a remarkable symmetry.

In 139 appearances for Blackburn Rovers, Blackburn Olympic and Everton, he scored 139 goals. He won three England caps – and scored three goals, and in his second – and sadly – final season for Everton he had completed nine matches and scored nine goals, when injury cruelly ended his career.

The injury sustained by Southworth in a match against Sunderland the following season was a grievous blow for the Blues.

In little more than a season and a half he had registered 36 goals in 32 appearances – but never played again . . . football that is.

Off the pitch Southworth proved just as talented as he had been on it.

In 1910 he became a member of the Pier Pavilion orchestra at Llandudno where he played the tuba. Later he joined the BBC Northern Orchestra.

He was also a scratch golfer, an expert billiards and snooker player and a crown green bowler who won several tournaments after the age of 80.

He died a couple of months short of his 90th birthday in 1956 at his daughter's home in Wavertree, still the proud possessor of Everton's individual scoring record.

THE FINAL CALL

———————×××⁄⁄⁄∧⁄‿×××———————

SATURDAY, MARCH 31, 1894

LESS THAN TWO YEARS AFTER GOODISON had opened its doors as the new home of Everton Football Club, its status as the country's leading club ground was confirmed when it was chosen to stage the FA Cup final. Since its inception in 1872 the FA Cup had become the most glamorous, prestigious football prize in the land. Before 1894 there had been 22 previous Cup finals, all but three staged at the Kennington Oval in London.

But with the professional northern powerhouses starting to take over from the amateur southern clubs and exert a stranglehold on the sport – after Old Etonians had beaten Blackburn Rovers in 1882 no club south of West Bromwich Albion had lifted the trophy – the decision was taken to relocate the final to the north-west.

Everton played in the 1893 final at Fallowfield in Manchester against Wolverhampton Wanderers in front of a then record crowd of 45,000.

But that was only an 'official' attendance figure. More than 60,000 spectators are believed to have crammed into the stadium, the over-crowding saw the kick-off delayed and fans spilled over onto the pitch several times during the match.

Having been knocked out in the first round of the following season's competition by Stoke City the Goodison board made representations to the FA and succeeded in having their new stadium, with its purpose-built stands, selected to stage the final.

Second Division Notts County and First Division Bolton Wanderers, the team who had been the first to grace Goodison two years earlier, were the finalists.

And in anticipation of another enormous attendance the Everton officials arranged for stands to be constructed on Goodison Road for the first time.

The Liverpool Mercury of March 26, 1894, five days before the final, detailed the changes which had been made to the stadium in preparation.

"The many thousands who visited Goodison Park during the past few days received practical testimony that some special event was about to take place there," it reported "one which would more than tax the normal accommodation.

"Having had their ground selected for the final tie of the English Cup competition – the annual blue ribands of the Association season which is celebrated next Saturday – the Everton executive, with their usual enterprise, promptly set about increasing the accommodations for the public.

"So as to be ready for whatever demands may be made, they are having constructed two additional stands.

"These are situated on the Goodison-road side of the ground and spring from the summit of the high cinder banks.

"They will be free of extra charge, and will hold 12,000 people so that it is computed the popular side will provide space for 25,000, all of whom will be able to see the play.

"The other three sides will accommodate in the aggregate another 25,000. If this vast number should assemble, the 'gate' of last year (£2,550) will be beaten.

"Thousands at Fallowfield saw scarcely any of the game, but there need to be no misgivings that such will be the experience at Goodison Park, which is so laid out with stands and banks that every spectator can see the play very fully.

"These who are willing to pay for comfort can do so as prices range from 10shillings to 2shillings for reserved places, the latter being the charge, for the covered stands behind the goals.

"Those who intend taking a reserved seat, however, should not delay, for, we understand, all the 10s seat have already been secured and that the less expensive ones are being taken eagerly."

An official attendance of 37,000 was recorded for a clash between sides described as "not of the highest class, but well matched and bound to supply a rousing game."

They did supply a rousing game, and an upset.

Jim Cassidy, who scored the first goal at Goodison Park in the exhibition with Bolton Wanderers two years earlier, showed how much he enjoyed Goodison with another strike. But it was only a consolation as second division Notts County became the first team from outside the top flight to lift the Cup, triumphing 4-1.

"The scene presented today at Goodison Park, Liverpool, proves to the full the hold football has upon the British public," reported the Yorkshire Press. "Before four o'clock, the time fixed for the start, thousands made their way to the Everton ground, which possesses stand accommodation without equal."

Despite the successful staging at Goodison Park, the FA took their final showpiece back to London the following year, to the Crystal Palace, where it remained until the First World War.

It was just as well, with Everton reaching the final again in 1897 and then winning the Cup for the first time in 1906.

Goodison was used again for a cup final, however, in 1910 when a replay was required between Newcastle and Barnsley. This time a staggering 69,000 crammed into the expanded stadium.

A VERY
SPECIAL RIVALRY

SATURDAY, OCTOBER 13, 1894

THE MERSEYSIDE DERBY HAS ALWAYS generated interest, intensity and excitement – right from the very beginning.

Two years after the infamous split which rocked football, the two fierce rivals met for the first time at Goodison Park.

The previous fixture staged at Goodison had seen 19,900 paying spectators watch Everton beat West Bromwich Albion 4-1. A week later 12,000 supporters had watched Liverpool held 2-2 at Anfield by Sheffield United.

But on Saturday October 13, 1894, a staggering gate of 44,000 – a new Football League record – was recorded as a fixture which would become the most played derby match in English football was staged for the first time.

Record gate receipts were taken, as the Liverpool Mercury reported: "The entertainment of Saturday surpassed in attractiveness every great event that had occurred before and Everton, who held the record of 'gates' for League matches, which was that of £735 taken the season before last when Preston North End were beaten so easily, have broken their own record, the money taken on Saturday being £1,026 which would show that the attendance must have been something like 40,000."

The Evening Express later clarified: "The announcement in the Sporting Express, which was published before the receipts were actually known, turned out to be perfectly correct. The amount of money taken at the "gates" was £1,026, and the attendance, including, of course, ticket-holders, and free admissions, exceeded 44,000.

"For League matches this furnishes the record in regard both to attendance and receipts.

"The previous best in the matter of money was credited to the famous match between Sunderland and Preston North End, but on that occasion the price of admission was raised, whereas on Saturday there was no increase in the charge, as for the attendance, nothing approaching it has ever been known in the history of the Football League."

An evocative description of the occasion was penned for the North Wales Chronicle by John Humphreys, a Bangor resident who watched the match from the Press Box but claimed to have no allegiance to either club.

He declared: "I never saw such a crowd.

"As early as one o'clock all streets, for miles around, leading to Goodison Park began to be thronged with men, women, and boys, all tramping to one place.

"As far away as the Pier Head every tramcar was loaded with excited intending spectators of the game, and these, together with a heterogeneous assemblage of omnibuses, wagonettes, drays, pony carts, hansom cabs, four-wheelers, and every imaginable description of wheeled vehicle, formed a huge possession stretching (to take one route alone) from the bottom of Scotland Road right up to the ground.

"Such was the throng of traffic that paying 3s 6d for a cab brought one no quicker to the scene of battle than threepence paid for a ride on a tramcar.

"The numerous entrances to Goodison Park were packed with throngs of eager applicants for admission, and the click of the turnstiles was for hours incessant.

"In the enclosure itself the spectacle was simply astounding.

"In a comparatively small space were packed (without, however, any approach to inconvenience, so ample is the accommodation of this magnificent playing ground) 44,000 people, the movement of whose faces as each individual turned momentarily this way or that, reminded one of the multitudinous ripples on the surface of the sea, while the hum, or rather roar, of their conversation was like the sound of the same sea restlessly dashing on its shores.

"It was a sight well worth coming a great distance to see, and will rarely be seen again."

His words were prophetic. With Liverpool relegated and forced to spend a season in the second division, it wasn't until the rivals clashed again at Goodison Park two years later that an even greater gate of 45,000 was recorded.

While the record crowd was filing in, Liverpool Schoolboys beat Nottingham Schoolboys 3-0 in an exhibition match – a scoreline which would be replicated by Everton.

Tom McInnes holds the honour of scoring the first Merseyside derby goal, after just 10 minutes – and Alex Latta doubled the home team's lead on the hour.

Liverpool wasted chances to reduce the deficit before Jack Bell sealed the first Mersey derby victory two minutes from time.

Such was the importance that the Everton directors had placed on this first derby against their upstart neighbours that the Everton players were offered, along with their normal win bonus, a silk hat valued at 20 shillings.

Whether they paraded the natty new headwear after the famous victory is sadly unrecorded.

GOALKEEPERS
ARE DIFFERENT

———✕✕╱╱⌒╲╲✕✕———

SATURDAY, SEPTEMBER 3, 1904

A CELEBRATED WELSH GOALKEEPER USING the Goodison goalframe as a resting place during a break in a match?

It happened earlier than you'd think.

The remarkable Leigh Roose not only beat his compatriot, Neville Southall, to an impromptu woodwork interlude by 80 years, he topped Southall's infamous 1990 half-time sit in by perching atop the Goodison crossbar during a break in play!

Leigh Roose was an extrovert personality.

Described by his biographer, Spencer Vignes, as "football's first playboy," he dated famous music hall stars like Marie Lloyd, refused to turn professional playing 'only' for expenses – which were considerable – and famously travelled by train to one match at Aston Villa in an engine he had commandeered himself, containing just one passenger – himself.

His Everton career was equally eventful.

Signed after he had announced his retirement at the age of 26 – to study bacteriology at King's College – he was asked by the Blues to answer a goalkeeping injury crisis.

Irish international Bill Scott was injured in a crazy 5-5 draw at Sheffield Wednesday in November 1904, his deputy George Kitchen had flu, so Everton asked Roose to don his goalkeeping gloves again for the first time in seven months.

The lack of match practice showed, as he made an uncharacteristic error on his Goodison debut against Sunderland and Everton lost 1-0.

The error marred an otherwise excellent return, but Roose showed he was also a public relations master as well as a fine goalkeeper.

Before his next Goodison appearance, a fortnight later against Derby County, the goalkeeper spent a quarter-of-an-hour before kick-off walking around the perimeter of the pitch shaking hands with spectators and apologising for his debut error.

Spencer Vignes, in his magnificent biography of the remarkable man, 'Lost in France – the life and death of Leigh Roose' wrote "as a public relations exercise, it was a masterstroke. Leigh went on to keep a clean sheet in a 0-0 draw, bowing and saluting to the crowd after several saves. His prodigious kicks, throws and punches drew gasps and applause from around the ground. During an injury enforced stoppage in the second half he even pulled himself up onto the crossbar and sat on the wooden beam until play resumed. Cue widespread laughter."

Billy Scott was by now fit again, but Roose was immoveable.

His arrival proved to be a turning point in the 1904/05 season.

From languishing in mid table, 12 wins and a draw from their next 16 matches put the Goodison side on target for a league and cup double.

Cup hopes were ended in an FA Cup semi-final replay defeat to Aston Villa, but with only six games left in the league Everton were four points clear.

Then fate conspired.

In November Everton's match at Arsenal had been abandoned with 13 minutes remaining because of fog, with Everton leading 3-1 and both teams reportedly happy to continue.

Everton bizarrely agreed to a replay on Saturday April 22, just 24 hours after a home match against Manchester City.

Presumably, way back in November Everton officials had no idea they would be involved in a title race.

But after losing 2-0 to City the tired players crammed into a London-train, a handful grabbed a few hours sleep in Leigh's London apartment in Camden, then travelled to Arsenal where they lost 2-1.

Leigh confronted club chairman Will Cuff afterwards and questioned the wisdom of playing two such important games in such a timeframe.

In an era of marked class divisions when footballers were supposed to know their place, Cuff instantly dropped Roose and recalled Bill Scott.

Roose refused to return north with his team-mates – and despite a letter of apology to Cuff once he had reconsidered his outburst, Roose's Everton career was over after five months and 24 matches.

But that wasn't the last the world would hear of the remarkable Leigh Richmond Roose.

After a colourful career which took in spells at Stoke, Sunderland, Celtic, Port Vale, Huddersfield, Aston Villa and Arsenal, Roose joined the war effort in 1914, despite being well above the age of the average recruit, and became a genuine war hero.

He fought off German flamethrower attacks in the trenches at Pozieres in 1916 – an act for which he was awarded the Military Medal – he was reported "missing presumed dead" after experiencing the hell on earth which was Gallipoli, and he did, eventually, lose his life – running at the enemy still firing his gun – at the Somme.

Yet when his ultimate sacrifice was ceremonially recognised – as one of the 72,195 names inscribed on the immense war memorial at Thiepval – it was misspelled. The name Leigh Roose does not figure on that incredibly moving monument.

Instead it is spelled L Rouse – an administrative error perpetrated earlier in the War, and an error which meant that for 87 years his family mistakenly believed he had died at Gallipoli.

His spell with Everton was shortlived – but contained enough drama to be remembered forever.

SOME LIKE IT HOT!

THE START OF SEPTEMBER 1906 SAW England sweltering in a heatwave – the most intense temperatures recorded in the 20th century.

It was weather for sunbathing, not sport, as the temperatures topped 32 degrees for four successive days throughout most of the country.

And no-one felt the heat more than Manchester City who were trounced 9-1 by the FA Cup holders in a result which remains Everton's record league victory.

The significance of the scoreline was not lost on the media. The Athletic News reported: "The Everton team created a new record when they defeated the unfortunate Manchester City by nine goals to one. They had previously scored seven and even eight goals, but never before had they gained nine in a League fixture."

Alex 'Sandy' Young, the centre-forward whose goal had won Everton the FA Cup five months earlier, scored four of the goals. Jimmy Settle, another legendary pre-War marksman scored twice, and Jack Taylor, Walter Abott and Hugh Bolton added to the tally.

The heat clearly paid a part.

The 1906/07 league season had kicked off on the Saturday, Everton drawing 2-2 at Middlesbrough and City slumping 4-1 at home to Woolwich Arsenal. Just 48 hours later, City had barely recovered. The Liverpool Courier reported: "Sympathy was extended to the City by the misfortune which befell them on Saturday when five of their players were rendered hors de combat by the terrific heat."

As a result City were forced to make significant changes to their line up for the second match of the season just 48 hours later, but Blues marksman Sandy Young clearly found the weather to his liking.

His hot streak continued all season. He ended the campaign as the division's top scorer with 30 goals in 33 games, following strike partner Jimmy Settle, who was the division's top scorer in 1901/02 and Jack Southworth in 1893/94.

Everton's reputation for prolific centre-forwards was clearly established in the early years of the Football League.

Young and Settle both filled their boots against City.

The Athletic News reported: "Young, the clever centre-forward, has certainly made a brilliant start to this season. Last year his efforts were of a spasmodic character, though brilliantly concluded when he obtained the only goal of the FA Cup final at Crystal Palace. But his play in the three matches already decided during this month has been incisive and full of energy."

Jack Taylor opened the scoring against City after just five minutes, before Settle added two and Walter Abbott made it four.

Young finally got in on the act before the break, as Everton went in for some much needed rehydration leading 5-0.

The sporting Goodison crowd greeted the returning City players after the interval "with a rousing cheer" which according to the local media "acted as a tonic to them for a few minutes."

After a brief rally Young made it 6-0 and then seven, when the home team, in weather more suited to cricket, effectively declared.

"The Toffeeites were now somewhat relaxing their efforts and as a result much of the interest went out of the game," reported the Liverpool Courier.

Fisher pulled a goal back for City as "spectators and players alike seemed to regard the match as a huge joke, the representatives of Toffee simply played with their opponents and had they been so inclined could have put on goal after goal."

They settled for two more, one from Hugh Bolton after Settle's shot had rebounded back off an upright and then Young's fourth of the fixture.

The Liverpool Daily Post & Mercury seemed more concerned with City's deficiencies than Everton's expertise.

"To have 13 goals scored against them in two matches discloses a deplorable state of affairs in the City ranks and unless there is an amazing transformation in the near future nothing can save them from the Second Division," they reported.

In the event City escaped relegation by five points, while Everton finished third behind champions Newcastle and Bristol City, and were denied back to back FA Cups by Sheffield Wednesday who won the 1907 FA Cup final 2-1 at Crystal Palace.

For once Alex Young wasn't on target, Jack Sharp scoring Everton's goal when Everton must have wished they had saved just some of their record rout of Manchester City for the Cup final.

GOODISON'S
BARN-STORMER

THURSDAY, APRIL 28, 1910

THE FA CUP SEMI-FINAL OF 1910 was one of Everton's unluckiest occasions. A stirring Cup run saw them drawn against Second Division Barnsley – at Leeds United's Elland Road ground – and held to an attritional goalless draw. The replay, four days later on a Thursday afternoon – because the Blues had a league match on the Monday against Bury to negotiate first, was staged at Manchester United's brand new Old Trafford stadium.

Everything that could possibly go wrong for Everton, did go wrong.

Club legend, the inspirational Jack Taylor, suffered a freak injury after just 15 minutes.

The centre-back was kicked in the larynx, was led off and didn't add a single appearance to the 456 he had already amassed. He remains seventh in the club's all-time appearance list. With substitutes still half-a-century in the future Everton were forced to continue with 10 men, until goalkeeper Billy Scott was also injured conceding the opening goal early in the second half – and also had to retire injured leaving Everton down to nine men.

He bravely returned, but was clearly hindered, and after conceding two more goals in the 85th and 87th minutes retired again to be replaced in goal for the last few seconds by defender John Maconnachie.

But even with 10 men, and then nine, Everton wasted opportunities – none greater than when captain Jack Sharp saw a penalty saved just before half-time with the score still goalless.

A contemporary report declared: "The result was certainly a surprise – Barnsley did not deserve to win, indeed they were somewhat fortunate. After Scott had returned to his posts there was a period during which Everton appeared almost certain to equalise."

But there was some consolation for the Toffees after such a traumatic defeat.

When Barnsley dew 1-1 with Newcastle United in the FA Cup final at Crystal Palace just three weeks later, it was decided to stage the replay in the North of England – and Goodison Park was chosen as the venue.

Not everyone agreed with the decision. The Manchester Guardian newspaper declared that the venue was unfair to Barnsley, because Evertonians in the crowd would be more likely to favour Newcastle, their own team having been beaten by The Tykes in the semi-final!

Regardless of their affiliation, plenty wanted to watch. Sixteen years after 37,000 had crammed into Goodison to watch Notts County defeat Bolton Wanderers in the Cup final, nearly double that number watched the 1910 replay.

Everton's record gate at that stage was 52,455 for an FA Cup third round tie with Bolton three years earlier.

This time a monster attendance of 69,000 crammed into what was described as "the magnificent enclosure of the Everton club."

Local police even had to deal with the drama of a large pre-match pitch invasion which had threatened to put the game in jeopardy.

The London Daily News stated: "Rain had fallen in Liverpool throughout the morning, and it was still pelting down when the crowd began to collect around the enclosure at one o'clock.

"Excursionists had packed into the city from all parts of the country, including trainloads from London, and a full hour before the time for the kick-off the ground was so densely packed that thousands of people broke the bounds of the cordon of police and stewards and swarmed over the playing pitch.

"The disorder had become so alarming before three o'clock that it appeared impossible for the game to be played, but a dozen mounted police were hastily summoned and they rendered such invaluable service that in half an hour the thousands of people who had scaled the low palings had been forced back into the enclosures."

The Liverpool Courier and Commercial Advertiser pointed out that despite the issues with the assembled hordes, the city had proven to be a worthy host, highlighting that the crowd was a record for any game outside of London or Glasgow and reported: "At Goodison Park every person who entered the gates could follow the progress of play without much difficulty. The remarkable figures suggest the enormous holding capacity of the magnificent enclosure of the Everton club."

Regarding the pre-match pitch invasion, they noted: "Matters looked ugly, and there were visions of interference with the game. The timely appearance of a detachment of mounted police worked wonders.

"Assisted by their comrades on foot and by officials of the club, the too impulsive spectators were quietly, but none the less firmly compelled to retire behind the barriers, so much so that when the players appeared on the field there was not the slightest sign of encroachment on the part of the crowd."

Those spectators saw two goals from Albert Shepherd take the cup to Newcastle for the first time, much to the delight of the watching crowd who had invaded the pitch again at the final whistle to watch the trophy presentation.

The trophy was presented by Lord Derby and the medals by the Lady Mayoress of Liverpool, but a speech of thanks by the MP for Barnsley Mr F E Smith was largely drowned out by the cheers of the crowd.

Maybe the Manchester Guardian had a point.

BY ROYAL APPOINTMENT

————✕✕⁄⁄⋀⟍✕✕————

FRIDAY, JULY 11, 1913

EVERTON HAD PLAYED IN ROYAL BLUE for more than a decade when they became the first football club to have their home ground granted a Royal appointment.

On July 11, 1913, King George V and his wife Queen Mary made a memorable visit to Merseyside, which included a trip to Goodison Park.

The Royal couple were in town to open the recently completed Gladstone Dock, then the largest in the world.

So it made sense that they would also pay a visit to the country's leading football arena, Goodison Park, just a short carriage ride away.

Everton's original historian Thomas Keates, in his Jubilee History of the Everton Football Club 1878-1928, wrote: "The arena was a riot of colour and animated charm; 1,920 elementary school children, prettily attired, sang the National Anthem as the Royal party drove round the ground, escorted by a squadron of King Edward's Horses.

"Ascending a platform, the Royal party witnessed a musical drill, physical exercises (executed with artistic precision) and a detachment finally formed a living model of a Union Jack. The King and Queen seemed to find the display a restful delight after an exhausting day.

"The enthusiastic cheering everywhere, added to the plethora of ceremonial and speech making at every stoppage, must have made the day an unusually tiring one. Goodison Park really seemed to be a restorative."

The visit wasn't all pomp and ceremony.

A wall collapsed at Prince's Parade near the landing stage, overcrowded with people anxious to see the Royal party, and three spectators were injured, one fatally.

While a Miss Jolly, secretary of the Liverpool branch of the Suffragette Movement, was arrested after hurling a poker through a shop window on the route of the Royal procession.

But they were isolated upsets on a significant occasion – one that wouldn't be repeated for another 25 years.

LADIES' DAY

SUNDAY, DECEMBER 26, 1920

ON BOXING DAY MORNING, 1920, A crowd estimated to be in the region of "nearly 40,000" gathered at Goodison Park for a match which proved to be both pioneering – and terminal.

The occasion was a ladies football, match – and such was the interest in a game between the celebrated Dick, Kerr Ladies and local rivals St Helens Ladies that, according to the Liverpool Courier, in addition to the huge crowd present, "large numbers were unable to gain admission."

The match was a fundraiser for the National Federation of Discharged and Demobilised Soldiers and Sailors – and a sum of £3,055 was taken in gate receipts (the equivalent of £160,000 today).

Dick, Kerr Ladies were a popular attraction at the time.

Established in 1917 by female workers at the Dick, Kerr and Company Ltd locomotive manufacturers in Preston their first match attracted 10,000 fans to Deepdale.

They continued to play regular charity matches – including continental tours – but nothing had been seen quite like the attendance they attracted to Goodison Park in 1920.

The Liverpool Echo's eminent sports writer Ernest Edwards, who wrote under the pseudonym 'Bee', wrote on Christmas Eve: "As the gate is for charity's sake I hope a four figure gate will be recorded."

In the event the attendance shattered the world record for a ladies match and set a mark which stood until Great Britain played Brazil at Wembley at the 2012 Olympics – 92 years later.

No official attendance mark was published, but all newspaper reports agreed that in the region of 40,000 were present.

Dick, Kerr's side triumphed 4-0, "superior in speed and stamina" to their St Helens rivals according to the Liverpool Daily Post and Mercury, with the same correspondent noting: "The game gave evidence of woman's capacity for taking hard knocks and woman's adaptability to shine in a man's sport."

The FA, however, thought differently.

The size of the Goodison gate had caught their attention and in the months that followed women's teams were tied by a host of new restrictions until finally, on 5 December 1921, the FA banned women's football.

They declared "the game of football is quite unsuitable for females and ought not to be encouraged."

The ban remained until 1971.

Dick Kerr's Ladies had been victims of their own success – but they had already proved on one memorable morning at Goodison Park that there was a huge appetite for women's football.

A BOBBY DAZZLER

SATURDAY, JANUARY 21, 1922

THERE HAVE BEEN 142 HAT-TRICKS CELEBRATED by Everton players at Goodison Park since Edgar Chadwick scored the first in 1893.

But none were quicker than the five-minute treble blitzed by Bobby Irvine on January 21, 1922.

The date was significant for two reasons.

Tittle winning skipper Hunter Hart made the first of his 301 heroic Everton appearances that day.

But for once Hart was eclipsed by Irish international striker Bobby Irvine in a remarkable match.

The media of the day was not known for sensationalism.

Yet the Liverpool Courier reported: "Everton's victory over Aston Villa is likely to be talked of for a long time to come, for nothing so dramatic has been witnessed locally for many a day."

The Liverpool Echo's 'Bee', declared: "The most amazing five minutes of football I have seen since the day Everton and Bolton met at Bolton in a cup tie and Everton were scoring while the Bolton players were kissing each other." (14 years earlier in 1908).

The Liverpool Daily Post simply restricted themselves to describing the clash as "sensational." For an hour there was little hint of the drama to come.

Billy Kirton gave Aston Villa a 20th minute lead and five minutes after half-time doubled the visitors' advantage.

Then Bobby Irvine stepped in. The Echo's 'Bee' takes up the story.

"This is surely a record in senior football for a player to perform the hat-trick in such a short space of time.

"The crowd went riotously wild as each goal was scored, the first at 62 minutes, the second at 66 and the third at 67.

"Unfortunately one of the worst scenes ever seen on the ground was associated with the second goal.

"Number one goal was scored from a corner and a second from a medley, Irvine having his first effort stopped by Barson on the goal-line. This led to a seeming goal, in which I seemed to see fists used." Bee was being diplomatic.

One newspaper reported: "Several players finished up on top of each other in the goal and were busily engaged thumping each other in the face without a bit of interruption."

While another wrote: "During the scoring of Everton's second goal there was an amazing scene, Barson and Jackson were on the ground freely exchanging blows with Irvine, Crossley, Downs and Fazackerley."

But the unseemly set-to was a side note on a day Bobby Irvine created a club record which still stands.

A WHOLE NEW
BALL GAME

THEY WERE THE GREATEST PLAYERS EVER to grace a pitch – but even the stellar line ups of the New York Giants and the Chicago White Sox couldn't convince an Edwardian English sporting crowd of the merits of American baseball.

On October 23, 1924, the highly paid stars of America's two leading baseball teams disembarked from the liner Montroyal in Liverpool and headed to Goodison Park to educate the locals on the intricacies of one of the United States' most popular sports.

It had been 11 years since the same clubs toured the globe.

And the whole purpose of this latest trip was to entertain – and educate.

"Baseball players make so much money during the season that the members of the two teams are not receiving any salary during the present trip. They look upon it purely as a holiday," said Mr Harry Grabiner, secretary of the White Sox.

They he went into detail about the riches on offer for his players.

"Quite a number of the players with us will receive £2,000 to £3,000 a season, and one or two will receive more than £4,000. On average they play about 10 or 12 seasons before they retire."

In post First World War England, while attendances were booming, footballers were restricted to a new maximum wage of £468 a year.

Not many football fans chose to spend their hard earned attending the exhibition.

One report estimated that 10,000 watched the Goodison clash, then the touring teams headed by train to London where 6,000 watched them play a second match at Stamford Bridge.

The Daily Express's war correspondent H.V. Morton was present at Goodison Park and detailed the events in light-hearted fashion.

"Ten thousand rather startled football fans had amazing escapes from thick ears, black eyes, and concussion when they watched the New York Giants play baseball with the Chicago White Sox on the Everton ground, Liverpool, yesterday," he wrote.

"Both teams trotted on the field wearing garments which some thought were riding breeches and others, more critical, considered almost plus fours – possibly plus six.

"They wore jockey caps and across the Shirts of the White Sox men was the one adequate scarlet word 'Chicago.' The New Yorkers wore the Stars and Stripes.

"As they appeared, a few lonely Americans became possessed of devils, shouting 'Sock it to 'em' 'Come on there raw beans!' and 'Come along pepper boy!'

"The cloth-capped Lancashire crowd just stood stolidly still like stalls of oxen, lit pipes and prepared to be bored. How mistaken they were!

"Before many minutes were over we were all to learn that in the primal passions self preservation comes before women, food, or money. The teams took up positions. The catchers wore leather gloves like gigantic pancakes.

"The luckiest man was the keeper of an invisible wicket. He was concealed in a quilt and a fencing mask and leg guards. The next luckiest man was the umpire, who looked as if he was going to a fancy dress ball as Joan of Arc.

"A man holding a thing like an Indian club hit a hard ball over the roof of a grand stand. All the players began to talk, shout and run. BIFF!

"Another ball hit the roof of the Grand stand. Phut!

"This time he had our range. We ducked. Two policemen ran for shelter.

"A half-witted old gentleman in the crowd tried to catch the projectile, missed, and it fell with a sickening crash into a place instantly cleared for it.

"For two hours this bombardment went on while the crowd ducked in its praiseworthy attempts to stay out of hospital. Many of us had not been so frightened since 1914.

"But when we had once awakened to the stern realities of baseball played without goal nets on a football field we actually began to enjoy the game. The crowd began to shout 'Atta boy!' with a Lancastrian accent. It is said that baseball is like rounders, which is like saying a child's pop gun is like a rifle. Baseball is rounders played with long range naval guns.

"A curious thing to us undefended civilians was was the fact that throughout the game, players shouted, yelled and ragged each other while one player, standing apart for the purpose, made funny remarks to the crowd, rather like a clown in a circus.

"Baseball seems to me to combine the less lovable characteristics of war with the best qualities of cricket, rounders, flat racing and football.

"It is certainly a great game played by tried gladiators.

"How it ended I cannot say.

"A left-handed player had my range to a nicety and I made an urgent appointment with a protecting wall.

"Later, I was told in confidence that the White Sox won."

H.V. Morton was not misled. The exhibition score was White Sox 16 Giants 11.

And while the exhibition and the subsequent follow up at Stamford Bridge may not have sparked a nationwide outbreak of baseball-mania, one young sports fan had his interest sufficiently piqued to launch a national crusade.

In 1933 John Moores, by then already a successful Littlewoods pools entrepreneur, spent a huge sum of money to launch a National Baseball Association and convince 18 teams locally to create a Liverpool League.

In 1936 the British NBA was restructured with Moores installed as President and Everton director Ernest Green appointed as vice-chairman.

Those intrepid tourists from the USA had planted a seed which eventually flourished.

LAW BREAKER SAM

SATURDAY, NOVEMBER 15, 1924

IT WAS ONE OF THE STRANGEST and most colourful moments of Goodison's long history, one which left perplexed fans scratching their heads in bewilderment – and an incident which led to the laws of the game being rewritten.

It was the day famous Everton winger Sam Chedgzoy saw his name make headlines nationwide – for taking a corner!

The roots of the story began in the summer of 1924, when the FA decided to amend their rulebook to allow players to score directly from a corner, a practice which had previously been illegal.

But the rewording of the law was vague and left a loophole which could be exploited.

By rewording Law 10 to allow players to score directly from a corner, a phrase which prevented a player taking a corner from touching the ball a second time was removed.

The omission was spotted by Liverpool Echo Sports Editor Ernest Edwards, who determined to expose the FA's error.

He initially approached Liverpool defender Don McKinlay with his cunning plan, who agreed but then got cold feet and backed out.

But Everton's England winger Sam Chedgzoy enthusiastically agreed and the pair pinpointed the visit of Arsenal on Saturday, November 15 1924 for the grand reveal.

Chedgzoy was commissioned to try and win a corner early in the match, and then dribble the ball all the way from the corner flag into the six yard box before scoring!

Chedgzoy tried to do just that – although didn't manage to end his unexpected dribbles by scoring.

It was only years later that Ernest Edwards' part in the ruse was revealed by Everton chairman Will Cuff.

Interviewed by the Echo, the legendary Mr Cuff recalled: "Bee offered a fee of £2 to Chedgzoy, with but one proviso: 'Get that corner in the first 20 minutes if possible as I want to feed my newspaper clients around the country with the full story, and if it arrives after then the wires I send will not reach London, Manchester, Preston, aye every big town, in time for publication.' "

As early as the first minute Chedgzoy was as good as his word, trying to dribble the ball in from the Park End corner flag to score.

According to Cuff the spectators, unaware of the arrangement "were getting waxier and yelled instructions as to what he should do with the ball!"

Referee Henry Griffiths allowed the dribbles, but then at half-time instructed Chedgzoy he would have to desist, only for Chedgzoy to dig out a rule book and point out the reworded law, with the referee reluctantly accepting his explanation.

Cuff added: "It was the funniest interlude for years. Chedgzoy was hanging onto the ball to try and force a corner kick. The crowd shouted 'Centre, Centre' but he wanted to hang on to force the ball onto a full-back's leg for a corner."

Edwards' match report of that day reported: "The crowd looked on with astonishment at such a procedure, but they were not exactly ignorant of the move because for a fortnight now this rule and its reading have been the subject of a big debate in Bee's Notebook (his weekly column in the Football Echo)." Catching on to Chedgzoy's cheeky manoeuvre, in the second half Arsenal's Jock Rutherford of Arsenal started to do exactly the same.

Ironically Arsenal won the match 3-2, with the winning goal coming from a corner taken in the traditional fashion!

The national newspapers did cover the controversy – although in later years the incident passed into popular folklore, with some history books claiming the incident took place at White Hart Lane and that Chedgzoy actually scored after dribbling the ball in.

He didn't, but the point had been forcibly made.

What was fact was that at half-time Edwards was allowed into the Everton dressing room area by Cuff, in order to visit Chedgzoy, where he duly handed over the £2 and remarked: 'Thanks for the fun.'

The rules were subsequently changed but not before the following ode was printed in the Liverpool Echo:

Little Jack Horner
Taking a corner,
Pulled out his rule book, quick
And found he could dribble
Right into the middle
Instead of the orthodox kick
So little Jack Horner
Dribbled his corner
Thinking he'd not get far
But the referee blew not
Jack got in a shot
Now we don't know where we are
And Little Jack Horner
All through this darned corner
Has got football fans all awry

Coincidentally, the loophole had also been exposed in another game the same afternoon. In a match between Preston and Nottingham Forest, Preston winger George Harrison (who used to play for Everton with Chedgzoy) also attempted Chedgzoy's dribble.

However, unlike Chedgzoy, Harrison was penalised, referee Charles Lines believing the dribble to be illegal and awarding Nottingham Forest a free-kick.

So it was Sam Chedgzoy's inventive corner routine which commanded the headlines and is still remembered today.

FLOODGATES OPENED

A MODEST GOODISON CROWD OF 25,000 were probably unaware they were witnessing a landmark moment in the dying days of March 1925.

An 18-year-old capture from Tranmere Rovers marked his Everton home debut with a goal – but little did anyone present know that it was a strike which opened floodgates which wouldn't be closed again for the next 13 years.

William 'Dixie' Dean's 27th minute shot heralded a goalscoring career the likes of which had never been witnessed before. It was the first of a staggering 383 goals in an Everton jersey.

It perhaps should have been 384.

On his Everton debut the week before Dean always maintained he should have been credited with a goal at Arsenal.

He wasn't alone.

A prescient letter to the Echo wrote: "There is something about his appearance and deportment that portrays the class footballer. He headed a fine goal and no-one yet seems to know why it was disallowed."

But that refereeing intervention at least meant that Dixie's first goal for Everton came at Goodison Park.

Despite that frustrating afternoon at Highbury on his debut, there was excitement in the Evertonian ranks surrounding the youngster's home debut.

"Dixie Dean, who made his debut at home, came in for a special little cheer all to himself," wrote Stork in the Echo.

Then the same writer described the historic moment for posterity.

Under the subhead DEAN MAKES GOOD he wrote: "The Villa adopted offside tactics, which is most unlike them, but that it did not avail them anything was proved when Kennedy bamboozled the Villa defence into the belief that he would allow the ball to go over and so claim a corner, instead of which he hooked the ball back to Dean, who slammed it clean into the net."

So Dean, who would become fabled for his heading prowess, scored the first of his 383 Everton goals with a fierce shot.

There was plenty of post-match analysis of Dean's performance.

The Daily Courier wrote: "Dean requires nursing until he gains more experience. That he has plenty of football in him, I am convinced. He seemed a trifle shy to let himself go all out on this occasion and he missed chances in consequence, but one could not fail to note useful passes and drives at goal. He heads the ball well, and on two occasions he diverted centres swiftly towards goal, suggesting that he will be useful in this direction. Dean will develop with more experience of first-class football. He has everything in his favour. He scored the first goal when he coolly placed a centre from Kennedy into the net."

The national outlet the Athletic News added: "Dean had good support and his goal, 27 minutes from the start, was very popular with the crowd."

While Monday's Echo wrote: "Kennedy was to my mind the "star" man of the line, for he schemed, shot, and used his speed to the best advantage.

"The first goal was due to his scheming. Most of the onlookers thought he would allow the ball to go over for a corner, but in the twinkling of an eye he changed his ideas and from almost off the line he hooked the ball back to the middle, where Dean met the ball before it touched earth and slammed it into the net.

"This was not the only thing Dean did."

Then in an entire section headlined ABOUT DIXIE DEAN, Stork wrote: "I liked the way he directed his passes to the wing. They were not square, but just far enough forward to enable his wing colleagues to take them on the run.

"Dean played really well, and with average luck would have had at least another goal to his credit."

Ultimately he had plenty more to his credit.

There were just another 382 to come …

DIXIE'S SIXTY

—⨯⨯/⋀⋁⨯⨯—

SATURDAY, MAY 5, 1928

OFFER ANY EVERTONIAN THE USE OF a time machine to witness one moment in Goodison's long and storied history – and chances are that Dixie Dean's 60th league goal will be the moment most would opt for.

Until Bayern Munich were battered, bruised and blown away in 1985 it was unarguably Goodison's greatest ever moment.

It is still undeniably the greatest individual goalscoring feat in English football history.

Another Prenton Park product, Thomas 'Pongo' Waring, managed 49 league goals in 1930/31. But that is as close as anyone has ever come to matching Dixie.

Erling Haaland's blistering start to his first campaign in English football in 2022/23 saw many commentators hinting that he could be the man to finally match Dean's mark.

But ultimately Haaland had to settle for a Premier League record of 35 goals – 25 short of Dixie's league tally, and 10 short of Dean's total in all competitions. Dean scored his 63 in League and Cup, while Haaland accumulated 53 in Premier League, FA Cup, League Cup and Champions League.

Like Haaland's Manchester City, Everton were crowned champions.

Despite having clinched the title for the third time a few days earlier, 48,715 fans still crammed into Goodison to witness Dean's bid to make history.

Aston Villa's 3-0 victory over championship chasing Huddersfield meant that the Toffees had clinched the league title before the visit of Arsenal on the season's final Saturday.

That placed all the focus on Dixie Dean – and whether he could pass the 59-goal mark set by Middlesbrough centre-forward George Camsell in the second division the previous season.

Everton's official matchday programme – a joint publication then shared with neighbours Liverpool, couldn't be accused of going over the top.

The Editor's Note Book opened, perhaps prophetically, with: "Twelve months ago Everton were in the depths, and now we hail them as the proud leaders of the Premier League, the most exciting competition in the realms of football!" This was a full 64 years before the EPL was formed.

Everton's about to be record breaker was only briefly referenced "Dean has, of course, been a grand leader among forwards" and it wasn't until seven pages in and a column entitled Breezy Briefs that the record bid was even mentioned!

"Dean will make his Continental tour accompanied with all good wishes. He has had a splendid season – splendid fellow that he is.

"Everton need a goal today to total the century. Who'll oblige?

"Can Dean pass Camsell's total and establish another record?"

Maybe they didn't want to tempt fate.

Dixie's team-mates and local media men were less reluctant.

Everton captain Warney Cresswell said: "I have been near the top so often that I feared I would never get this great prize. Now we all want Dixie to get some on Saturday – and thus break all the records."

The Echo's correspondent called Bee, buzzed: "At Goodison Park tomorrow, the sting of the League game would ordinarily have left the game, but the bonus and the natural desire of Everton to wind up with a victory and, more than all, to see Dean pass all existing English League records, make the day a gala day in the history of the city's football marks.

"In many clubs, success such as one man (Dean) has won would have been fatal; there would have been petty jealousies, but at Everton that is not the case; they all recognise Dean's worth and his great help, and naturally they are as keen as Dean to see Camsell's record go by. It is an alluring prospect, and with the presentation to follow, the game becomes an historic one in the history of the Everton club."

Bee had no idea quite how historic the day would become.

Dean came out of the blocks like a sprinter, levelling Camsell's record inside six minutes.

After just three minutes a Ted Critchley corner was headed on by George Martin to Dean, who headed it into the extreme left corner of the Gwladys Street goal.

Just three minutes later Arsenal midfielder Jack Butler ran across Dean and tripped him. Most thought it was an accidental collision, but the referee, perhaps caught up in the excitement, pointed to the penalty spot and Dean coolly dispatched his first penalty of the season.

Dean was the only cool-headed man in the stadium.

Contemporary reports wrote: "The crowd's roar knew no bounds. They were crazy after this inspiring turn round in the score sheet."

But Dean still needed one more for the outright record.

And there was a player in the Arsenal ranks who was intent on raining on Dean's parade.

Arsenal defender Joe Hulme later said: "We were aiming to stop him (Dean), but that was easier said than done."

Charles Buchan, the legendary Arsenal inside-forward who scored 224 goals in 413 appearances, was making his farewell appearance before retiring to pursue a career in the media.

Legend has it that the jealous Charlie was the only player in the 22 who wouldn't shake Dixie's hand after his 60th goal.

Dixie was more magnanimous. "I can't understand it," he said. "They never leave me alone, these defenders: yet here is big Charlie standing unmarked for a corner kick. How does he kid them to leave him as if he weren't the best man in the world for a corner kick? That's what beats me."

That attention from defenders was underlined when the record-breaking goal finally arrived, eight minutes from time, via an Alec Troup corner.

Reports describe Dean's vivid black mop of hair rising from a "ruck of probably 14 players" and heading the ball past Willie Paterson "with unerring accuracy, into the extreme right hand side of the goal."

The reaction was widely reported and is worth repeating.

"There has never been such a joyful shout at Everton," read one report. "It was prolonged for minutes and went on to the end of the game.

"The crowd never stopped cheering for eight solid minutes and Dean was hugged by all his comrades, and indeed there was a threat of the crowd breaking onto the field of play. In fact, two men rushed across through the barrier of police and the referee had to bundle one man off and out of the way of trouble.

"It was a memorable scene."

When another corner was awarded after play restarted Arsenal goalkeeper Paterson took the opportunity to shake Dean's hand. So, too, did Joe Hulme, who had tried so manfully to thwart Dean's record-breaking efforts.

The remarkable moment was recorded in all the national newspapers.

Under the headline "AMAZING SCENES AT LIVERPOOL" the Sunday Post reported: "Amazing scenes of enthusiasm were witnessed at Goodison Park when Dixie Dean performed the hat trick against the Arsenal.

"When Dean scored his third goal a few minutes before the finish tremendous cheering took place. Hats were thrown in the air, excitement continued until the close."

The Athletic News followed up on the Monday with: "There was expectancy in the air."

The next day's Daily Courier wrote: "Memorable scenes marked the final match between Everton and the Arsenal at Goodison Park, when two records were made.

"Dean became the champion English goal-scorer passing Camsell's figure of 59 by one, and his club set up new goal-scoring figures of 102, their greatest total in a season of League games.

"It was well on the second half before 'Sixty' Dean made history. A sporting incident was that John Butler, the Arsenal international centre-half, who had been doing his utmost to spoil 'Dixie's' ambition, took the opportunity of going up and giving him a hand-shake.

"The history-making game was not one of Dean's most spectacular in a way although it was characteristic of him, for when the ball came in from a corner Dean was in the midst of a bunch of players – friend and foe, and when it was a case of whose head was going to reach the ball first it was a foregone conclusion it would be Dean's.

"He nodded the ball into the right hand corner of the net.

"The air was full of electrical disturbances after that, and it was just possible the crowd might have over-run the ground as they saw Dean's colleagues hugging him.

"Instead, the crowd cheered themselves out for more than five minutes without stopping. A small boy wriggled by policemen and officials and succeeded in reaching Dean in the centre of the field and giving him a handshake.

"Then an excited supporter rushed on waving his arms wildly until he reached Dean, and likewise gave him a hand grip. Not content with that, he proceeded to ruffle Dean's hair as a further mark of affection before Referee Harper, not too gently, seized him by the scruff of the neck and the pantaloons and pushed him into the hands of a policeman.

"Fortunately the crowd refrained from over running the ground."

It was a moment in time which has still never been eclipsed.

The 100th anniversary of the feat will soon be upon us – which suggests that perhaps it is the one football record which will never be beaten?

Regardless it remains perhaps Goodison's greatest ever moment.

GOODISON'S GOAL GLUT

—⤬⤬⁓⌃⁓⤬⤬—

SATURDAY, OCTOBER 17, 1931 TO
SATURDAY, NOVEMBER 28, 1931

IT WAS THE GREATEST GOAL GLUT Goodison has ever witnessed.

On November 28, 1931 Everton demolished Leicester City 9-2. If that scoreline alone wasn't astonishing enough, it capped a staggering four match sequence of 33 goals scored by the Blues in just FOUR matches.

The power of Goodison had never been so stark as during Everton's title winning season of 1931/32.

By the culmination of the campaign Everton had won 18, drawn none and lost just three of their 21 home games.

And in those 21 Goodison games they scored 84 times – an average of exactly four goals a game – conceding 34.

The home form contrasted vividly with Everton's record on the road – where the Blues lost more matches than they won and ended with a negative goal difference, 32 goals scored compared to 34 conceded.

But at Goodison, Everton were majestic.

None more so than during that spell from mid-October to the end of November, when the delirious Everton supporters were treated to matches boasting an average of more than 10 goals a game, most of them scored by their own team.

The remarkable results read Everton 9 Sheffield Wednesday 3, Everton 8 Newcastle 1, Everton 7 Chelsea 2 and Everton 9 Leicester 2 – interspersed by a goalless draw at Huddersfield, a 2-1 win at Grimsby and a 4-2 defeat at West Ham.

For the Everton players of the day Goodison truly was home, sweet home.

With Dixie Dean spearheading the forward line at the peak of his powers, either side of Tommy Johnson and Tom White and wingers Ted Critchley and Jimmy Stein, Everton's forward line was unplayable.

After the second match in the sequence, when Newcastle were beaten 8-1, the local press reported: "Everton have developed into a wonderful scoring machine. It was one of those games where everything goes with a swing and the opponents are helpless."

After Leicester City were demolished on November 28 the superlatives flowed in the media.

"Who is going to stop Everton?" asked the Echo. "Some of the League's best sides have been at Goodison and they have all suffered the same fate. Sheffield Wednesday, Newcastle, Chelsea and Leicester City have yielded 33 goals to this wonder team of ours. It must be confessed that there was much good football in the City make up but it could not live against the progressive play and deadly marksmanship of Everton …. a team that astonishes the football world."

The correspondent called Stork was even stuck for words. He wrote: "I am stumped for adjectives! I have worked them all out but you know the reason of Everton's success as well as I – it is team work, one mighty whole."

While Pilot (D.M. Kendall), in the Liverpool Evening Express, extolled: "Everton were irresistible. If you have any doubt about Everton's astonishing ability this season, ask Leicester City. Yes, ask McLaren, who had nine goals put past him and yet gave one of the most brilliant goalkeeping performances of the season. He did not get the proverbial dog's chance with any of the shots that beat him. What a team!

"Their 33 goals in four successive home matches is, I think, without parallel in the annals of First Division football. Where is it going to end?"

The answer was in an FA Cup tie at Goodison against our neighbours from across Stanley Park, when Liverpool scored a shock 2-1 victory.

But in the First Division Everton continued to sweep all before them.

Pilot pointed out before the visit of Middlesbrough that "White, Dean and Johnson, the Everton inside forwards, are within reach of another goalscoring record. If they score three goals they will not only have the distinction of being the first inside trio in the Football League to obtain 50 goals between them, but in doing so in 18 minutes will create a post-war record as far as the competition is concerned."

The Blues missed out on the clock record, going behind to Boro and only levelling through Tommy White before half-time.

But they reached the half-century with second half goals from Dixie, Tom Johnson, White again and another from winger Ted Critchley for good measure.

Everton clinched the League Championship uncharacteristically, with a 1-0 victory over Bolton Wanderers, Dixie Dean scoring the decisive goal in the first half.

But Everton had been so far clear of the chasing pack and their goal average so superior that challengers Arsenal actually sent a message of congratulations, via Bee at the Liverpool Echo, to the Goodison directors with the title still not statistically won!

With four matches remaining Everton needed three points to mathematically confirm their fourth league title, while The Gunners had to win all of their remaining matches.

In the event Arsenal won three and drew one of their remaining four, meaning that the message from their legendary secretary-manager Herbert Chapman did not leave him with egg on his face.

"I would like to be associated with a message of congratulation to the Everton FC who are a team who always play football of the best type," he wrote. "They are a pleasure to meet both on and off the field as an example of all that is best in the game. Congratulations to them, the result of real, good, enthusiastic work both on the part of the team and the management."

Job done, Everton promptly failed to score in their remaining two matches – but it had been a goalscoring season like no other, capped by that remarkable autumn scoring blitz.

GREATEST CUP TIE
EVER STAGED?

WEDNESDAY, JANUARY 30, 1935

TEN GOALS, A MANAGER 'ESCORTED OFF the pitch' by the referee, chaotic scenes in and around Goodison Park – and "a blind man, a boy and a man minus a leg making their exit into the players' tunnel" – no wonder Everton's 1935 FA Cup classic against Sunderland was described as "one of the most thrilling in the history of the Cup."

It was a fourth round replay – the teams had drawn 1-1 at Roker Park four days earlier – and despite the 2.30pm kick-off time for the Wednesday afternoon replay the crowd was huge.

Later editions of that day's Evening Express reported: "Thousands of people were unable to gain admission to the Everton ground and for a long time hundreds stood outside the closed entrances on the chance of room being found for them.

"Many fans who arrived at the ground about 2pm and waited in a queue found themselves unlucky and by the time they reached other entrances they found these closed as well.

"Tramcars from town, packed to capacity were still arriving until almost three o'clock half an hour after the kick off. The Priory-road tramwaymen and civilians stood on the roofs of tramcars trying to catch a glimpse of the game.

"Early on, one of the corners of the ground broke through, and a blind man, a boy and a man minus a leg were seen to make their exit into the players' subway, but by degrees the crowd was replaced in its proper position."

The 59,213 crowd witnessed a match which was subsequently referred to, decades hence, as Goodison's greatest.

"It was a match of a lifetime," wrote Bee (they used pen names then, instead of their own).

"One international player of years gone by told me he had never seen anything to approach this historic struggle; incident upon incident; goal upon goal; a home victory seemingly settled a quarter of an hour from the finish of 90 minutes; only for a rallying force by Sunderland fighting back to accomplish the seemingly impossible."

The Liverpool Post and Mercury's John Peel wrote: "There have in the past been many exciting Cup-ties played on Merseyside, but never has there been a more thrilling struggle than that in which Everton defeated Sunderland yesterday in the fourth round replay by six goals to four. Whatever Cup-ties are talked about in years to come this one will hold a prominent place in competition history."

While Pilot wrote in the next day's Evening Express: "Everton won what I consider their greatest cup-tie at Goodison yesterday in beating Sunderland by six goals to four in the fourth round replay after extra time. As one who saw the match I will never forget it.

"The pace was a cracker from start to finish and thrill followed thrill throughout the 120 minutes of play. 59,213 spectators who paid £4,382 for admission were kept on tenterhooks to the last minute.

"Mr. W. C. Cuff, the Everton chairman, said to me: 'It was a wonderful day and one we will never forget as long as we live.' "

Unusually, in a game featuring 10 goals, was the absence of Dixie Dean from the scorers' list.

Indeed none of the 10 goals were headers.

Everton scored twice through Jackie Coulter, after 13 and 31 minutes, Bert Davis pulled a goal back for Sunderland before Alex Stevenson gave Everton what appeared to be an insurmountable 3-1 lead with 16 minutes remaining.

But Sunderland refused to lie down and struck again through Jimmy Connor after 78 minutes and then in the last minute through Bobby Gurney to force extra-time.

Coulter completed his hat-trick two minutes into the extra half-hour, Dean heading the ball across goal for Coulter to score with a terrific drive from close range. Connor equalised yet again "with the best shot of the match" before Albert Geldard struck twice to finally seal Everton's place in the last 16 – and win a match which is still being talked about today.

GRANDSTAND
EXIT FOR DIXIE

———⋙⟋⟋⋀⟍⋘———

DIXIE DEAN ALWAYS DID THINGS IN the grand manner.

A hat-trick to break a Football League scoring record, pulling on a number nine shirt for the first time in a Cup Final at Wembley – taking his last breath during a derby match at Goodison Park.

So it was fitting that the day Goodison Park was eventually completed as Britain's first stadium to feature double-decker stands on all four sides, he would bring the curtain down on one of football's greatest scoring sequences.

Dixie's last goal as an Everton player was scored at Goodison Park, on the day the Gwladys Street Stand was unveiled to an admiring Everton public.

Arsenal were the visitors on August 28, 1937 and the extra fans who could be accommodated by the new stand meant that an attendance of 55,711 crammed into Goodison. That was some 40,000 more than the crowd who had watched the final home match of the previous season, a 2-2 draw with Charlton!

Sadly Dixie couldn't script a victory.

His 383rd – and final goal – for the Blues, was an equaliser – but ultimately came in a 4-1 defeat thanks to a Ted Drake hat-trick and a Cliff Bastin strike.

Sadly there is no record of whether the strike came at the newly extended Street End or not.

But Everton's bid to become the owners of a four-sided two-tiered stadium had actually been more than 20 years in the making.

Goodison's original stadium architect, the celebrated Archibald Leitch, completed his last act of a near 30-year Goodison Park project, once a 23-year obstacle had been removed!

Everton's ambitious board had planned two-tiered stands on all four sides of the ground way back in 1914.

But World War interrupted their plans initially – then one stubborn Street Ender stood in their way until January 1937.

He was an ex-soldier called William Fraser – and while Everton had diligently bought up all of the houses on the stadium side of Gwladys Street in order to demolish them to make way for the new stand, he refused to move on.

In a precursor to the saga of the Mason sisters, two Anfield residents who prevented neighbours Liverpool from extending the Kemlyn Road Stand for many years, private Fraser refused to budge.

The saga eventually came to a head on January 26, 1937.

The Daily Herald reported: "Another "home victory" for the Everton Football Club – which has not lost a home game this season – achieved at a cost of £25 "transfer fee" means accommodation for 13,000 more spectators at Goodison Park.

"And the right-outside – right outside the ground in fact – has proved the key man.

"The story began 23 years ago when the Everton club bought a row of 24 houses in Gwladys Street to demolish and extend one of their stands.

"Then came the war (First World War) – and there was no necessity to extend the stands.

"Later the various slumps and the Rent Acts secured the tenants of the doomed houses a further extension.

"But two years ago Everton decided that the time was ripe to give 13,000 more fans an opportunity to watch their famous team.

"Accordingly the tenants of one half of Gwladys Street were asked to find other accommodation and given £25 each to help in their search.

"But one man – Mr William Fraser, an ex-soldier who is now a patient at the Ministry of Pensions Hospital in Park Avenue, Mossley Hill, refused to leave.

"The Everton club was beginning to get anxious. Plans for the new stand had been submitted to the authorities and it was hoped that the stand would be ready for next season.

"Now at last everything is well.

"Mr Theo Kelly, Secretary of the Everton club, said: 'Everything has now been amicably arranged and Mr Fraser and his family are willing to leave the house as soon as suitable accommodation can be found. The stand, which will increase our accommodation by about 13,000, should be ready for next season.' "

Everton didn't hang about.

A tender was submitted by Archibald Leitch to an Everton Board meeting the very same day, January 26th 1937.

The club minutes recorded: "After discussion and consideration it was resolved that the Gwladys St. Double Decked Stand as planned and specified by Mr. Leitch, be proceeded with forthwith; and that the Architect be constructed to accept the steelwork tender of Francis Mortons of Liverpool and place the order for the said steelwork forthwith.

"Offers of premises for Mr. W. Fraser of 32, Gwladys St., were reported from Messrs T. Percy and E. Harrison. It was agreed that if necessary, we subsidise the tenancy of 14, Oxton St., at 1/6 per week for 3 years."

At a board meeting on June 3, 1937 – at the Exchange Hotel in Liverpool, it was minuted that work was about to start on the new construction.

Archibald Leitch spoke of the determination of the Board to see that the estate was kept right up to date and how, in accordance with that policy, work had now began on the erection of a new double-decker stand on the site of the Gwladys Street property, which had been bought as long ago as 1914, with this specific object in view. The increased accommodation was likely to be available for the opening match of 1937-38, and nothing now remained but to provide a team worthy of the ground and of the support that had been given for years past.

A follow up board meeting resolved the issue of the proximity of St Luke's Church to the new stand.

"June 19 1937.

"St. Luke's Church The Rev. Gibbs along with his Church-wardens and Mr. Archibald Leitch, met the Directors, and inspected the site of the suggested new wall, joining up the New Stand to the Church Building.

It was agreed by the Sub-Committee that the Board be recommended to undertake the cost of the erection of the said wall, as it would add to the appearance of the Gwladys St. portion of the estate."

The new construction was completed promptly.

On July 28, the Echo's Stork reported: "Instead of the cheering and the sighing for a goal the only noise I heard at Goodison Park yesterday was that of iron against steel.

"It was an uncommon experience for me, for my visits to Goodison have usually been on match day when the air has been charged with electric currents.

"I must tell you of the progress being made with the Gwladys Street stand although I know you will be much more interested in the building of the Everton team."

That team kicked off in front of the new Gwladys Street for the first time on August 28, 1937 – and the building of the Everton team was just as impressive.

Dixie Dean might have scored his last goal for the Blues, but a stunningly talented young successor had already been secured in the shape of Tommy Lawton.

The young centre-forward finished the campaign as the First Division's top scorer, then repeated the feat the following season as Everton were crowned champions for the fifth time.

GOODISON'S RECORD GATE?

——⋈⁄⁄⋀⋋⋈——

THURSDAY, MAY 19, 1938

THE 78,299 WHO CRAMMED INTO GOODISON Park in 1948 has officially been declared the stadium's greatest ever gate.

But there have been more spectators inside Goodison Park – at least if newspaper estimates were accurate – a decade before that statistical record breaker.

The occasion was a Royal visit, the second to have graced Goodison.

On May 19, 1938, King George VI – 25 years after his father visited Goodison – and his wife Queen Elizabeth (the future Queen Mother) were at Goodison Park.

Their visit was to present the new colours to the Liverpool-based 5th Battalion the King's Regiment and the Liverpool Scottish (Queens Own Cameron Highlanders) – and the city was gripped by excitement.

According to local newspaper reports – which were remarkably accurate when it came to estimating football crowds before official numbers were presented – there were around 80,000 people inside Goodison for the military parade.

A report in the Liverpool Echo captured the excitement on the streets from the people of Merseyside for the royal visit.

"Tumultuous scenes were witnessed when the King and Queen departed from the Town Hall for the Everton football ground," read the report. "Thousands of voices took up the cry 'we want the King! We want the Queen!' followed by more cheers.

"The route to the football ground (Dale Street, Byrom Street, Scotland Road, Kirkdale Road, Everton Valley, Walton Lane, Goodison Road) was lined with cheering crowds.

"One of the best views of the procession was obtained by a gang of workmen engaged on a house chimney in Kirkdale Road, who used the scaffolding as a grandstand."

It would be the last appearance of a King at Goodison Park... at least until Johnny and Andy pulled on Royal Blue jerseys!

OFFICIALLY GOODISON'S RECORD GATE

⸻⸺✕✕╱⌃╲✕✕⸺⸻

SATURDAY, SEPTEMBER 18, 1948

GOODISON'S RECORD ATTENDANCE WAS ONCE 74,721 – for a match which did not include Everton! There was a boom in post war crowds as the nation relished the return of competitive football once again following years of regional wartime action.

And in January 1948 an enormous gate of more than 74,000 crammed into Goodison Park to watch champions Liverpool face FA Cup holders Manchester United in an FA Cup fourth round tie – with an estimated 10-15,000 more locked out!

United had been drawn at home, and with Old Trafford still being repaired from bomb damage sustained during the Second World War, the Red Devils had chosen to play the cup tie at Goodison.

The record stood for 239 days – until Everton entertained Liverpool in the third league derby to be hosted at Goodison since the First Division had resumed.

As ever, it was an eagerly anticipated – and important showdown.

Six defeats in Everton's opening eight matches of the season saw Theo Kelly's side rooted to the bottom of the table.

Liverpool were a little better off, in 14th, but the teams' respective league positions did not diminish the enthusiasm of the local fans.

Local reports at first struggled to pinpoint the exact number of supporters who had swarmed into the stadium.

The Evening Express initially suggested "a record crowd of 76,599" had packed in. A figure of 78,599 was then reported – before the club tempered that number slightly and issued an official figure several days later of 78,299, which has stood the test of time.

Those fans witnessed a dramatic affair.

In a bid to stabilise their league fortunes, Everton boss Theo Kelly had turned to the "old guard" – six of the team who had won the club's fifth league championship in the final season before World War brought a halt to league football – in 1939.

Wally Boyes and Stan Bentham were making their first appearances of the season, the legendary T.G. Jones his sixth, Alex Stevenson only his third and Gordon Watson just his second.

Goalkeeper Ted Sagar had been the only ever present from the title winning season.

But typically of their fortunes that season, defensive leader Jones limped to the touchline to receive attention to an injury in the 79th minute, and while they were down to 10 men the Reds took advantage scrambling a goal by Joe Fagan.

For six minutes the home fans licked their wounds, then in the 84th minute a penalty was awarded and Ephraim 'Jock' Dodds, having sat out the previous four matches, stepped up to slam home the equaliser.

"Everton confounded the critics," wrote Stork in the Liverpool Echo. "Not only had they played grand football but the 'old guard' lasted it out to the bitter end."

"Each section of the ground looked to be well and truly packed, and there were many thousands outside. There were many casualties and some swaying in parts of the paddock."

The record gate – and the spirited display – was not enough to save Theo Kelly's job. Two days later it was reported that "Mr Clifford S. Britton, manager of Burnley FC, has been appointed manager of the Everton Football Club, and will be taking over his duties shortly. The appointment is great news for Everton followers, for Mr Britton is one of the greatest of all post-war managers and as whole-hearted an Evertonian as one could find anywhere."

At last Mr Kelly bowed out in a match which made history.

FOREIGN AFFAIRS

————✕✕╱╲✕✕————

WEDNESDAY, SEPTEMBER 21, 1949

GOODISON PARK HAS HOSTED MANY OF English football's historic firsts – but there is one that our national team's governing body actively tried to disown!

In the 77 years which had elapsed since England faced Scotland in football's first international football match, the men with the Three Lions on their chest had never been beaten on home soil by a foreign side.

Until September 21, 1949, when Ireland crossed the Irish Sea.

Just a year previously the Republic of Ireland Act had declared Ireland to be a republic – effectively declaring the visitors as 'foreigners'.

Yet not everyone was quick to embrace the new republic's status.

The English FA refused to call the visiting team Ireland, instead calling the touring team the FA of Ireland.

Pathe, the pre-eminent newscaster of the day, were not so sniffy. In the news bulletins shown in cinemas nationwide they described Ireland's 2-0 win as "the soccer sensation of the season" and "England's first ever home defeat by a foreign team."

Goodison Park was a fitting venue for such a significant success.

The closest English city to the Emerald Isle geographically, Liverpool had long been the most Irish of cities culturally.

Long dubbed Ireland's second capital, many emigrants, intending to cross the Atlantic for a new life in the United States, crossed the Irish Sea to the embarkation port and decided to stay. By 1891 more than 10 per cent of the city's population had been born in Ireland.

And links between Everton and Ireland were already extensive. The first match between Everton and an Irish team had taken place as far back as 1885 – a Boxing Day visit of Ulster FC to Anfield, quickly followed by the visit of Limavady United. And when Everton signed Val Harris, the celebrated Irish international in 1907, ties were further strengthened.

So extensive was Everton's scouting system in Ireland, that they signed nine players from across the Irish Sea between 1945 and 1952.

One of them scored the match clinching goal in that historic 1949 showdown.

After Con Martin had given Ireland the lead from the penalty spot, Everton captain Peter Farrell sealed victory with a late second goal fired in at the Gwladys Street End.

He later recalled: "The large number of Evertonians amongst the crowd showed their loyalty towards their own players by cheering equally as much as if it had been a goal for England."

Farrell had been joined in the Irish starting XI by club-mate Peter Corr, uncle of future chart-topping band The Corrs.

He later said: "It was the biggest thrill of my life. Playing for the Republic was always a great honour. It was a day when our pride was as big as our hearts."

And brilliantly captaining the Irish that day was Manchester United defender Johnny Carey, who became Everton's manager nine years later.

Hundreds of Irish supporters had made the ferry crossing over for the match, but, as Farrell remembered, many Evertonians in the 51,847 crowd cheered along with them.

The reaction to the defeat in the English newspapers was not quite so warm.

One wrote: "To think that Eire, who had extreme difficulty in raising eleven men of sufficient calibre for such a match should be the first 'outside' country to beat us on home ground. It shows plainly how far we have fallen from the all-conquering England of a few seasons ago. They have fairly put the cat amongst the England selectors' pigeons."

England's sense of superiority and self confidence was encapsulated by the Daily Express sportswriter Henry Rose, who wrote before the match: "Anybody who thinks the Irish have any chance should make an appointment with a Harley Street psychiatrist."

It meant that defeat brought disbelief.

Indeed, so great was the shock that the English essentially went into denial that it had happened at all.

Instead, in the popular mind, it was only in 1953 that England first lost to a 'foreign team', when they were defeated 6-3 by Hungary at Wembley Stadium.

Those present at Goodison Park on September 21, 1949, knew differently.

THE FESTIVAL
OF BRITAIN

SATURDAY, MAY 19, 1951

A CROWD OF 52,686 CRAMMED INTO Goodison Park on a late Spring afternoon in 1951 – without an Everton footballer in sight!

England were facing Portugal in a showpiece international to celebrate The Festival of Britain.

Described as a 'tonic for the nation', the Festival was a spectacular cultural event intended to raise the spirits of a country still in the grasp of post-war austerity and rationing, and undergoing severe social and economic reform.

And Evertonians needed a pick me up more than most.

Only two weeks earlier The Toffees had been relegated to the Second Division for only the second time in the club's history.

But the crushing disappointment did not diminish local enthusiasm for the international extravaganza.

A large gate of more than 52,000 – only the Lancashire derbies with Blackpool, Bolton and Liverpool attracted more – gathered for the friendly.

And they were royally rewarded.

Tottenham's Bill Nicholson had replaced the legendary Billy Wright – and enjoyed the distinction of scoring with his first touch in international football.

The Liverpool Echo reckoned it came after 16 seconds; the FA Yearbook claimed 19 seconds, while other media outlets more conservatively assessed 30 seconds.

But all agreed it was a spectacular strike, arrowed left-footed from 20 yards into the top corner.

More was to follow.

Inside a minute Portugal had levelled through Patalino, and before the 10th minute had elapsed Jackie Milburn restored England's lead.

If the first half had been entertaining, the second 45 minutes was thrilling.

Hesitancy between Alf Ramsey and Jim Taylor allowed Albano to slip the ball past Bert Williams to level the scores again.

Portugal began to look increasingly dangerous and threatened to follow Ireland's lead of two years previous and inflict another home defeat by a foreign team.

But with 15 minutes remaining England decided to launch their own festival of goals.

Tom Finney, in one of his most devastating moods, scored the decisive and killer goal in the 76th minute. It came with a superb swerving left-foot shot from the touch-line.

Portuguese spirits broken, further goals followed from Milburn again and Harold Hassall – each time assisted by Finney.

At a post-match banquet the entire Portuguese party stood and toasted "Mr Finney, the Master."

Whether the seven goal thriller put smiles back on the faces of the Evertonians in the crowd is unrecorded, but gate receipts of £10,734, 16 shillings and sixpence helped ease the furrowed brow of exiting secretary Theo Kelly.

A BLOODY HERO!

———✕✕╱╱⌒╲╲✕✕———

SATURDAY, FEBRUARY 14, 1953

LESLIE EDWARDS WAS ONE OF MERSEYSIDE'S finest and most respected sports writers.

He served the Liverpool Daily Post and Echo for more than four decades and reported on Everton centre-forwards from Dixie Dean to Joe Royle.

So when the Echo's doyen described the events which unfolded at Goodison Park on Valentine's Day 1953 as "Everton's finest hour-and-a-half" what had unfolded was clearly memorable.

It was another centre-forward who was at the centre of the commotion – the dashing and the swashbuckling Davey Hickson, who thrilled the second largest gate ever to cram into Goodison Park.

A staggering 77,920 spectators watched an Everton team lying 13th in the Second Division beat reigning First Division champions Manchester United, with their warrior centre-forward Dave Hickson living up to the legacy of predecessors like Dean and Tommy Lawton.

After a stirring 2-1 victory, in which Hickson returned to the fray with stitches in a head wound still pumping with blood, to score the winning goal, Mr Edwards wrote: "This was Everton's finest hour-and-a-half. It will be recalled as nostalgically as that famous 6-4 victory against Sunderland on the same ground. Maybe more nostalgically because although goals were fewer, the football was better; and because Everton, in humbler days, had to do so much more this time, when they beat the best Manchester United I have ever seen.

"The crowd, too, had its part in this great performance. Nearly 78,000 of them roared almost continually – and well they might. When the game ended with Cummins all but getting his side's third goal, the uproar was such that referee Beacock's whistle could not be heard. But he made the signal to the players and once it was seen that this really was the end the Everton roar of relief and realisation must have been heard miles away.

"Dancing dervishes then appeared from nowhere. Police patrolling the touchlines were powerless to prevent these fanatics from giving homage to Everton heroes. They kissed them, hugged them, slapped them and cut ecstatic capers with them. And not surprisingly, Everton players joined the frenzy.

"Dave Hickson, blood stained from a deep cut over his right eye and the day's most gallant representative of walking wounded came in for special treatment.

"The thrills of this game came so continuously and were so spine tingling they had the huge crowd swaying and surging, sometimes rather dangerously, almost from start to finish. I confess the spirit and drama of the game and its beautiful football registered on even a spine hardened like mine."

So what had transpired to move even a hardened old cynic like Leslie to such emotion?

Everton had started the 1952/53 season badly, their second campaign in the second tier of English football since relegation in 1951.

After three defeats and a draw in their opening four matches Cliff Britton's side started to revive and from the start of the New Year found renewed spirit and optimism.

And in the FA Cup they garnered a sense of togetherness and momentum.

The inspiration came from the Goodison fans. More than 42,000 saw them beat Division Three South side Ipswich Town 3-2 in the third round. More than 48,000 saw second division rivals Nottingham Forest eclipsed 4-1 in the fourth round – then Davey Hickson warmed up for his Manchester United exploits by scoring a hat-trick in a 5-0 demolition of player-manager Tommy Lawton's Brentford.

Such had been the upturn in fortunes that local reporters were suggesting Everton were capable of causing an upset – but when Jack Rowley gave the champions a 27th minute lead those predictions looked wide of the mark.

Tommy Eglington scored a riotously received equaliser seven minutes later, but in making a flying header which struck the post Hickson sustained a cut above his eye which instantly started to pour with blood.

In the days before substitutes he was led off five minutes before half-time and when he failed to reappear after the interval, Evertonians were grimly resigned to playing the champions for the entirety of the second half with 10 men.

But it transpired that the delay was to allow the flaxen haired firebrand to have more stitches inserted into the wound. A minute after the restart the blond bombshell emerged from the tunnel to a deafening roar, clutching a white handkerchief which quickly turned red as he dabbed it to his head wound.

Hickson continued to launch his head recklessly at the ball – and twice the referee suggested he should leave the pitch for further medical attention.

"Dave waved him aside like a tee-totaller refusing a drink," reported Monday's Echo.

The winning goal, from Hickson's boot, came in the 63rd minute.

"The move began with a long ball from Clinton near the halfway line," related Monday's report "which went over to Eglington, who wasted no time in squaring it to Hickson. He appeared to have little chance with two men in attendance but chasing the ball he beat one man, side-stepped another and then screwed back an oblique shot which Wood failed to reach."

Davey didn't rest on his laurels.

A fortnight later he scored a 75th minute matchwinner in the quarter-final, too, but this time his heroics were at First Division Aston Villa, watched by an army of travelling Blues fans.

But his feats of February 14, 1953 at Goodison Park are still – quite rightly – talked about today.

BACK AT THE TOP

—————✕✕⁄⌃⁄✕✕—————

WEDNESDAY, AUGUST 25, 1954

NO FOOTBALL CLUB HAS PLAYED MORE seasons of top flight football than Everton – and appetite for action in the top tier, be it Premier League or First Division, is unmatched.

After three seasons spent in the wilderness of Division Two, Cliff Britton's side achieved promotion back into the top division on April 29, 1954.

The fixture list for the 1954/55 season was eagerly anticipated.

The Blues were handed an opening day trip to Yorkshire on the opening day of the new campaign, and a stunning 5-2 victory at Sheffield United only heightened expectation and excitement for the first top flight match staged at Goodison Park for three years – against Arsenal.

It was a Wednesday night match, 6.30pm kick-off, and it was raining.

Yet the crowd scenes were still described as "extraordinary."

More than 10,000 were estimated to have been locked out, with the official attendance still 69,034.

The Liverpool Daily Post, under the banner headline Packed Crowds Struggle in Streets near Goodison Park, reported: "Extraordinary scenes outside Goodison Park marked Everton's first home game since their re-entry to the First Division last night, when an estimated 10,000 supporters were turned away.

"Gates were closed more than ten minutes before the 6.30 kick-off and many of those who did manage to get inside the ground left long before the game was over. They claimed they could not see the game.

"A police official told me 'the only time I have ever seen anything approaching this was a few years ago when Everton played Manchester United in a cup tie. But I think this has been even worse. I am sure at least 10,000 people must have been turned away.' "

Queues started to form at three o'clock in the afternoon and by kick-off time it was impossible for vehicles to get within half a mile of the ground.

Those that did get in found it difficult to see the action on the pitch such was the over-crowding, swaying and surging.

As a result Tommy Eglington's winner was the greatest goal many never saw.

The Daily Post described it in detail for those who didn't see it.

"What a goal! Seven minutes had gone and Everton were shaping well when Donovan began the move carried through with such inevitability that one sensed a great goal before the ball sped, finally from the head of Eglington into the net. Hickson's flick of the ball was a touch of genius; that Eglington anticipated it to make the glorious final move in a lovely round of passing was equally out of this world. This was a goal which deserved to be the counting one."

After back to back victories, and such incredible crowd scenes, Everton officials urged supporters to turn up early for the visit of Preston North End three days later.

The fans largely listened to that advice and as a result the stands were full and the turnstiles closed 75 minutes before kick off, and 76,839 squeezed in to witness another 1-0 win.

The season ended with an average attendance of 46,394, the biggest in Goodison history until the title winning season of 1962/63.

THE LIGHT SHOW

————✕✕╱╱╲╲✕✕————

WEDNESDAY, OCTOBER 9, 1957

GOODISON UNDER THE LIGHTS IS AN emotive experience.

The bright glare of the lamps accentuates the green of the grass, electrifies the crowd and casts atmospheric shadows around the players. It creates something magical – and a very different occasion to daytime football.

But it was more than 65 years after Goodison first opened its doors that the floodlights were first switched on.

Everton had first experimented with floodlit football as long ago as 1890, when Anfield was our home. We were even nicknamed the Moonlight Dribblers.

A game against Sheffield United on January 9, 1890 attracted 8,000 spectators to see the 5-2 victory.

"16 Wells Patent Lights were erected 25 feet above the Anfield ground and the matchball was painted white so it could be more easily picked out in the ghostly glow," explained contemporary reports.

Two days later another floodlit match against Lancashire Nomads attracted only 3,000 and the evening games on Merseyside went into cold storage for another 60 years.

Until October 9, 1957.

Fittingly, neighbours Liverpool were the first visitors.

The Liverpool Echo headlines the previous night proclaimed: GOODISON FLOODLIT GAME MARKS BEGINNING OF A NEW SOCCER ERA.

Ranger wrote: "Tomorrow will be a memorable day not only in the history of Everton, but of the Liverpool club as well and Merseyside football generally.

"It marks the beginning of floodlit football in this city, and we could have nothing better to usher in the new era than a meeting of our two senior sides.

"At one time Everton considered inviting a leading Continental team over for the occasion, I am glad they decided otherwise. We shall see the Continentals later."

A special edition of the newspaper was published the following day to commemorate the occasion which attracted 58,771 fans.

The lights were estimated to have cost Everton almost £40,000 – around a million pounds at 2024 prices. To put that sum into perspective, 12 months later Everton broke their transfer record to sign Bobby Collins from Celtic for £23,500.

The four towering floodlight pylons erected in each corner of the ground were considered state of the art.

Ranger added: "The pylons are 160 feet high, plus 1½ feet in the foundations, on top of which the square 'frames' occupy another 24 feet, making a height of 185½ feet from ground level. This is the tallest installation in existence in this country."

Floodlights had been in existence elsewhere in the country for some years, but both Everton and Liverpool remained initially suspicious.

"Many people have wondered why neither Everton nor Liverpool, whose solid and loyal public support, irrespective of how the teams are faring, is the envy of almost every club in the country, did not get in on the ground floor when floodlighting first began to become the rage some years ago," continued Ranger.

"The reason was that both waited to see whether night football had come to stay, or was just a novelty which would soon pall."

The match to herald the arrival of floodlights was termed a friendly – but the Liverpool County FA, celebrating its 75th anniversary, commissioned a handsome silver gilt cup worth £300 to be presented to the winners and for some the Liverpool Floodlit Cup became a popular addition to the fixture list (Everton and Liverpool were in different divisions at the time).

The next night's Echo carried the headline THE GOODISON GLITTER and Ian Severns reported that "Enough electricity to last an ordinary house for six months will be used at Goodison Park tonight."

He added: "The incredible business of lighting a football pitch is really a large-scale extension of the simpler problem of lighting a billiard table. If skyhooks were available that is exactly how it would be done. But skyhooks haven't been invented, and towers – the next best thing – have to do.

"The higher they go the better the lighting. Everton's towers are 185 feet high the highest in the country."

On the night Everton were ALL LIT UP BY THOMAS GOALS – an Eddie Thomas brace giving Everton a two-goal lead to take to Anfield for the second leg three weeks later.

But with it being a derby match there was controversy.

"One, did Referee Mitchell of Whiston, err when he disallowed (a minute from the interval) what Liverpool claimed was a perfect goal by Rowley?" asked Leslie Edwards in his report, adding: "Two, was Thomas, the scorer of Everton's second goal, offside when Hickson slid the ball over to him to plant with no opposition into an empty net? These were crucial points on which the issue depended."

Perhaps most crucially, floodlit football was deemed a success.

A week later, Goodison Park's first competitive match under lights took place when Arsenal were the visitors.

The Blues twice came from behind to level the score at 2-2 in front of 52,000 supporters.

The Daily Post's Leslie Edwards described it as a "match with everything in Technicolour".

Several months later, 20 lamps were added to each tower – doubling the luminosity – and Goodison night matches have been here ever since.

GOODISON
GOALFEST

————— ⟩⟩⟨⟨ ⟩⟩⟨⟨ —————

SATURDAY, APRIL 28, 1962

ON AN EXHILARATING APRIL AFTERNOON IN 1962, Harry Catterick's emerging Everton served notice of the shape of things to come. Imminently as it turned out!

The group of players who would be crowned champions 12 months later scored eight goals to relegate Cardiff City and serve notice of the attacking intent which would fire them to their sixth league championship the following season.

Most impressively of all, six of the 10 outfield players got their names on the scoresheet.

Alf Ramsey's Ipswich had just won their first league title, Everton trailing the Tractor Boys by five points in fourth.

But the Daily Post's Horace Yates prophetically declared: "Ipswich have just been crowned champions, a wonderful feat worthy of the highest commendation and congratulation, but I doubt if even they would claim to possess the glittering brilliance of this Everton side on a day such as this.

"City's defence was not only cracked, it was split wide open by an attack which danced daintily and devastatingly in the fulfilment of its mission. Alex Young and Roy Vernon are artists in their own right, a delight to watch and a nightmare to oppose.

"Their passing, positioning, tip-tapping and finishing mark down the Welsh-Scottish combination as among the most eye-catching and entertaining in football. They are a feast in themselves and plainly Everton lean heavily on their artistry for their attacking splendour."

Vernon celebrated his first hat-trick of the season – taking his tally for the campaign to 26 goals.

But he was joined on the scoresheet by all four of his striking partners (football still lined up with two wingers, two inside forwards and a centre-forward in 1962) and a midfielder.

Alex Young opened the scoring, Mel Charles equalised for Cardiff, Derek Temple "all but broke the net" to make it 2-1, Vernon lobbed in the first of his hat-trick but Tony Pickrell reduced the arrears before the interval with a shot Gordon West should perhaps have dealt with better.

After five first half goals no-one expected the tally to be eclipsed in the second period, but that's just what happened.

Derek Stevens missed a sitter but then made amends to restore Everton's two-goal lead, Billy Bingham made it 5-2 then Vernon scored his second from the penalty spot.

Pickrell scored Cardiff's third of the afternoon, before Vernon completed his hat-trick and Jimmy Gabriel completed a rout two minutes from time.

Again, somewhat prophetically, the Echo's Leslie Edwards added: "If only Everton could match this sort of inspiration from Young's leadership in away matches, you can depend on another trophy arriving to supplement the one Liverpool will receive tonight at Anfield."

That trophy was the Second Division championship which the Reds were presented with. The following season Everton picked up the First Division prize at Goodison Park – with Young scoring 10 of his 22 league goals away from home.

RIVALS
REUNITED

———————⋙⁄⌃⋘———————

SATURDAY, SEPTEMBER 22, 1962

GOODISON HADN'T HOSTED A LEAGUE DERBY for 12 years.

It had been seven-and-a-half years since an FA Cup fourth round tie between the city's closest rivals at Goodison attracted 72,000.

So when Liverpool's promotion from the Second Division in the spring of 1962 ensured a revival of one of football's greatest rivalries, interest was unparalleled.

The fixture list staged the Goodison derby first, on September 22.

And a full three weeks before the big showdown Everton striker Alex Young was already talking about the clash in his weekly Liverpool Echo column.

On Saturday September 1 he wrote: "It is still 21 days and five matches away but already Merseyside seems to be buzzing with excitement and anticipation of the clash between Everton and Liverpool at Goodison Park on September 22."

Two days later Everton officials declared the match would be all-ticket, in a bid to avoid over-crowding issues which had beset other fixtures.

The Echo's Michael Charters suggested: "The ground record of just under 79,000 must be in danger of being beaten."

But on Friday, September 7 Everton announced that a crowd limit of 73,000 would be set.

Tickets sold out quickly.

That allowed the build up to begin in earnest, with Alex Young, Ron Yeats and Roy Vernon all using their Daily Post and Echo columns to disparage the opposition and predict victory for their sides.

The night before the showdown Everton skipper Vernon even went so far as to describe the match as a "home banker!"

"I doubt if there has ever been a match we are more confident of winning than tomorrow's derby," he wrote. "All the lads feel the same way. Their only regret is that we can only play Liverpool twice for, quite apart from the points this game will yield, the Everton players will have a handsome bonus as a result of the 73,000 crowd.

"All leg pulling apart for a moment, let me put the position quite squarely. Suppose Liverpool were visiting Goodison Park tomorrow under any other name, did you think they would be given the slightest ghost of a chance of winning by anybody?? Look at their form and look at ours. This should be the best home banker of the day. Only the fact that it is a derby game gives Liverpool any hope, and I know that form is not always the most reliable guide in these circumstances."

Even 60 years ago the formbook was flying out of the window at derby matches!

For the first time since the original clash in 1892, all 22 players were making their derby debuts.

And predictably, the clash was wrapped in controversy.

Leslie Edwards had written pre-match: "In 40 years of watching soccer in this football-crazy city I can't remember a game between the teams which created so much talk and conjecture a week in advance. Or one looked forward to with such eagerness."

There was plenty to talk about afterwards.

Liverpool striker Ian St John failed a late fitness test and had his

place taken by Kevin Lewis, which would ultimately prove significant.

But in the very first minute Everton striker Roy Vernon thought he
had given his side the lead, only for referee Howley to rule a foul on
goalkeeper Jim Furnell.

Michael Charters reported: "The atmosphere was electric and within
seconds of the start there was a sensation when Vernon appeared to
rob Furnell of the ball near the penalty spot and pushed it over the
line for what looked a fantastic goal. But Mr Howley considered that
Vernon had fouled Furnell and Liverpool were given a free-kick."

Vernon himself was adamant.

After the match he used his Daily Post column to declare: "Whether
Furnell was unlucky enough to get a bad bounce, whether the ball
struck his foot as he bounced the ball or whether he just had a fit of
nerves, I cannot say. But I do know that the ball bounced clear of him
straight to me. I whipped round and put it into the net.

"I was staggered when the goal was disallowed for there was never
anything approaching a foul. That I can say with absolute certainly for
the simple reason that there was never any contact between Furnell
any myself.

"When Ron Yeats dashed up to Furnell and told him it was not
a goal, his face lit up with a smile. It is true that Furnell received
attention from the trainer, but what it could have been for I have
not the slightest clue. The only way he could have injured himself,
was when he fell to the ground and seemed to beat the turf with big
hands."

That was only the appetiser for an incident packed match.

Mr Howley was centre of attention again in the 25th minute when
he awarded Everton a penalty.

A Dennis Stevens shot struck Gerry Byrne's arm. Liverpool claimed
the contact was accidental, the referee deemed otherwise and Roy
Vernon firmly fired in his fifth penalty of the season.

After 38 minutes Kevin Lewis, handed his chance by St John's absence, hooked in an equaliser and the sides trooped in level at the interval.

Seventeen minutes after the restart, however, Everton restored their lead – from a player who had crossed the park in a controversial transfer just a month earlier.

Bill Shankly was furious when his directors allowed Johnny Morrissey to join Everton – and his reaction when the winger scored Everton's second after a Vernon shot had been blocked by Yeats was happily unrecorded!

But with just a minute remaining and Everton fans starting to celebrate, Roger Hunt ended the match as sensationally as it had started by ramming in an equaliser.

The match had lived up to pre-match expectations.

The Daily Post's Horace Yates reported: "This was a rip-roaring, tension packed, excitement laden and full-blooded return to reality – and how the capacity 73,000 crowd loved it.

"I would not argue with any contention that there have been more spectacular, more classical exhibitions of football in 'derby' encounters, but for sheer thrills and unrelenting drama this battle zooms to a very high place in the list of matches which have excited me most.

"It had almost everything required for complete entertainment. In the beginning we had a sensational goal scored and disallowed, and in the end there came another goal, this time legitimate and honour saving."

His counterpart on the Echo, Leslie Edwards, was just as excited.

"A just verdict – but only just! That, in a sentence, sums up the memorable game at Goodison Park," he reported. "It was hard, exciting, entertaining noisy, tense and fluctuating. Seventy-three thousand people (rather too many, I would say, on the terraces) gave this first League Derby for eleven years an extraordinary back-cloth of sound and movement. They were never still, never silent. They swayed: they roared: they cheered: they chanted. Almost from first to last, Ever-ton! Liverpool!"

One of English football's greatest rivalries had been restored.

THE DUN DEAL

———✕✕/⋀✕✕———

WEDNESDAY, OCTOBER 24, 1962

SOME OF GOODISON'S GREATEST MOMENTS HAVE come in European competitions.

The occasions are usually distinguished simply by the names of the opposition. THAT Bayern night. Fiorentina. The Moenchengladbach shoot-out.

But it all began on an October night in 1962. Against Dunfermline. A small Scottish club just 185 miles north of Goodison Park.

It wasn't meant to be that way initially.

On their first appearance in the Inter Cities Fairs Cup (the predecessor of the UEFA Cup and the Europa League) Everton were initially drawn against Salonika of Greece.

But just six weeks before their European debut the Greeks withdrew from the competition, and Dunfermline Athletic were accepted as replacements, having finished fourth in the Scottish First Division the previous season behind Rangers, Celtic and champions Dundee.

European football was still in its infancy. This was just the fifth season of the Fairs Cup.

But some of the traits for which early European clashes would become known were already being established.

The match was christened the "Battle of Goodison" with experienced press hacks horrified by what they witnessed.

The Daily Post's Horace Yates wrote: "Everton won the battle of Goodison Park last night by the only goal of the game, if one can call it a game and still lay claim to accuracy, for it developed into a foul-a-minute exchange in the second half, with football completely impossible and sportsmanlike thrown to the winds.

"It was the most nakedly ill-tempered match I have ever seen, and I shudder to think what may happen in the second leg of the first round of the Inter-Cities Fairs Cup competition unless there is firmer control."

The referee hailed from the Republic of Ireland and Mr Yates added: "Patently the game passed clean out of his control. Players did as they liked and the amazing thing was that 22 men were still on the field at the end, even if Thomson, a first half casualty, limped off. The Scots left to an outburst of boos and the slow hand clap from all parts of the ground. They were pelted with peel, paper but they replied with arms to the air in an expression of complete satisfaction with a mission carried out to the letter."

The Echo's Leslie Edwards was even more distraught.

"If last night's miserable exhibition is any indication of the shape of things to come in the inter-city Fairs Cup they can keep the Cup – and the competition," he wrote. "A more dissatisfying 90 minutes of 'football' would have been hard to devise. Some blamed the referee, Mr. Meighan, of Eire.

"He might have taken more drastic action instead of issuing cautions and booking players, but does anyone think he was mainly to blame for all the hacking and tripping and kicking? I don't. You have to have players of goodwill on both sides and there were precious few of them around in the Everton v Dunfermline match."

At least five players were booked, in an age when offences had to be significant for officials to take action – Callaghan and McLindon for the visitors, and Bingham, Stevens and Young from the home side.

The match was played against the backdrop of the Cuban Missile Crisis, with all the tensions the threat of imminent nuclear war created.

And despite a 1-0 win courtesy of a Dennis Stevens header, Edwards signed off with some gallows humour referring to the United States' escalating diplomatic stand-off with the Soviet Union by claiming a friend of his overheard the following conversation...

Evertonian: "Who do you fight next week mate?"

Fifer: "We'll nominate you for Cuba!"

Dunfermline won a more firmly controlled second leg 2-0, with a late strike dumping Everton out.

Manager Harry Catterick was far from despondent, claiming: "One can feel relieved that Dunfermline did us a good turn when they defeated us in the Fairs Cup. At least we were relieved of those extra games."

Dunfermline played three more matches in the competition, losing 4-0 at defending champions Valencia, but rubbing out the deficit in a remarkable 6-2 second leg.

A deciding rubber was required on neutral ground, which Valencia won 1-0, before going on to retain their crown.

Everton went on to win their sixth league championship.

ALEXANDER
THE GREAT

—————— ⚡/⋀⋀⚡ ——————

SATURDAY, APRIL 20, 1963

ALEX YOUNG STOOD JUST FIVE FEET eight-and-a-half inches tall in his stockinged feet.

Even with a halo he wouldn't scale six feet.

Yet the black and white newspaper image of perhaps his most celebrated goal is staggering.

The Golden Vision, as Alexander the Great was nicknamed, appears to be levitating as he outjumps Tottenham defender John Smith to meet a Roy Vernon cross. His feet are fully four feet off the ground as he skilfully directs a header over goalkeeper Bill Brown.

Young was renowned for his skill, for his shooting power, for his fluid movement and for his dribbling unpredictability.

But on that April afternoon in 1963 he showed off his astonishing spring.

It yielded a matchwinner in a match between two teams challenging for the 1962/63 League Championship. Tottenham and Everton were locked on 50 points but the Londoners were fractionally ahead on goal average.

Young's soaring strike left Everton's title destiny in their own hands – and the Daily Post's Horace Yates described the crucial goal in minute detail.

"The match, as events turned out, was won in 17 minutes and it was Tony Kay who opened up possibilities for Roy Vernon," he said. "There are not many players in the game who can pin-point long distance passes with more devastating accuracy than the Welshman, and here was the perfect example of his art.

"Up and across went the ball, dropping invitingly in front of goal, just far enough out to put Brown in two minds. Marchi had momentarily handed over the policing of Young to Smith (J.) and the Scot, more than a foot higher than his opponent in the air nodded Vernon's centre beyond Brown into goal."

It was the only goal of a thrilling afternoon, watched by an all-ticket sell out crowd of 67,650, and helped cement Young's legendary status.

With five matches remaining of a thrilling title chase after Spurs' visit, the showdown wasn't quite a title decider. But it was certainly pivotal.

With two wins and a draw from the three matches played over the Easter weekend, Everton were breathing down the necks of their title rivals. Leicester led the First Division by a point from Spurs and Everton, but had played a game more.

Spurs edged Everton into third by goal average – just one tenth of a goal separating the sides – meaning, according to the Friday night Echo headline, the "Stage is Set for Match of the Season at Goodison."

The winner would have the destiny of the title in their own hands and Young's soaring header ensured that it was Everton who ended the match in the driving seat.

Horace Yates went on to celebrate Young's art.

"Alex Young, a controlled fighting fury, is another reason why I believe Everton's troubles are behind them. Here is a player of almost unrivalled potential, one of the most skilful controllers of a ball in the game with the ability to outleap in the air rivals towering inches above him, but not always has he demonstrated his arts convincingly.

"Slowly over the last few games. Young has shaken off whatever it was that was preventing him from realizing his vast potential and undoubted class, but he gave Marchi a regular nightmare of an afternoon. Young in this mood, and that is what Everton demand to the season's end, is a weapon of rare and decisive strength."

This title winning Everton team was packed with outstanding talent, one of whom had only signed from Sheffield Wednesday in a British record transfer deal four months earlier.

Tony Kay was making only his 16th appearance in a Royal Blue jersey against Spurs, but after a mixed start to his Goodison career was beginning to show the class which had prompted Harry Catterick to spend £60,000 on his signature.

It wasn't just Alex Young that Post writer Yates was impressed by.

"Towering above them all, not in stature, but in spirit, ability enterprise and example, was the ginger-headed Kay," he reported.

"I suggest the last has been heard of any sniping there may have been against this pocket battleship.

"Kay was the man who taught Everton beyond doubt that not only were Tottenham fallible, but that here was the chance to prove it – and prove it they did.

"White never came into the reckoning at all for he hardly had an earthly chance of making anything of the technically faultless tackling of the remorseless Kay, who was always a move ahead, with the situation so completely in hand that his mastery suggested an almost casual supremacy.

"He had the pace and timing to halt movements in their tracks and decide at leisure where best his pass could be employed. More than anyone he was alive to possibilities for he was quick to realize that Vernon was finding the open spaces, surprisingly left repeatedly by Tottenham and it was Kay's feeding of his skipper that helped Vernon to come right out of the shell into which so much of his talents have been hidden in many disappointing frustrating games.

"Here was Kay, surrounded by international talent, and capping them all. Not once was he guilty of an unseemly action, or anything remotely approaching an unworthy deed, and the inevitable result was that his class outshone anything else on view."

Yates also suggested that England boss Alf Ramsey might also have found a solution to his midfield problems – two years before a certain Nobby Stiles received his international call up.

"Surely a Kay in this form is not only Everton's answer to their moment of trial, but the solution too, to an England problem so terribly acute," he added.

"The crowd were not slow to react to his brilliance, and although I maintain that Kay had done enough and more in previous outings to stop the critics in their tracks, here was the piece de resistance, the crowning vindication of a signing which has converted strength in the position to well nigh invincibility."

Tragically the future for Tony Kay lay in a very different direction … but on that April afternoon the possibilities for him and for Everton were boundless.

THE TITLE PARTY

—————×✕/⌃∖✕×—————

SATURDAY, MAY 11, 1963

GOODISON HAD NOT HOSTED A LEAGUE title party for almost 25 years.

But the people who were packed inside a vibrant, heaving old stadium on May 11, 1963 believed that the atmosphere generated on that dazzling day harked back even further.

The Liverpool Echo's Michael Charters had only joined the newspaper five years earlier, so he sought the counsel of some "old-timers" for his Monday report.

"Has there ever been an atmosphere, an excitement, a thrill, sports-wise in Liverpool, to equal that at Goodison Park on Saturday?" he asked, before continuing "old-timers who have seen the great football moments in this city over the past four decades say there has been nothing like it since Dixie Dean broke his goal-scoring record in 1928 in the last match of the season on the same pitch.

"It was a privilege to be in the historic ground again this time to see Everton win the Football League Championship by crushing Fulham 4-1 to the accompaniment of the roaring acclaim of 60,000 delirious fans."

A stunning end of season run of five wins and a draw from their previous six matches had left the Blues knowing that victory over Fulham would guarantee their sixth league championship – and first since 1939.

Two Roy Vernon goals in the opening eight minutes ensured it would be a procession.

A Johnny Key goal for Fulham in the 20th minute threatened to puncture the party atmosphere, but when Alex Scott restored the two goal lead eight minutes later the celebrations were back on in earnest.

And when Roy Vernon completed his hat-trick seven minutes from the end, the celebrations began. They would go on so long after the final whistle that the players were forced to return to the pitch from the dressing room to take the acclaim. It was a memorable occasion.

"The players, the crowd, everybody, entered into the carnival spirit when the game, and the championship had been well and truly won," reported Mr Charters. "A massive ring of policemen prevented any wholesale, surge onto the pitch by the supporters – apart from a dozen or so youngsters hotly pursued by the law – and the team were able to make their lap of honour as the huge crowd stood and cheered themselves hoarse.

"If the Pier Head pigeons were disturbed by the noise I would not be surprised. It was a shattering ear-shaking approval for the Everton team and management who had come through to the title with a magnificent home straight run in which they had taken 20 out of the last 24 points at stake.

"Not a soul moved out until the lap of honour was ceremoniously completed, and the on-pitch congratulations had been joyfully exchanged between team and supporters.

"Then the crowd turned their attention on the occupants of the directors' box, calling 'We want John Moores.'

"The hatless chairman – he lost his hat when he threw it up after Everton's second goal – acknowledged their applause and then the fans wanted to see the team again.

"As they sipped champagne in their dressing room the cry went up 'We want the Blues.'

"On and on it went and hardly anybody among the vast throng left their places. Only the seats in the directors' box were vacant, as the demand for opportunity to pay further tribute to their favourites continued.

"They saw them, led by Roy Vernon, still in their playing strip, champagne bottles in hand with Tony Kay doing a war-dance of joy in front, smoking the biggest cigar I've seen outside of Winston Churchill.

"The crowd loved it, and the only time they were quiet was to hear Vernon pay tribute to the supporters, the rest of the team and the management.

"This is what the skipper said: 'On behalf of the players and myself I would like to thank you for your wonderful support throughout the season and the management for the grand way in which they have backed us up. I hope this will only be the start and that we shall have many great games and highlights at Goodison Park.'

"So ended another wonderful day in the club history.

"It was one big happy family – the sort of feeling one gets out rarely and which only sport can provide on these truly great occasions."

INTER THE
EUROPEAN ARENA

———————×××⁄⌒⌒⁄×××———————

WEDNESDAY, SEPTEMBER 18, 1963

EVERTON'S REWARD FOR THEIR FIRST LEAGUE title triumph in a quarter-of-a-century was entry to the fledgling European Cup.

The introduction to what quickly became Europe's most celebrated cup competition couldn't have been more glamorous – or tougher.

After winning our first league title for 24 years in May 1963 – the only criteria by which clubs could then qualify for Europe's pre-eminent competition – Evertonians eagerly awaited the identity of our opponents in the first European Cup tie to be staged on Merseyside.

It was a humdinger.

In an open draw – no seeding in 1963 – Everton were plucked out to face Inter Milan, the reigning Italian champions and the team who would go on to win back to back European Cups.

History shows that Everton went out to the only goal scored in 180 minutes of pulsating action.

But Harry Catterick's side gave Helenio Herrera's legendary team their most testing assignment in the 1963 competition, and but for a hastily raised linesman's flag history might even have been different.

117

A Sunday Times expose more than a decade later revealed that match fixing and corruption had been rife in European football in the 1960s, with then Inter secretary Italo Allodi and Hungarian 'fixer' Dezso Solti at the centre of a tangled web.

Borussia Dortmund, later in the competition, and Liverpool famously the following season, are believed to have suffered in semi-finals from the influencing of officials in Inter's favour.

But while Roy Vernon had an 80th minute 'winner' in the first leg disallowed for an offside decision which BBC cameras later showed to be incorrect, no evidence was ever unearthed that the Hungarian officials that evening had been coerced.

And in the event, few of the 62,408 gate who watched the match disagreed that Inter had been the better side at Goodison Park.

The Everton crowd created a memorable atmosphere – but sportingly applauded the Italians off the pitch at the final whistle.

Coach Herrera had visited Goodison Park on a spying mission 11 days earlier – to see Everton beaten at Goodison for the first time in two years, 4-3 by Burnley – and declared: "It will be a hell of an ordeal, for us at Goodison, for I have seen just what a din the local crowd kicks up.

"They are tireless and sometimes turbulent – quite an effective 12th man for a very strong team.

"I demand every ounce of effort from my men, every inch in the straining for speed, every residue of courage they can muster from their boots upwards.

"Believe me; I'll be happy to settle for a draw there."

That is exactly what the Milan Maestros, as they were christened by the local media, achieved, in front of a crowd which generated record receipts for an English club match outside of the FA Cup final, of £31,450. The previous record of £27,500 had been set by Tottenham Hotspur and Rangers for another European Cup tie at White Hart Lane.

Despite the absence of goals, there was no shortage of excitement –

but Inter always looked more fluid, more assured and more comfortable with the demands of European football.

The Echo's Michael Charters declared: "On the evidence of the thrilling game, Everton's chances of achieving anything at Milan next Wednesday are very slim indeed.

"The Inter-Milan coach, Helenio Herrera, pulled one of the confidence tricks of the age when he said, pre-match, that his intention would be to play a defensive game. Instead, the 62,000 crowd saw some superb attacking play from the Italians, particularly in the first half.

"They parked their defence when they had to, but their play was so fluid, so slick in turning defence to attack, that they were much the better team."

But still there was that disallowed goal.

Mr Charters added: "The great talking point of the match was Vernon's disallowed goal in 80 minutes. Was it a goal? My view was not good enough for me to be dogmatic, it seemed near enough to raise hopes of it being allowed to stand.

"One reader, after seeing the incident on TV, rang me up to say that the cameras proved beyond doubt the legality of the goal. It is a matter of history now and the referee's decision, right or wrong, must stand."

The decision did stand – and Everton lost the second leg a week later by a single goal, an occasion famously marked by the senior debut of a young man who would become one of Goodison's greatest servants, Colin Harvey.

But Merseyside had witnessed European Cup football for the first time – and relished the experience.

BEST OF BRITISH

———— ✕⁄∧⁄✕ ————

MONDAY, DECEMBER 2, 1963

JOHN HURST FAMOUSLY HOLDS A PLACE in the record books as Everton's first substitute.

Which isn't quite the whole truth.

The yeoman Hurst was undeniably the first player introduced from the bench … in a Football League match.

But there had been an Everton substitute prior to his breakthrough appearance, in a match which was never granted 'official' status – even though it was for a Best of British title and attracted more than 40,000 fans to Goodison Park.

Colin Harvey was the young footballer who enjoyed the distinction of becoming Everton's first senior substitute, in a British Championship match against Glasgow Rangers.

But the occasion became more memorable for the antics off the pitch rather than on it.

A week earlier Everton had won the first leg of the first British Championship match 3-1 in front of 64,006 largely rabid Rangers' fans.

The first leg deficit may have diminished the number of Scottish supporters who travelled south for the second leg – but not their passion!

The Echo's Leslie Edwards painted a colourful picture.

"Fun and games at Goodison Park of the kind we've never seen before in the long history of football crowds in this city," he wrote. "The cult of The Beatles is only an extension of the cult of Glasgow Rangers. To hear the small, but gigantically vocal Rangers contingent singing their 'Follow, follow!' in competition with Everton's Z-Cars theme song and, at the interval, in competition with The Beatles' Yeah, Yeah, Yeah was quite something.

"Add to the scene Scottish standards and Union Jacks waved by fans standing on each other's shoulders: police constables mingling among the Scottish contingent (what a chance those coppers took) and the whole topped off with Scotland's national spirit and effervescence and you have something which riveted one's attention almost as much as the game.

"With the inevitable bottle – this time a broken one-tossed on the pitch to add to Everton's embarrassment and make our own spectatorial misdemeanours seem almost in the Sunday School picnic category.

"Despite the far-from-capacity attendance this was an occasion.

"Just as well Everton went into it with a solid two goals' lead from the game at Ibrox: just as well we had fewer than 1,500 Rangers fans instead of the promised 10,000. I think the police and the Everton team did a grand job."

But despite the efforts of the Merseyside constabulary, many of the Everton fans were unimpressed and flooded the local media with letters of complaint.

Mr. P. Lamb, of Oriel Road, Bootle's correspondence was typical.

"Having the ill-luck to be a spectator at Monday's Everton-Rangers game, the added misfortune to be standing where Rangers supporters were thickest, and having heard that this match could become a seasonal fixture regardless of League championship, I am forced for the first time ever to write in papers that this particular team and its supporters should never come here again," he wrote.

"I am a fervid Everton supporter missing few games over the last 18 seasons and looking forward to many more seasons of viewing. This is one fixture I don't ever intend attending again.

"The Scots are supposed to be fitba daft, I didn't hear one sentence of criticism or praise constructive or otherwise from any Rangers supporters for the whole 90 minutes, but my ears were deluged with profanities and unholy chants.

"Having no religious bias and having heard none in any football ground this side of the border their people appal me.

"Please Mr Moores, let's have no more."

There would be one more meeting with Rangers – in Dubai – a quarter of a century later, when ironically Colin Harvey was the Everton manager.

Back in 1963, Harvey trotted on for another senior appearance after just 35 minutes, just 10 weeks after his San Siro debut, to replace the limping Jimmy Gabriel.

He played his part in a 1-1 draw which clinched an aggregate victory – but the undoubted man of the match was young goalkeeper Andy Rankin.

"Everything hinged, mid-way through the first half, on two fantastic saves by young Andy Rankin, the Bootle boy whose goalkeeping dynamics make him the find of the season," reported the following night's Echo.

"To put it shortly Rankin broke Rangers' hearts in two minutes of goalkeeping magic which even a Scott, a Hardy or a Sagar could not have bettered.

"Ritchie in Rangers' goal had punched a long clearance from hand plumb down the centre of the field, three parts of its length. Heslop, misjudging the arc of the ball as it dropped, let in Miller and that hefty bundle of football skill, hit his shot on the volley with all the considerable power at his command. Somehow Rankin saw this one coming: somehow he got his hands to it and turned it to Brand on the left whose gallop with the ball was promptly stopped.

"The murmurs of wonderment at such a save (which if it had not been made would have taken the aggregate 3-2) had scarcely died when little Henderson, roaming to outside-left made a glorious jinking run which enabled him to cross the ball to McLean to shoot, at point-blank range and still find those trusty hands of Rankin reaching out to make contact in yet another stupendous save."

Those saves, and a soaring Alex Young headed goal, at least gave the home supporters something other than the antics of the visiting fans to focus on!

BATTLE OF GOODISON

———— ✕✕/⋀\✕✕ ————

SATURDAY, NOVEMBER 7, 1964

GOODISON PARK HAS WITNESSED MANY FAMOUS footballing firsts – but not all have been celebrated.

On November 7, 1964, a seething Goodison gallery was witness to a scene described by the media at that time as "spine-chilling", "disgraceful" and "an unhappy day for English football."

It was the infamous Battle of Goodison, an ultra-aggressive showdown with Leeds United so charged and so volatile that referee Ken Stokes took the unprecedented step of leading both teams off the pitch to cool down.

After 36 minutes.

There had been precious little hint of the carnage to come.

Everton and Leeds would become fierce rivals later in the decade, challenging for titles and meeting in an intense FA Cup semi-final – but the seeds of the clubs' most notorious battle had been sown the previous season, when Leeds were a Second Division side on their way to promotion back into the top flight.

The sides were drawn in a fourth round FA Cup tie at Elland Road, which Everton won after a replay, but Everton players had bristled at a perceived overly-aggressive approach from their opponents.

It was a reputation which would follow Don Revie's side for the rest of the decade, with his talented team re-christened "Dirty Leeds."

Adding fuel to the fire, was the presence in the Leeds side that November afternoon of Bobby Collins, a diminutive footballing genius jettisoned by Blues boss Harry Catterick in 1962 as being past his best.

Collins had a score to settle with his old manager, but it was Johnny Giles, a gloriously creative midfielder with a notoriously cynical streak who lit the blue touchpaper just 48 hours after Bonfire Night.

Only four minutes had gone when he launched a studs up challenge on Everton defender Sandy Brown, a 'tackle' which left six-inch grazes on the players' stomach – as later revealed to Daily Mirror journalist Dave Horridge.

Brown swung a punch at Giles in retaliation and was sent off, the only Everton player to receive his marching orders that season.

"I have been playing top-class football for eight years and I have never been provoked like this before. I have never known anything like it. I'm really sick about the whole business, I lost my head," Brown said later.

The dismissal stoked an already agitated crowd, a toxic atmosphere which deteriorated when Leeds took the lead against the 10 men after 15 minutes.

Coins and missiles were hurled onto the pitch. Any Leeds player brave enough to approach the touchline was targeted.

According to the Liverpool Echo's Michael Charters "then followed foul after foul with so many free-kicks that there was no continuity in the game."

Charters added: "Bremner and Vernon were having a personal duel of the worst kind. Bremner fouled Vernon and Vernon was lucky not to be in trouble with the referee for what happened immediately after the whistle had gone."

Perhaps happily, the Echo journalist did not detail exactly what had happened after the whistle had gone!

Then after 36 minutes the pin was plucked from the hand grenade.

Leeds left back Willie Bell and Everton striker Derek Temple collided when running at pace. For once there appeared to be no vicious intent on either side, but the collision was sickening and during lengthy treatment the players were subjected to a barrage of coins and missiles thrown from the crowd.

During this break in play referee Stokes was struck by a coin – which possibly prompted his fateful decision.

He led both sets of players off the pitch. For 11 minutes.

During the break in play there were repeated calls for calm over the public address system, referee Stokes visited each dressing room and warned the teams to start playing football or he would abandon the fixture, Leeds' officials were jeered in the Directors' Box and the Echo's Charters reported: "Fights were breaking out in the crowd while they waited for the game to resume and this incident was the most sensational, I have seen in my years of watching football.

"Altogether there was a delay of 10 minutes from the time the referee went off with the players until he came out again to restart. The Leeds players were first back onto the pitch, and before the Everton team appeared the crowd started a chant of 'Dirty Leeds.'

The mood did not improve after play restarted.

"Rees was guilty of a very bad foul on Collins and really it was a miracle that the referee had not sent off two or three players by now," added Charters.

The players managed to get to half-time and another – this time scheduled – break.

An uneasy truce existed in the second half, before the final whistle blew and a temporary ceasefire declared … until incredibly the sides were drawn to face each other again in the FA Cup just two months later!

By then Sandy Brown had served a two week ban, Everton had paid a £250 fine to the FA for failing to control their supporters and the president of the Football League, Joe Richards, had claimed growing player wages were at the root of the problem.

The footnote was delivered by the Echo's Leslie Edwards on the Monday evening.

"What we were supposed to see was a football match between Everton and Leeds United," he wrote "what we saw was a crime against football and against sportsmanship and good sense.

"One cannot comment on it as a game, because there was no game – just a series of reckless, feckless scrimmages between two teams of eleven men masquerading as footballers."

Quite.

TEENAGE RAMPAGE

---✕✕／∧＼✕✕---

MONDAY, MAY 3, 1965

THE POWER OF GOODISON HAS ALWAYS inspired all teams who pull on the Royal Blue jersey, regardless of quality, sex or age.

On April 28, 1965, a small Highbury crowd of 5,000 watched Arsenal's youth team grab a 1-0 first leg lead in the FA Youth Cup final against Everton. It was the first goal the exciting young Everton team had conceded in that season's competition.

But the Liverpool Echo's Paul O'Brien prophetically reported: "Arsenal, a good footballing side, will not be beaten easily at Goodison Park, but given the right backing from the Everton crowd Everton can give their fans one success to shout about."

Five days later a staggering crowd of 29,908 turned up at Goodison Park to roar on the youngsters – six times the number who had watched at Highbury – and they were not passive viewers!

"There was no doubt that this was just what the Evertonians, who have been taking a back seat over the weekend, had been waiting for," reported the Echo "and they really let themselves go.

"Thousands raced on to the pitch to mob the Everton players, as so great was their enthusiasm that at least two members of the successful side had their shirts ripped from their backs.

"Up in the main stand, hundreds more swarmed across to the centre to get a glimpse of the players and cup in the directors' box, and it was about 10 minutes after the final whistle when someone decided to put on the 'Z-Cars' record, and the spectators took the hint and started to make their way home."

So what was all the excitement about?

Liverpool had lifted the FA Cup for the first time on the Saturday afternoon and 48 hours later, on the Monday night, Evertonians were also eager to celebrate a trophy the club had not won before.

And this Everton team was packed with exciting potential, featuring several players who would soon become familiar faces in the first team.

Jimmy Husband and John Hurst would soon become first team regulars and mainstays of the 1969/70 title winning team. Frank Darcy also featured five times in that title winning season, while goalkeeper Geoff Barnett made 10 appearances in the first team the following season and Gerry Glover and Aiden Maher also went on to feature in the first team.

The young guns had sparkled throughout the Youth Cup campaign.

After a 5-0 December thrashing of a Manchester United side featuring five players who had helped win the Youth Cup the previous season, the Echo reported: "Everton gave one of their best displays in Under-18 football for many years when they beat a strong Manchester United side 5-0 in the second round of the F.A. Youth Cup at Goodison Park last night."

And after 11,025 fans witnessed a 4-0 defeat of Burnley, the next day's report read: "A sparkling display by Everton against Burnley, in the fourth round of the FA Youth Cup last night, helped to clear away the gloom which had descended on Goodison Park during the previous two Tuesday evenings, when the club were knocked out of the FA and Fairs Cups."

Sunderland were dispatched just as commandingly in the semifinal, before young Arsenal striker Doug Baker beat Barnett for the first time in the competition at Highbury in the Youth Cup final first leg.

The huge crowd which gathered for the second leg saw a Cup classic.

"The amazing thing is that although Everton dominated the game territorially, the trophy was within 60 seconds of going to Highbury," wrote Paul O'Brien.

Everton had levelled the scores on aggregate when Tony McLoughlin maintained his record of having scored in every round of the competition, knocking the ball in after goalkeeper Ernie Adams had parried Maher's powerful shot in the 41st minute.

But The Gunners equalised on the night and restored their aggregate lead from a rare breakaway 20 minutes after half time, John Radford who would go on to become a Gunners' legend, pouncing.

Everton dominated but Arsenal clung grimly on. As the seconds ticked away the Blues were awarded one of their many free kicks of the second half, 10 yards inside the Arsenal half.

Young England international Gerry Glover accepted the responsibility of taking it and placed the ball perfectly into the penalty area, where Aiden Maher, described in the local press as "the other half of that famous former Liverpool schoolboys double act" rose high to head it brilliantly beyond goalkeeper Adams.

"To judge by the noise made by the 29,908 spectators, one would have thought this goal had clinched the First Division championship," reported the Echo. "The crowd continued their chant of 'Everton, Everton' right through to the end of the short break allowed by referee K.H.Burns of Worcestershire, before extra time."

The Cup winning goal came five minutes after half-time in extra-time.

Showing the trickery and ability to run with the ball he would soon be displaying for the first team, Jimmy Husband was upended inside the penalty box, then John Hurst, displaying the leadership and authority he would soon be showing for the senior side, stepped up to smash the spot kick in off the underside of the crossbar.

The excitement wasn't quite over.

With a minute remaining Arsenal forced a corner kick, Radford rose to bullet a header goalwards only for Barnett to pull off an equally brilliant save to push the ball over.

He then safely gathered the following corner and the FA Youth Cup came to Goodison for the first time – and Evertonians showed their ability to celebrate any success by a side wearing Royal Blue.

1966 & ALL THAT

TUESDAY, JULY 12, 1966 TO
MONDAY, JULY 25, 1966

PELE, GARRINCHA, EUSEBIO, THE KAISER HIMSELF Franz Beckenbauer … and Pak Doo-Ik.

Some of the most legendary names in football history graced Goodison Park during the 1966 World Cup tournament.

But they were all almost upstaged by a previously unknown North Korean striker!

The eighth World Cup tournament was staged in England for the first time in 1966.

And while Wembley Stadium offered the backdrop to English football's finest moment, Goodison Park played host to some of the tournament's most dramatic showdowns.

The Grand Old Lady had been given a facelift for the World Cup. The Park End stand was reconstructed at a cost of £160,000, providing seating for 2,500 fans. The pitch was extended by five yards to meet World Cup requirements while 900 seats were removed from the Goodison Road stand to make way for the typewriters and telephones for 700 journalists from around the world.

The evening after England kicked off the tournament with a goalless draw at Wembley against Uruguay, reigning world champions Brazil, featuring some of the most charismatic names in world football, loped out of the Goodison tunnel in their iconic yellow, green and blue strip to face Bulgaria.

An expectant crowd of 47,308 Merseyside spectators saw the widely acknowledged greatest player in the world, Pele, open the scoring, and the man acknowledged as the greatest dribbler of all time, Garrincha, seal victory.

Street parties were organised around Goodison Park to celebrate the tournament, with bunting draped from houses – but having thrilled to the sorcery of the brilliant Brazilians, just 72 hours later the local fans had new heroes to thrill to.

And after England had laboured to that goalless draw at Wembley, the events at Goodison belatedly vindicated England's hosting of the tournament.

Pele missed the next match staged at Goodison on July 15, rested after being brutally buffeted by the Bulgarians, but the magical Magyars of Hungary more than filled the void created by the absence of the world's greatest player.

"Take into account the absence of Pele and the fact that the Brazilians did not enjoy the conditions, and even then it is difficult to diminish the magnificence of the Hungarians' victory," Eric Todd wrote in Saturday's Guardian. "Not often have I seen better team work. Not often have I had such welcome confirmation of the belief, old fashioned though it may be, that there is nothing like honest, uninhibited attacking football."

The Observer's Hugh McIlvanney was just as enthused.

"It was an incredible occasion," he wrote "filled with the archetypal elements of the great game – skill, heart, atmosphere, an awareness of immortality being earned."

And in response to the cynics who had sneered following England's blunt introduction to the tournament, he added: "Now no one will dare to ask what all the fuss is about. Friday night at Goodison Park gave a gloriously comprehensive answer."

However, Hungary's thoroughly deserved 3-1 victory left pre-tournament favourites Brazil in danger of failing to qualify for the knockout stages.

The final Group game pitted two of the all-time greats of world football against each other – Eusebio versus Pele.

The gate of 58, 479, the highest at a World Cup group game outside of Wembley, indicated the excitement generated.

Eusebio scored twice, Pele was still inhibited by the injury he had received in the bruising opening encounter with Bulgaria and Portugal's 3-1 triumph confirmed an unexpectedly early exit from the tournament for the world champions.

Enter the darlings of the tournament. North Korea had travelled to England as 1,000-1 outsiders – odds which seemed justified by their 3-0 defeat by the Soviet Union in their opening match.

But they rallied to draw with Chile then in the shock of the tournament beat Italy 1-0 at Ayresome Park with a goal from Pak Doo-Ik to reach the quarter-finals and set up a showdown with Portugal.

North Korea's progress had taken even their own management by surprise, with no accommodation prebooked for the knockout stages. That meant the team stayed in a Jesuit retreat ahead of the biggest moment in their nation's football history.

What then transpired at Goodison Park was one of the greatest matches in World Cup history and one of the most spectacular showdowns ever staged at Goodison Park.

North Korea tore into Portugal with style and verve. Pak Seung-Zin crashed a searing drive into the roof of the Park End net shortly after kick-off. Chances came and went at either end before Li Dong-Woon pounced from close range to make it 2-0. When Yang Sung-Kook fired a third after 25 minutes the nation's newspaper wires were chattering with tales of perhaps the greatest upset since USA had shocked England 16 years earlier.

The legendary Eusebio pulled one goal back inside two minutes, then after yet more chances were either fizzed past the post or parried by the goalkeepers – at either end – he stepped up to smash a penalty high to the goalkeeper's right.

After a wildly entertaining 45 minutes North Korea's lead was slender. And it was cancelled out in the 56th minute when Eusebio raced onto a pass to unveil his venomous shooting power once again, firing high into the Gwladys Street net.

As Portugal coach Otto Gloria observed afterward: "We do not like defence. Attack is our best defence. We do not like to play on defence. We do not know how to play on defence."

Neither did North Korea. They continued to create chances, but Portugal were growing in confidence and stature and when Eusebio was fouled not once, but twice, he stepped up to take his second penalty of the match and fired a carbon copy of his first high into the net – his fourth goal of a striking masterclass.

Centre-forward Jose Torres finally interrupted Eusebio's scoring streak when he headed the fifth 10 minutes from time to end the North Koreans' resistance.

"We were not disturbed at any time," Portugal captain Mario Coluna said afterwards. "We knew we would beat Korea."

At 3.25pm there were plenty inside Goodison Park who did not share his confidence.

After the giddy roller-coaster ride of an astonishing quarter-final, Goodison still had a World Cup semi-final to look forward to. But with the local spectators dismayed by the FA's decision to renege on a promise that England would play their semi-final against the Portuguese on Merseyside, just 38,273 turned up to watch West Germany beat Russia.

Goodison had already witnessed its World Cup show-stopper. And one of world football's greatest names had been given a suitable stage on which to display his majesty.

When he returned in 2009 for a Europa League visit of Benfica,

Eusebio declared: "Sorry, I don't speak good English. But today for me, for my family, it's a good day for Benfica to play here. This stadium for me is the best stadium in my playing life."

His performance that July afternoon was undeniably one of Goodison's greatest.

INCREDIBLE
TREBLE

SATURDAY, AUGUST 13, 1966

WHAT HAPPENED AFTER THE WHISTLE BLEW to kick-off the 1966 Charity Shield was underwhelming.

But the parade before kick-off was unique in the history of English, if not world football.

Everton and Liverpool put on a display of treasure which even Buckingham Palace would have struggled to match.

Everton captain Brian Labone trotted around Goodison Park proudly holding the FA Cup. Liverpool counterpart Ron Yeats held the League Championship trophy.

While forming a priceless vanguard, Everton World Cup winner Ray Wilson and his England team-mate Roger Hunt held the Jules Rimet trophy won at Wembley just a fortnight earlier.

The Daily Express's Jack Rowe articulated the uniqueness of the scene celebrated by more than 63,000 Mersey football fans.

"It can scarcely happen again in this country," he wrote "that on one ground two teams from the same city will do a lap of honour with the captain of one carrying the FA Cup, the captain of the other the

League Championship Cup and in front of them a player from each side carrying aloft the most prized National trophy in the world, the Jules Rimet Cup.

"What else is there we can offer to the soccer loving fans of this city of Liverpool? Apart from a conquest in Europe and an FA Cup final at Wembley between our two clubs. I can think of nothing else.

"They've pretty well seen the lot and every one of the 63,000 spectators at Goodison Park on Saturday left the ground with the inner glow of satisfaction that they can boast they watched history made."

The pre-match scenes are still talked about even now on Merseyside.

The match itself less so.

After Liverpool's 1-0 win the Guardian's Eric Todd wrote: "The game itself was not a particularly inspiring one, but 63,329 Merseysiders – there were no outsiders surely? – no doubt felt that their £18,000 entrance money had been well spent for the pleasure of seeing the trophies of war that their teams had won or had helped lesser mortals to win.

"Before the match the World Cup, the FA Challenge Cup and the Football League Championship Cup were paraded before the drooling fans. After it, Liverpool generated sufficient strength to do a lap of honour with the Charity Shield, and finally miniature cups were presented to the Liverpool and Everton representatives in the World Cup squad."

In the match itself Liverpool had 22 efforts at goal, 13 on target, Everton just three, with Gordon West having to make at least three outstanding saves.

The only goal was scored by Liverpool striker Roger Hunt after nine minutes, with Todd adding: "Thereafter the proceedings deteriorated in quality and interest, although as I wrote earlier, the crowd were more than compensated by the sight of all that booty."

Jack Rowe offered a prophetic insight into what Everton needed to do to improve on their Charity Shield performance: "The truth is that their attack was pretty much non existent and unless it is capable of lifting itself to a height of ability which will make a mockery of Saturday's outing, then there must be replacements."

There was.

It was the last match an Everton team would play before a flame-haired talisman breathed fire and brimstone into their ranks.

Forty-eight hours later they signed Alan Ball.

WHO IS THE GREATEST OF THEM ALL?

SATURDAY, AUGUST 27, 1966

A WEEK IS A LONG TIME in football.

So a fortnight? A football club's entire trajectory can shift in that timescale.

Just 14 days after Everton had been well beaten by Liverpool at Goodison Park in the 1966/67 season's Charity Shield curtain raiser, Harry Catterick's men welcomed their neighbours again.

But this time they had Alan Ball in their team.

The World Cup winner wrote about his second Goodison experience as an Everton player – he had made his home debut four days earlier against Manchester United – in his 2014 autobiography Playing Extra Time.

"The noise from the packed crowd as we ran out was staggering," he recalled. "Manchester United at home had been deafening but this had an extra edge to it. I remember looking up at the Goodison Park clock in the corner of the ground. It was three o'clock and there were no nerves. I was loving every moment of it as if this was my stage.

"I had a fear of nobody and I knew that this was what I wanted for the rest of my life. The image of that famous old clock will never leave me because when I looked at it again it was 12 minutes past three and I had scored two goals. The whole place was jumping."

Ball's presence wasn't the only change from the starting line up which had been well beaten in the Charity Shield – Fred Pickering and Johnny Morrissey were also available – but the World Cup winner's presence 10 days after his £110,000 transfer from Blackpool was the most significant.

Just nine minutes into his derby debut, Ball darted onto a pass from Johnny Morrissey and cracked a shot past Tommy Lawrence.

Four minutes later a free-kick by Colin Harvey caught Ron Yeats and Gordon Milne in two minds – and in their uncertainty the ball bounced off Milne's shins for Ball to pounce and rocket the ball into the roof of the net.

Goodison erupted.

He later said: "I was running back to the centre circle after I scored the second goal against Liverpool and pure elation welled up inside me. I remember thinking, 'I just love this place – I want this place forever.' "

Tommy Smith pulled a goal back in the 43rd minute then the match degenerated into a series of squabbles and fouls and recriminations – a typical Merseyside derby, then.

But there was still time for another slice of Mersey football history to be made.

Substitutes had been introduced into the Football League at the start of the previous season – and Everton had used the new innovation on nine occasions, but no-one had managed to come on in a match and influence the outcome sufficiently by scoring a goal.

That all changed in the 99th Merseyside derby.

Sandy Brown had replaced injured centre-forward Fred Pickering in the 58th minute, and 25 minutes later Alex Young headed Ray Wilson's cross back across goal where Brown nodded the match-clinching third past Lawrence.

It was a piece of derby folklore often overshadowed by another headed goal scored by Sandy at Goodison Park, into his own net.

But there was no doubt that the 99th Merseyside derby was dominated by one man.

Already the subject of instant hero worship following a winning goal on his debut at Fulham, this was the match which elevated Ball to Goodison God-like status.

It's a reputation he still enjoys today.

BALL OF FIRE

———— ✕✕／⌒＼✕✕ ————

SATURDAY, SEPTEMBER 17, 1966

NINE GOALS, A THREE-GOAL LEAD SQUANDERED, late penalty drama – and the confirmation of a new terrace idol, the visit of West Bromwich Albion on September 17, 1966 provided one of Goodison Park's most thrilling league clashes.

Games with The Baggies often provided rich entertainment in the 1960s. In nine visits to Goodison Park from February 1959 the Goodison gallery witnessed 43 goals – often equally shared – but the September showdown in 1966 eclipsed even the usual entertainment value the two sides routinely produced.

The Liverpool Echo's experienced observer Michael Charters declared: "Well we won't see another game like that for a long time."

He then went on to detail the bald facts of a riotously entertaining afternoon.

"The bare statistical facts of this nine-goal epic in technicolour and high drama are these:

"Everton went ahead in seven minutes; Everton moved superbly to a 4-1 lead just after half-time; found themselves pulled back to 4-4 with 13 minutes to go; hit the winner from a penalty when their supporters had given up hope."

Evertonians had already fallen head over heels in love with their new signing from Blackpool, and another inspired afternoon from "little curly Alan Ball" simply confirmed that the adoration would be enduring.

A gate of 45,165 watched Ball thread a pinpoint pass through for Alex Young to equalise Jeff Astle's seventh minute opener.

Ball then "sent Temple away for the finest goal of the lot."

After two assists he took a backseat while Johnny Morrissey made it 3-1 shortly after half-time then "Ball sent the score to 4-1 with a cheeky individual effort down the right, rolling the ball into the net from an angle after beating four men, including the goalkeeper."

Four-one up with almost the entire second half still to come, an expectant Goodison gallery sat back and waited for even more goals to rain in.

They did – at the opposite end of the pitch!

Doug Fraser reduced the arrears in the 50th minute, Bobby Cram made it 4-3 with 15 minutes left and then two minutes later a disbelieving Goodison crowd saw John Kaye pull the scores level.

Enter a man made for moments like this.

"It took Ball, the outstanding performer on a day when so many individuals were so brilliant to bring Everton both points," reported Charters.

"He worked his way through into the penalty area, was pulled down rugby style by Collard and hit the winner from the spot in precision style sending Sheppard one way and the ball the other."

That nerveless penalty kick came with just seven minutes remaining.

The Echo concluded: "No-one left the ground early on this day. No-one wanted to miss a moment of this magnificently entertaining spectacle.

"There will be those who will point the finger of criticism at the defences. It was true that there was some amazingly slipshod work in this department by both teams but it did allow some breathtaking attacking play and this, surely, is what thrills and delights spectators.

"Both Everton inside men played superbly, with Ball particularly giving a non-stop display of the highest class.

"This was inside forward play in the textbook style – hard work in midfield to create the openings, fine running with the ball, artistry in tight situations to get out of difficulty, accurate finishing, indeed the lot."

And a match which lived long in the memory of all who witnessed it.

THE SILVER
SCREEN

———— ⋙⁄⋀⋙ ————

SATURDAY, MARCH 11, 1967

NOT EVEN WEMBLEY STADIUM WAS BIG enough to stage a
Cup tie the world wanted to see in March 1967.

In the 1966/67 season Everton were the FA Cup holders. Liverpool
were the reigning league champions – and the two sides boasted three
World Cup winners between them.

So when they were drawn to meet in the FA Cup fifth round there
wasn't a stadium big enough to accommodate the fans who were
desperate to witness a titanic collision.

Goodison could accommodate 65,000. Such was the demand
for tickets that when they went on sale at Goodison Park, more
than 100 people were hurt in a scramble and 30 taken to Walton
Hospital.

At another selling point, the old Liverpool Boxing Stadium, sales
were halted for an hour while police reinforcements were called to
handle the crowds.

One enterprising Evertonian, Paul Gray, even offered his 1957 Ford
Consul motor car, worth £50, in the pages of the Liverpool Echo in

exchange for a match ticket. He was successful, receiving a ground ticket face value five shillings and sixpence!

Such was the demand to see the game – in an age when the only televised club match ever screened was the FA Cup final – a novel solution was sought.

Liverpool's outstanding administrator Peter Robinson explained the logistical difficulties.

"We were all somewhat taken aback when the draw came out," he said, speaking 20 years later. "At the time we'd been averaging something like 100,000 spectators a fortnight between the two clubs. It was obvious that everyone would want to see the game, and equally obvious that we couldn't fit them all in.

"The suggestion for a closed circuit relay came from Granada Television."

Liverpool arranged for eight giant screens to be erected at Anfield where closed circuit television could relay images from Goodison.

The installation of scaffolding platforms to mount the screens meant that capacity had to be set at 40,500.

So 65,000 at Goodison (the official attendance on the night was recorded as 64,851) and 40,500 at Anfield – and still it wasn't enough.

"We had no idea what would be involved (in the closed circuit TV relay) because we were, in effect, complete amateurs," added Mr Robinson. "I know we did things then that wouldn't be allowed now – for example sitting a projector in the middle of the Kop.

"The screens were only installed the day before the match and so we had sold all the tickets before we had a chance to test the system.

"With that many spectators there was a marvellous atmosphere, even though the pictures were only in black and white. There's no doubt that it was a success. The cost to us was only £5,000 – but we realised how much of a gamble it was when the gale, which had been gathering strength all evening, blew two of the screens away only half-an-hour after the match finished!

"I don't know how we would have coped if that had happened with

40,000 people in the ground and no provision for giving them their money back."

The wind caused problems for the players, too, at Goodison Park.

The kick-off was set for 7pm to ensure the best conditions for the TV audience – but what they witnessed was a tense, scrappy, contentious clash. A typical derby, in fact.

Everton manager Harry Catterick said afterwards: "I thought we had just that little edge in skill in very difficult conditions with a high wind and a dry ball.

"Once I saw the conditions I realised that good football was virtually impossible. I have played many times on this ground and I know only too well that the wind does not blow right down the field but because of the stands swirls all over the place. It is terribly difficult."

Of course, Everton possessed one player capable of mastering any conditions – and as he so often did against Liverpool, Alan Ball made the difference.

The pivotal moment came a minute before half-time.

Gordon Milne was pressed into a hasty back pass to his goalkeeper, defending the Gwladys Street goal, and Jimmy Husband raced in to challenge before Tommy Lawrence could gather.

The ball span loose and Ball was the quickest to react, flicking the ball with the outside of his right boot wide of a gathering melee of players, galloping after it and volleying it sweetly into the net from a tight angle.

The Liverpool Daily Post's Horace yates wrote: "It is my firm conviction that there was not another player on the field and very few anywhere in the country, given the same opportunity, who would have converted it into a goal."

Ball himself recalled afterwards "I just gambled and went after it. I smacked the volley from an acute angle and I've never hit a volley as sweet in my life. I finished up right in the corner by the flag and I don't think I got away from there for about three minutes.

"I can remember thinking when they decided to put the television screens up at Anfield that this was the stage for me."

It might have been the perfect stage for Alan Ball – but another star of the stage and screen was less cheery.

Liverpool supporting comedian, Jimmy Tarbuck, was trudging away from Anfield having watched the closed-circuit relay – with his usual gap-toothed grin wiped off his face by Everton's victory.

One enterprising Evertonian spotted him and quipped: "Don't worry Jimmy, it's only a film!"

WINNING THEIR
TITLE SPURS

———⋈⁄‿⋈———

SATURDAY, MARCH 14, 1970

JUST AS IT HAD DONE SEVEN years earlier – and just as it would do a decade-and-a-half later, a title-winning Everton campaign pivoted on a thrilling clash with Tottenham Hotspur.

Or in this case, two.

On Wednesday, March 11, 1970 Everton won a rearranged league fixture at White Hart Lane 1-0, thanks to an early Alan Whittle goal.

The significance of the strike was enormous.

It took Everton back to the top of the table for the first time since mid-January and left the destiny of the title in their own hands.

Carry on winning and Don Revie's Leeds United couldn't catch them. But the forthcoming fixture list contained a trip to Anfield, the visit of third-placed Chelsea – and an instant rematch with Spurs.

Just three days after that White Hart Lane win, Bill Nicholson's side were back at Goodison – and the showdown was as thrilling as it was significant.

Just as he had in midweek, Alan Whittle opened the scoring to give Everton a deserved lead. But three minutes later Alan Gilzean equalised.

Five minutes before the half-time interval Alan Ball was given the opportunity to restore Everton's lead from the penalty spot after Mike England had fouled Joe Royle. He made no mistake.

With Everton holding a slender lead and the 51,333 crowd growing increasingly anxious, Everton were given another chance to soothe everyone's anxiety with a second penalty 10 minutes into the second half. Mike England fouled Joe Royle again, Alan Ball stepped up again – but despite striking the ball cleanly and accurately, Pat Jennings dived full length to pull off a superb save.

The significance of the stop was highlighted when, in an isolated raid, Tony Want centred, Roger Kenyon pulled back Gilzean by the shirt and referee D.J. Lyden of Birmingham awarded his third penalty of the afternoon.

Dennis Bond made no mistake, firing past Gordon West to level the scores.

This was in the 73rd minute – but the Goodison crowd was deflated for barely two minutes before they were celebrating again.

Mike Charters reported in the Liverpool Echo: "Royle had the crowd on their feet cheering a great goal. Ball chased down the middle and made contact with Brown's cross to touch the ball inside to Royle. The centre-forward, although covered, turned and hit a great low shot which Jennings half-saved but could not stop rolling over the line."

With title rivals Leeds in FA Cup semi-final action against Manchester United the same day, the victory took Everton three points clear – but despite Everton now having played a game more, Leeds' commitments were starting to prove damaging.

The FA Cup semi-final would take three matches to resolve, while Don Revie's side also defeated Standard Liege over two legs to reach a two-legged European Cup semi-final against Celtic.

Everton, meanwhile, had their focus solely on the league title.

"This had been one of the most exciting games at Goodison this season and the importance of it to Everton was made clear in every move they made," concluded Charters.

THE SCHOOL
OF SCIENCE

————✕✕╱∧╲✕✕————

SATURDAY, MARCH 28, 1970

SEVEN GOALS, AN EXULTANT ATMOSPHERE AND a strike after 14 seconds – the day league leaders Everton faced third placed Chelsea on a cold Easter Saturday afternoon in 1970 was an occasion few who were fortunate enough to be there have ever forgotten. Alan Hudson played in it and he hasn't forgotten. He was on the receiving end.

"Ball, Harvey and Kendall was special," he said. "That day they absolutely hammered us. They had big Joe Royle up front, who of course was a handful. We were a couple of players short through injury, which is not an excuse by the way. If we would have had 15 players that day, Everton still would have tortured us."

There were still two victories and five days to go before Harry Catterick's thrilling young Everton side could officially be crowned champions for a seventh time – but Goodison was impatient, and confident.

"Champions! Champions! Champions!" was the roar from a 58,337 crowd throughout a magnificent afternoon – and their confidence was understandable. Title rivals and FA Cup finalists Chelsea were demolished in a comprehensive display of power and glory.

152

Howard Kendall opened the scoring in 14 seconds. Before the hour mark Everton had scored FIVE without reply.

It was a decisive demonstration of Everton's title credentials.

The Daily Post's Horace Yates wrote: "This exultant roar of acclaim for a feat still to be finalised swept Goodison Park with the force of an explosion.

"Not since the Cup-winning glory days have we heard the like of it, but imagine the scene when near certainty is converted into unassailable fact as it may well be on Wednesday night.

"The position could hardly have been better stage-managed, for if the mighty omnipotent Everton sweep Stoke City out of their path today (they did) and the wounded lions of Leeds succumb to Derby County (they did), Everton's concluding home game with West Brom on Wednesday provides the opportunity for Championship-clinching in the grand manner.

"The way is cleared. Only the final few unfaltering steps remain to be taken and probably the most spectacularly successful season in the club's history will be crowned with unchallengeable triumph."

The title ceremony had been set up by the resounding performance against Chelsea, a result which confirmed Everton's status as deserved champions.

"Poor Chelsea!" declared Yates. "Cup Finalists they may be and until Saturday given an outside chance by their manager of pipping both Everton and Leeds for the Championship, but they took the knock-out punch on this relentless day of reckoning.

"Two goals down in the first four minutes, the first in 14 seconds, would have shattered any side. This was annihilation in the grand manner.

"The greatest display of the season? That is the verdict most fans took away with them but once again perfectionist Harry Catterick, jubilant as he was entitled to be, remained the typical hard taskmaster. 'I think they were better in the early days of the season when they were sharper and more decisive,' he said.

"Admittedly this was the period in which spectators became almost lyrical in praise of Everton but is it, I wonder, not just another case the old days always having something the present day cannot rival?

"A fan with fifty years of Everton memories insisted 'This is the greatest team of them all. They have never been better.' "

The writer asked Harry Catterick for his own thoughts, surely no better judge.

"I remember the 1938 side," said the Blues boss. "They were a wonderful outfit and because of the war they never achieved their true potential.

"But we have not seen the best of this side yet. They are all young. They should go better yet. Their peak is still to come."

It could be argued that the halcyon afternoon against Chelsea was the day Catterick's second great title winning side peaked.

"A blistering performance by Everton, including two goals in the first three minutes paralyzed Chelsea at Goodison Park this afternoon," wrote Michael Charters in that day's Football Echo. "Although Chelsea tried to get back into the game they were no match for the pace and skill of Everton who produced a championship style performance, with the whole team moving like clockwork."

The Post's Yates was typically more lyrical.

"The fount of greatness undoubtedly was the control, creative skills and consummate artistry of the most talented midfield trio in football, Ball, Harvey and Kendall, for this was the occasion on which Harvey turned back the clock to something approaching his finest hours enjoyed before his eye affliction took him out of the game.

"This was decisively Harvey's best comeback display and lording it over them all with his impish talent and creative flair was Ball, the man who has played a tremendous part in laying the table for the forthcoming Everton feast."

For the record: "Those who had the misfortune to blink their eyes twice missed the first goal. It came in 14 seconds when Brown returned Dempsey's clearing header into the middle. Momentarily Harvey and Kendall competed for possession, Harvey gave way and Kendall, swooping past three defenders into the penalty area, pushed rather than thumped a precision placing into the net off the inside of the post.

"That was surprise enough but Chelsea reeled and Goodison shook before the enthusiasm that acclaimed goal No.2 in just under four minutes.

"This time Wright cleared a Chelsea corner kick to midfield where Whittle pulled down the ball and set Morrissey racing up the left wing. Over came the defence clearing kick and Ball simply nodded into the net."

With John Hurst off the pitch for 15 minutes having a head wound stitched and Everton playing with 10 men, Royle headed an Alan Ball corner past Chelsea goalkeeper Hughes to make it 3-0.

Two minutes after the restart, with Hurst patched up and back "It was Royle again when Morrissey and Ball laid the foundations before Kendall short passed in front of goal. Royle had to make a complete turn before hammering the ball just inside the post in really great opportunist fashion.

"Then Alan Whittle stabbed a Morrissey express centre past Hughes in 57 minutes at which stage Everton declared."

Chelsea pulled back two goals before the final whistle, one in the last minute, but no-one demurred.

And some good did come out of Chelsea's defeat. Hudson went on to become one of the finest midfield generals of his generation – and pinpointed that afternoon as part of his learning curve.

"Bally was on another planet and I realised that day I had to improve my game. I had never been on the field with anyone like that. He was unbelievable," he explained.

"Without those two goals Everton would have been able to match Leeds' record of goals against, but at this stage nobody believes that scoring averages are likely to decide the outcome of the title," wrote Yates.

He was spot on. Two days later Everton were officially champions.

THE WHITE
PELE STRIKES

WEDNESDAY, APRIL 1, 1970

IT WAS ONCE WRITTEN OF COLIN HARVEY, that people didn't count the number of great matches he played in the Royal Blue of Everton, they counted the number of great seasons he produced. Entirely true. But when it came to goals, the reverse was usually the case.

The man memorably nicknamed 'The White Pele' on one supporter's banner was not renowned for the quantity of his goals – just 24 in 388 Everton appearances – but the quality meant they were usually worth waiting for.

And one of Colin's finest strikes came on the night Everton clinched their seventh league championship on April 1, 1970.

Already leading West Bromwich Albion 1-0 thanks to Alan Whittle's 19th minute poacher's goal – the sixth successive match in which the white-haired whippet had scored – Harvey's superb solo goal after 65 minutes started the celebrations in earnest.

"It set up a succession of exultant chants that persisted for the rest of the match," reported the Daily Post's Horace Yates, before describing the strike in detail.

"What a goal it was by Harvey. First he moved towards goal, changed his mind and veered out as though to bring Morrissey into play. Seeing Morrissey was doubled back to the edge of the penalty area, and while on the run, Harvey sent a crashing drive soaring into the net with Osborne leaping spectacularly but vainly across goal."

Goodison exploded.

It was an unseasonably cold April evening, with wintry showers gusting around the ground. But the atmosphere on the terraces was white hot.

In 1963, the Liverpool Echo's Michael Charters reckoned Goodison had not witnessed an atmosphere which greeted the Blues' sixth title triumph since Dixie Dean broke the Football League's scoring record 35 years earlier.

Seven years on, the reporter then known as "Mike Charters", was inside the press box again for the next title clincher against West Brom – and he believed the atmosphere which celebrated the club's seventh championship was even more intense.

"The fans created an atmosphere of happy anticipation and adulation for their team, much greater than seven years ago," he declared. "It was not only the Gwladys Street fans who roared their team on to triumph. This was total unreserved acclaim of the champions from every section of the crowd."

After a stunning run of six successive victories, including a win in the Anfield derby and an annihilation of FA Cup finalists Chelsea, Everton knew that victory would clinch their seventh crown.

On the Saturday Everton had thrashed Chelsea. Forty-eight hours later, Easter Monday, an Alan Whittle goal earned a hard fought 1-0 win at Stoke. That created the platform for the Wednesday evening visit of West Brom – and the coronation.

The same XI started – and finished – all three matches: West; Wright, Kenyon, Hurst, Brown; Ball, Harvey, Kendall; Whittle, Royle, Morrissey.

And with West Brom naming a young starting XI, it was effectively a title party.

"Everton sparkled in their play to the sparkle of their fans' applause," wrote the Echo. "They clinched the title to a non-stop roar of chants. including 'Ev-er-ton.' 'We are the champions.' 'We're on the way to Europe.' 'Send our team to Mexico' and even a couple of choruses of 'When You're Smiling.'

The performance was worthy of such acclaim.

"Champions ... and they played like it," added Charters. "Everton's performance was full of the brilliance which has established them as a superb footballing side, a side which plays the game with a skill and speed as fine as anything we have seen for many years.

"I consider them a better team than that which won the title seven years ago. The championship is harder to win these days but Everton thrilled and entertained crowds up and down the country with football of the highest quality. It was fitting that they should delight their own deliriously happy fans in their last home game of the season with a title-clinching display which contained all the joys and delights of their skills in one smooth, effective package."

Such was Everton's lead in what had been a fierce title race until Catterick's men surged clear in the spring with six successive victories, the Football League agreed to have the trophy on hand at Goodison Park in Everton's final home game of the season, for a title presentation.

"The lap of honour began in decorum but ended in a wild display of enthusiasm as hundreds of fans spilled onto pitch, despite appeals to keep off. Then came the touch which completed this wonderful night," added the Echo.

Mr. Louis Edwards, chairman of Manchester United and a member of the League Management Committee, was at Goodison Park to present the trophy which had been collected in secret from the previous season's champions Leeds United a couple of days earlier.

The players appeared in the directors' box one by one, each to be greeted with individual roars of acclamation. Alan Ball, captain in the injured Brian Labone's, absence, received the trophy from Mr. Edwards, who also handed the players their medals.

The usually reserved and composed Catterick allowed himself the indulgence of racing onto the pitch at the final whistle to hug his players and hoist first Alan Whittle, and then Alan Ball, into the air.

The Post's Horace Yates concluded: "Everton put a fine show that will carry their fans through hopefully to next season. I think they realise what a lucky lot they are, for no crowd in the country has been treated to more skilful or exciting play."

PENALTY
PRIZE GUYS

EVERTON AND GOODISON PARK WERE AT the birth of a piece of heart-stopping football drama in November 1970. For fifty-four years now, penalty shoot-outs have climaxed some of football's biggest occasions. Three World Cup finals, two European Championship finals, three FA Cup finals and 11 European Cup finals have all been decided by the ultimate test of nerve and technique.

But one of its first unveilings came at Goodison Park, the night before Bonfire Night in 1970.

The penalty shoot-out had been adopted by FIFA on June 27, 1970 to replace the unsatisfactory method of drawing lots or flipping a disc to decide the outcome of drawn ties.

The idea was proposed by the president of the Israel FA after his national team had been 'beaten' in an Olympic quarter-final by the drawing of lots.

It was first used three months later, on September 30, when Honved of Budapest beat Aberdeen 5-4 in the first round of the European Cup Winners' Cup.

But it made its debut in the European Cup at Goodison Park.

So unfamiliar was the new format that one radio commentator actually ended his broadcast and returned to the studio after Joe Royle saw Everton's opening kick saved, thinking the home team had lost on sudden death!

Fortunately his producers restored the link – for the climax of one of Goodison's greatest nights.

The headline in the following night's Echo was A MATCH OF GUTS, GLORY AND HEART-STOPPING DRAMA, while vastly experienced reporter Mike Charters described the showdown with German champions Borussia Moenchengladbach as one of the most thrilling in the old stadium's long history.

"The Goodison legend persists that the 6-4 Cup replay between Everton and Sunderland 34 years ago was the greatest game ever seen on the ground," he wrote. "Well, if it was more exciting, more dramatic, more tense or more compelling than the epic at Goodison last night, then it must have been the greatest match of all time.

"Last night's game was the thrill of a football lifetime for me and, I suspect, the 42,744 who will never forget every thrilling moment of it."

After a 1-1 draw in Germany a fortnight earlier, Everton scored after just 23 seconds when what Johnny Morrissey surely intended as a cross deceived German keeper Wolfgang Kleff who stood flat-footed, before belatedly diving as a ball which looked like it was curving past the post suddenly drifted back into the goal.

It was the only false step the big goalkeeper took all night.

He produced an inspirational performance to keep the Everton forward line at bay – and allow Herbert Laumen to level the scores in the 34th minute.

Chances came – and went – at either end.

Moenchengladbach were still relatively unknown to an English audience, but contained stars who would soon become household names, like Gunter Netzer, Jupp Heynckes and Berti Vogts.

But Everton outplayed their visitors, only to find the big goalkeeper an immoveable object.

Goalkeeper Kleff was subsequently overshadowed in his home country by the legendary Sepp Maier, but at Goodison Park he was truly inspired.

Unfortunately for him, his Everton counterpart proved even better.

Andy Rankin had received four stitches in a cut over his right eye in a League defeat at The Hawthorns four days earlier – but fortunately for the Blues was declared fit to face the Germans, and take his place in an historic penalty shoot-out.

After Royle had seen the first kick in the shoot-out saved by Kleff, Rankin was beaten by Sielhoff. Alan Ball comfortably slid his penalty into the Gwladys Street net, then Herbert Laumen shot wide.

Johnny Morrissey, Howard Kendall and Sandy Brown all scored. So did Jupp Heynckes and Horst Koppel, before Ludwig Muller stepped forward, towards a Gwladys Street End encouragingly chanting Andy Rankin's name.

Rankin responded by plunging to his right to push away Muller's shot and spark joyous celebrations.

Everton manager Harry Catterick wasn't exactly exultant. "I still say these penalties to decide a match are like a circus," he said afterwards. "But I can't think of a better answer apart from a third game."

But Evertonians loved the circus act.

Strangely, the act of missing the first kick in a shoot-out became something of a lucky omen for Everton teams.

Everton endured a long sequence of losing shoot-outs, and the only times they were successful came after missing the first kick!

David Unsworth in a 2002 League Cup tie at Newcastle, Steve Watson seeing his opening effort saved at Bristol City in the same competition, Tim Cahill firing over the crossbar at Wembley in an FA Cup semi-final and Leighton Baines missing in an FA Cup tie at Stamford Bridge.

Joe Royle really did start something!

GOODISON'S GREATEST GOAL?

———————×××/∧\×××———————

SATURDAY, JANUARY 16, 1971

IN 2011 LOUIS SAHA SMASHED EVERTON'S 5,000th Goodison goal – in a thrilling 5-3 victory over Blackpool.

To commemorate the historic landmark the Liverpool Echo newspaper asked its readers for their all-time favourite Goodison goal.

The usual contenders were all represented, Graeme Sharp against Spurs, Trevor Steven against Sunderland, James McFadden against Charlton and Andy King v Liverpool.

But there was one unexpected contender which cropped up over and over again.

It seems Jimmy Husband might just have scored the greatest goal Goodison has ever seen.

It came in 1971, in a match between the reigning league champions and the FA Cup holders Chelsea.

And even 40 years on, plenty of older Evertonians still recalled the strike vividly.

One wrote: "It was versus Chelsea, '70-71 season, we won 3-0. A sublime goal from Jimmy Husband. John Hurst won the ball in our penalty box, passed to Harvey standing on the edge of our area and he hit a 20 yard pass to Bally wide out on halfway line (standing in front of the players' tunnel).

"On the half volley he immediately passed it on to Husband running towards the Chelsea box and as the pass landed, Jimmy hit a superb first-time half volley past (I think) Bonetti. Cue delirium in Goodison. A sensational goal."

Another fan was more succinct.

"There was a goal scored by Jimmy Husband (against Chelsea I think). Colin Harvey played it forward from defence and Jimmy Husband at full pace looked up as the ball came over his head and struck it on the volley as it dropped – a brilliant goal."

That was how supporters recalled the moment four decades later – and it seemed it wasn't just fans indulging in a little rose-tinted nostalgia.

The headline on the back page of the Daily Post newspaper on the morning of Monday, January 18, 1971 carried a ringing endorsement from a man who had seen more spectacular Goodison goals than most.

He'd even scored some of them.

"One of the best goals I've ever seen, says Catterick."

The Liverpool Echo's Michael Charters agreed with the Everton manager's assessment.

"Everton took the lead with a Husband goal that deserved to be put on film for the majesty of its creation and the power of its finish," he reported.

The Post's Horace Yates, then a venerable sage of the press box, added: "I doubt I will see a more brilliant goal than that with which Everton lit up the scene after only eight minutes. It was poetry of motion from the moment Hurst brought the ball out of his own area to send Harvey up the middle.

"If Harvey's pass out to Ball on the right was a demonstration in slide rule accuracy, how then to describe Ball's transfer to Husband?

"The ball, like a bullet homing to a bull's eye, dropped on Husband's chest. Breasting it down on the turn, Husband hit the ball as it fell and away it soared, unstoppably, into the roof of the net. Goodison was roused as it has not been all season."

It was clearly something very special – and it set Everton on the road to a handsome 3-0 win.

And in answer to the question 'was it Goodison's greatest ever goal?' the most ringing endorsement came straight from the horse's mouth!

Phil Claire e-mailed the Echo in 2011 to say: "All the lunchtime regulars at the Royal British Legion in Newport Pagnell have voted and said yes, it was the best goal ever.

"We voted this way as Jimmy Husband himself told us it was and as he drinks with us every day, it would be rude not to agree!"

Enough said.

END OF AN ERA

SATURDAY, NOVEMBER 20, 1971

IT WAS A SYMBOLIC LAST HURRAH. The last defiant twitch from the corpse of Catterick's second great title winning team – and the final Goodison goal for the iconic Alan Ball.

Everton's 8-0 victory over Southampton on November 20, 1971 was a wonderfully vibrant afternoon.

But it was a dramatic – and unexpected denouement.

No top flight team had scored eight times in a league match since Blackburn won 8-2 at West Ham to celebrate Christmas 1963.

And in 1971/72 Everton had not exactly been potent.

They ended the campaign scoring just 37 goals – only one team scored less, rock bottom Huddersfield.

Yet improbably eight of them came on one wintry afternoon against Southampton!

Jimmy Gabriel – a remnant of the free-scoring 1963 title winning team – was in the Southampton side.

While Catterick's team contained eight members of the team who had lifted the league crown just 18 months earlier, scoring 72 goals: West, Wright, Kendall, Kenyon, Ball, Royle, Hurst and Whittle.

John McLaughlan, Peter Scott and David Johnson offered evidence that Catterick was trying to initiate another evolution – but of that trio only Johnson could ultimately be described as a success, and even he was prematurely sold to Ipswich.

The young Scouser, he'd only just celebrated his 20th birthday, scored a hat-trick against The Saints. Joe Royle was only two years his senior but he went one better, hitting four.

But it was the goal a minute before half-time which proved the most poignant of the day, Alan Ball scoring the 79th and final goal of his glorious Everton career.

It was a memorable strike, too.

Seconds before the interval Ball scampered a full 60 yards upfield before sliding the ball past Eric Martin. That made the score 5-0 at the end of 45 wonderful minutes for the Blues.

At the time no-one knew the significance of the strike.

Ironically on the morning of the match the Liverpool Echo had carried a picture feature on Saints goalkeeper Eric Martin.

Under the headline 'The Saviour of the Saints' it showed how Martin had helped keep Everton's goal count down to four in a 4-1 victory in December 1970.

Eleven months later he shipped twice as many.

Once David Johnson's fierce low angled shot made its way into the Gwladys Street End net, Martin's dismal day began.

The match had kicked-off in a heavy snowstorm and it was Everton who clearly relished the conditions more than the opposition. Three minutes after Johnson's opener, Royle scored the first of his awesome foursome, his well-placed shot from an Alan Whittle pass giving Martin no chance.

Just before the half-hour, Kendall and Whittle combined to set up Johnson who finished clinically from 12 yards. With Southampton now on the rack, Royle also made it a personal brace with goal number four on 40 minutes via a close-range flick from an uncleared Kendall cross.

Royle's hat-trick strike was also a beauty, the forward netting a superb 18-yard half-volley from a Johnson pass on the hour as Everton made it 6-0.

And six became seven on 72 minutes, Royle adding his fourth of the afternoon through a glancing header.

If the Saints thought their misery was at an end, they were sadly mistaken, as five minutes from time Johnson made sure he also had a hat-trick to celebrate applying a cool flicked finish to complete the rout. It was Johnson's first, and only career treble for the Blues.

Everton's new electronic scoreboard had traditionally spelled out the names of the goalscorers. On this occasion there wasn't room!

Under the legend Everton Eight Southampton Nil the scoreboard operator listed the numbers of the goalscorers: 7 9 7 9 8 9 9 7.

They had clearly used up all their goal luck. Everton then failed to score in their next four matches.

But for one night only they were inspired.

BELFAST'S NEW HOME

―――――――×××∕⁀＼×××―――――――

SATURDAY, MAY 12, 1973

SEVEN YEARS AFTER A MERSEYSIDE CROWD was cruelly deprived of the prospect of watching an England team in international action at Goodison Park in the 1966 World Cup, Sir Alf Ramsey's men were belatedly invited to step out on Merseyside.

But this time there was precious little appetite for the occasion.

Republican threats made to visiting British teams to Belfast during The Troubles meant that Northern Ireland's 'home' fixtures in the annual Home International Championships were transferred across the Irish Sea to Goodison Park.

The British Home International competition had been a feature of the football calendar since the 1883/84 season, England, Wales, Scotland and Northern Ireland facing each other in an annual end of season round robin.

But by 1973 appetite for the tournament was waning.

Scotland had won the previous year's tournament – one of only two occasions that England had not proved triumphant since 1964.

And England kicked off their bid to reclaim the trophy on May 12,

1973 with a 2-1 victory over Northern Ireland at Goodison Park. Only 29,865 spectators watched – the Goodison average for the season had been 34,540 – and most spent the afternoon calling for local heroes Howard Kendall and Kevin Keegan.

After England struggled to build on an early gift goal, Pat Jennings fumbling a Martin Chivers header into the Park End net, the Merseyside crowd booed, slow handclapped, chanted "Get back to Wembley!" "We want football!" and finally "Ireland, Ireland!"

There were cheers when referee Clive Thomas awarded a hugely contentious penalty to the visiting 'home' team and Dave Clements, just two months before he signed for Everton, clinically converted an equaliser from the penalty spot.

But eight minutes from time Northern Ireland defender Terry Neill slipped and Martin Chivers took ruthless advantage to score his second goal of the game and the winner.

The victory did little to improve Daily Mirror columnist Frank McGhee's mood.

Watching from the Goodison press box he wrote: "The crowd made it clear, by staying away in large numbers, that they didn't rate the match as attractive as their own parochial affairs. The attendance was thousands below the League average in this city.

"But for me it was the Irish attitude throughout most of the match that presented the convincing argument for abandoning the home international championship in its present form – perhaps even slitting its throat and quietly burying it."

A week later there was a less emotive but even more articulate argument for abandoning the tournament when a paltry crowd of 4,946 watched Northern Ireland beat Wales 1-0 at Goodison Park – Bryan Hamilton maintaining the future Evertonian link by crashing in a sweetly struck matchwinner at the Gwladys Street End, three years before he signed for the Toffees.

It would be another 22 years before international football returned to Goodison Park – but then the desire to see the Brazilians of

Rivaldo, Roberto Carlos, Ronaldo and co. proved very different to the days Northern Ireland crossed the Irish Sea to play their home games at Goodison Park.

DUNCAN MCKENZIE IS MAGIC!

SATURDAY, DECEMBER 18, 1976

EVERTONIANS WERE HOLDING OUT FOR A hero in the winter of 1976.

The initial promise of Billy Bingham's managerial reign had become dogged by inconsistency.

It quickly became evident that a spectacular 4-0 opening day victory at the previous season's runners up QPR was just an illusory false dawn.

And the manager's own future was increasingly becoming the subject of cruel speculation.

So the Everton manager decided to give Evertonians a little festive cheer. A fortnight before Christmas he made a double swoop in the transfer market – splashing out on silk and steel.

The steel came in the shape of renowned resolute midfield hard-man Bruce Rioch from Derby County. The silk was Supermac.

DUNCAN MCKENZIE IS MAGIC!

A £200,000 capture from Belgian side Anderlecht, Duncan McKenzie had already built a reputation as a footballing entertainer at Nottingham Forest, Leeds and on the continent.

His debut came on a frozen pitch at Coventry – and despite a 4-2 defeat, the watching BBC TV cameras captured enough flicks, feints and moments of magic to whet fans' appetites.

The Goodison Box Office reported a £3,000 boost in the sale of season tickets following the twin swoop.

And it wasn't just fans who were gripped by excited anticipation.

Renowned BBC sports reporter Bill Bothwell wrote: "Everton Manager Billy Bingham's double coup this week in bringing Duncan McKenzie and Bruce Rioch to Goodison is about the best thing that has happened to Everton in a very long time …. BBC colleague Bryon Butler asked me last Saturday whether success or entertainment was the greater crowd puller. I had to plump for entertainment and charisma as the crowd pulling qualities. And this is what McKenzie can provide.

"Although, to some ears it might sound like heresy to suggest that he is another Alex Young, I have seen this fellow pull out football skills that left you gasping not only at his ability but at his impudence in the face of top class opposition. Brian Clough, no mean judge of a player, regarded Mac as something special.

"English football, at this time of dull conformity and, in places, plastic efficiency needs entertainers; it needs players with the charisma that surrounded Alex Young. And I'll be surprised if McKenzie doesn't give them that. Generations of Evertonians have been brought up to regard Goodison as the school of science. In recent years that edifice has been in decay. McKenzie is a scientist while Rioch is the man to give that science an end product. Between them they can make a lot of sweet music at the turnstiles."

Ahead of McKenzie's home debut against Birmingham City on December 18, 1976, the Liverpool Echo's Charles Lambert expressed similar sentiments: "I confess I am really looking forward to the match at Goodison Park on Saturday for one reason, summed up in two words: Duncan McKenzie.

"We saw enough on Match of the Day on Saturday to know that the grins that appeared on the faces of Evertonians when the McKenzie transfer was finalised were not out of place.

"The man has flair; he is exciting to watch. It has become a truism to say that our game contains too many artisans and not enough artists. A glimpse of the McKenzie skills gives new meaning to the statement. The flick that set up the move leading to Everton's first goal was magic.

"That is the kind of thing I like to remember from football matches – the same kind of magic performed by Mr. Causio when he set up Italy's second goal against England in Rome.

"Saturday, of course, is the Saturday before Christmas, the day when many football fans desert the terraces to go shopping. I won't be joining them, pushing through the hordes in Church Street and fuming while old ladies nudge to the front of the queue at the cash-and-wrap. The Christmas shopping will just have to take care of itself. I'm going to the match."

Lambert's use of the word 'magic' was prescient.

Within 90 minutes the Gwladys Street had adopted a new anthem: "We all agree, Duncan McKenzie is magic!"

The new striker scored twice against Birmingham City – but it wasn't the end product which excited Evertonians so much, it was the artistry and the impudence he displayed which thrilled them.

The Liverpool Echo reported: "McKenzie started off in inspired mood, displaying a range of flicks, dummies and back-heels which had the fans almost beside themselves with delight. Later he demonstrated his ability to beat a man, again drawing gasps of admiration as he ambled forward almost at walking pace, then danced round his man as a defender imprudently jumped in."

Afterwards a relieved Billy Bingham said: "There was a little bit of magic there and it was the first time I've seen people standing up to applaud a player at Goodison. They certainly took to Duncan and it was a tremendous performance from him."

While skipper Mike Lyons added: "People have been saying that he (McKenzie) is reminiscent of Alex Young, and there was no greater hero for Everton fans than Alex.

"Maybe the supporters need someone to idolise, like the Liverpool fans have Kevin Keegan. We have got Bob Latchford, but he is not in the same mould as Keegan, and I think Duncan might fit into the part."

He did. He certainly did.

GORDON'S GREAT ENTERTAINERS

———×✕╱⌃╲✕×———

SATURDAY, NOVEMBER 26, 1977

THROUGHOUT THE 1977/78 SEASON, GORDON LEE'S Everton were the top flight's great entertainers.

They ended a once highly promising campaign in a disappointing third place, but still finished as the division's leading scorers with 76 goals, seven more than champions Nottingham Forest.

Bob Latchford, revelling in the service provided by new winger Dave Thomas, was enjoying his celebrated 30 goal season. Andy King and Martin Dobson were midfielders who loved to cause mayhem in and around opposition penalty areas while Mike Lyons was a centre-back who was equally as comfortable operating as a centre-forward.

But if Lee's Everton were the division's most attack-minded team, Gordon Milne's Coventry weren't far behind. Just one goal, in fact, by the season's end.

Playing an expressive 4-2-4 formation, they were from the school of thought that was happy to give up a chance to create one of their own.

While their 75-goal total was only one behind Everton's, the 62 goals they conceded ultimately cost them a place in Europe.

But when they came to Goodison Park in late November they were riding high in the table in third, just one place behind Everton.

What came next, in front of 43,309 agog Evertonians, was a joy to behold.

The Liverpool Echo's Charles Lambert was one of those excited observers and two days later he wrote: "Football is the greatest game in the world, and when teams play the way Everton and Coventry City played on Saturday it is easy to see why.

"Excitement flowed round the ground like an electric current throughout the afternoon, and for the Everton fans and those who were simply fans of football the day had everything they could wish for.

"A 6-0 victory against your closest challengers to second spot, a hat-trick from Bob Latchford, including one brilliant goal, some scintillating wing play by David Thomas, the match had everything.

"Everything, that is, apart from a small amount of justice for brave Coventry. They attacked throughout the game, playing 4-2-4 with two wingers, had Everton worried for a long spell in the first half, and never deserved to go down to a heavier defeat than those 5-1 hammerings Everton inflicted on Leicester and QPR.

"For the sake of football we can only hope that this result does not deter Coventry from continuing their attacking policy. It was wonderful to see them prepared to attack the home team, and on another day it could easily have been they who scored a hatful of goals."

But they didn't. The day was Everton's – and Bob Latchford's.

Fresh from his England debut against Italy just a fortnight earlier, Everton's adored number nine headed goals in the 42nd and 44th minutes, but it was the goal which completed his hat-trick in the last minute which was celebrated most riotously.

With Everton leading 5-0 – Martin Dobson, Andy King and Jim Pearson the other marksmen, Coventry winger Donato Nardiello was still trying to attack the Everton rearguard and feed his forwards.

But his ambitious pass was intercepted by Mike Pejic, one third of a celebrated Everton left flank trio, who dribbled away from trouble then prodded the ball to Dobson. The left midfielder shuttled the ball onto the left winger, and Dave Thomas did exactly what he did best, sprinting half the length of the field before arrowing over a cross of penetrating accuracy and simplicity.

Gerald Sinstadt, commentating for ITV's Sunday afternoon highlights show, described the moment vividly.

"Acres of space for him. Two men to cross to.

"Laaatchford!!! What a glorious goal!"

Goodison erupted as Latchford raced away to celebrate with his equally excited manager who had run out of the dug-out.

It was a day for everybody to get a little carried away. Sinstadt hollered: "That's the goal of a Championship side."

Nottingham Forest's extraordinary consistency meant that the title didn't materialise, but Evertonians were still treated to some sparkling football in that 1977/78 season.

THE DAY BOBBY
WALKED ON WATER

———————— ✕✕ ╱╲ ✕✕ ————————

SATURDAY, APRIL 29, 1978

EVERTONIANS HAD HAD PRECIOUS LITTLE SILVERWARE to celebrate during the frustrating decade of the 1970s – but Blues fans did have the feats of a buccaneering centre-forward in the club's very finest traditions to express their adulation for.

The veneration for big, bustling Bob Latchford verged on the religious – well the Gwladys Street did claim that he walked on water.

And on one spring afternoon in 1978 Bobby Latchford gave Evertonians an afternoon they would never forget.

It was April 29, the same date that the club's most celebrated centre-forward, Dixie Dean, wore number nine for the first time and scored in an FA Cup final at Wembley 45 years earlier. It was just six days shy of the 50th anniversary of the culmination of Dean's record-breaking 60 goal season.

In six successive seasons Latchford topped Everton's club goal-scoring charts, but it was in the 1977/78 season, when he topped the nation's scoring charts, that Latchford really fired the public imagination.

Concerned by the apparent demise of out and out goalscorers, the Daily Express newspaper offered a £10,000 prize to the first man to score 30 League goals in a single season.

The previous man to reach such a daunting total had been Manchester City's Francis Lee – seven years previously – who included a record 13 penalty kicks in his haul.

Latchford took just two in his 30-goal season – and only when the prize was within tantalising reach.

The forward had started the season slowly, just two goals in his first seven appearances after missing the opening day clash with Nottingham Forest through injury.

But then his partnership with wing wizard Dave Thomas clicked.

One precisely whipped in corner against Manchester City gave Latchford the opportunity to bullet a header into the roof of the Gwladys Street net. He added another three days later against West Brom, then four days later scored FOUR in a 5-1 rout of Queens Park Rangers, the second from another laser guided Thomas cross.

A hat-trick against Coventry, two more from Thomas crosses kept Latchford's tally ticking over, then over Easter Latchford pressed hard on the goalscoring pedal.

He scored on Good Friday, Easter Saturday and twice on Easter Monday – Everton winning all three matches against Newcastle, Leeds and Manchester United – then added another the following Saturday against Derby County.

His 27th came against Coventry – with four matches still remaining – and with the prize in sight Latchford claimed penalty talking duties from Trevor Ross and duly hammered one into the roof of the Ipswich net with three games to go.

But as the pressure – and the tension – tightened, Latchford drew blanks at Middlesbrough and West Brom.

That meant two were required in the final match of the season, at Goodison Park, against Chelsea.

Almost 40,000 excited Evertonians crammed into the stadium –

including the greatest centre-forward in the history of the club, Dixie himself, to see if Latchford could achieve the feat.

The only problem was that everybody else was getting on the scoresheet ahead of Bob!

Neil Robinson scored the first goal of his professional career, so did Billy Wright.

Latchford hadn't had a sniff.

There were only 18 minutes left when Everton won a corner at the Gwladys Street End, Dave Thomas swung it in – and the double act which had worked so effectively all season clicked again.

"I got on the end of it and I knew then the other would come," said Latchford later.

It did. Eventually.

Stuck tantalisingly on 29 goals another Thomas corner swung his way. But Mick Lyons nipped in to score instead.

"Goodison produced this roar-cum-groan and I told Mick to bugger off back into defence and stay there," Latchford later joked.

Lyons actually apologised for scoring and tried to convince referee Peter Willis to award a penalty for an imagined foul on him.

Willis didn't listen. Neither did Lyons, who was back in the penalty area five minutes later and this time made a meal of a challenge on him by the towering Micky Droy. This time Mr Willis did point to the penalty spot. Up stepped Latchford. His second-ever penalty.

"I struck it okay," he explained "not great, but it went past Peter Bonetti's right and the place went berserk.

"It was the 78th minute in 1978 and it was Everton's centenary year — formed in 1878.

"The stars were aligned and to top it all, the great man, Dixie Dean, was there, 50 years after his 60 goals."

On the final whistle the pitch was invaded and Latchford chaired off in celebration, a blue and white cap placed on his head. One over-enthusiastic supporter, perhaps with a passing interest in horticulture, grabbed a chunk of turf from the penalty spot.

Hundreds of fellow pitch invaders followed suit, so that Goodison's previously lush green surface started to resemble a golf fairway with patchy divots everywhere.

After much champagne, as he was leaving the Goodison reception area, Latchford bumped into the legendary Dean.

The legend of 60 league goals quipped: "Well done son. But don't forget. You're only half as good as me!"

KING OF
GOODISON

———————⋙⋀⋙———————

SATURDAY, OCTOBER 28, 1978

THE BRIGHT AND UNSEASONALLY WARM AUTUMN morning of October 28, 1978 was derby day on Merseyside – and Evertonians woke up to the knowledge they had not beaten Liverpool for seven long years.

Such was the class of Bob Paisley's multi-trophy winning side that any improvement on that statistic didn't look likely.

Reigning European champions, the Reds were on their way to their 11th league title, with a degree of dominance previously unparalleled in top flight history.

By the end of the campaign they would achieve a record points haul (68), score 85 goals at a ratio of more than two a game – and staggeringly concede just 16 goals.

They went into the Goodison derby with the remarkable record of played 11, won 10, drawn one, 35 goals scored and just four conceded!

But this was also a very good Everton team.

Everton were also unbeaten in 11 matches from the start of the season – a sequence they would extend to 19 – had made progress in the League and UEFA Cups – and had an unpredictable maverick at the heart of their midfield who took great delight in riling the Reds.

Two of the paltry 16 goals conceded by the Liverpool defence that season were scored by one man.

Andrew Edward King.

An effervescent, sparky midfielder with a voracious appetite for goals, Andy King finished the 1978/79 season as Everton's top league scorer – but none of the 12 goals he celebrated with infectious enthusiasm was more sweetly struck than the venomous volley dispatched into the Park End net that afternoon.

It became a much loved goal – and gave rise to an enduring joke.

Evertonians everywhere asked puzzled Red rivals afterwards: "Everyone knows where Queens Drive is, but where's King's drive?"

To which they would gleefully retort: "In the back of Clemence's net!"

In the seven years since David Johnson's 1971 matchwinner, Everton had only scored one league goal against the Reds – a Martin Dobson consolation in a 3-1 defeat at Anfield.

But King's matchwinner which ended that long winless drought earned him cult hero status amongst Evertonians.

After the match he explained: "Mickey Pejic played a long high ball that Martin Dobson nodded down. I remember as it fell to me I saw Graeme Souness showing his foot so I hit the shot first time with the outside of my boot.

"Graeme said afterwards that I mishit it. It was one of those that commentators call great goals but I call lucky goals.

"It could have gone anywhere. When this one ended up in the net I made a beeline for the bench and Micky Lyons because he was the all-time Evertonian. I knew how much he had wanted to play, and I knew what that goal would mean to him."

Big Mick – the bluest of bluebloods – was sadly missing – victim of seven stitches received in a knee injury the previous Saturday.

"There were stories even on the Friday that I was going to play," he recalled "but really I had no chance. You'll say anything because you're so keen to be there, but the truth was I could hardly walk. So I had to go on the bench with the other lads.

"It was certainly a game I'll never forget. When I sat down I was wearing a watch that meant a lot to me then – I'd bought it on a trip to Singapore – but at the end of the match it had gone. I never saw it again."

Mick was even denied an opportunity to make a couple of quid on the match.

Liverpool skipper Phil Thompson later revealed: "For several seasons Mick and I had always had a £5 bet on the outcome. So I'd become quite a rich man! But that year he didn't want to bet. Perhaps he was skint!

"More probably I think he may have felt it was becoming a little bit of a burden. And with the injury keeping him out of the game he most wanted to play in, maybe he felt it would change his luck.

"Anyway he lost the chance of getting some of his money back."

Mick didn't mind. He revelled in a derby victory replayed on that night's Match of the Day programme.

John Motson's commentary became iconic amongst Evertonians.

"It's going to fall for Andy King," he screamed in that trademark, high-pitched timbre. "Oh yes he's done it! Andy King has scored. Everton have taken the lead. A typical King goal. And Goodison Park goes absolutely mad. Would you believe it?"

At least Motty's words were transmitted.

BBC Look North presenter Richard Dukenfield tried to grab a post-match interview with the man of the moment, only to be manhandled off the pitch by an over eager policeman!

The footage was canned until it emerged several years later on the popular It'll Be Alright on the Night outtakes programme.

Richard explained: "I was working for 'Grandstand', the BBC Saturday afternoon sports programme and covered the North West teams. We were allocated 90 seconds for a match report.

"If there was an outside broadcast team there, we might want an interview after the game with a player or the manager. That was the case on that day because it was a Derby game.

"The obvious person to speak to that afternoon was Andy King because he scored the goal that gave Everton victory, something that they had been denied for seven years.

"I was situated on the side of the pitch near the players tunnel, so I caught hold of Andy as he was coming off which meant at that moment, we were standing on the pitch, just over the touchline.

"I started to ask a question when a Police Inspector, who later became quite famous for the incident, swept me off the pitch. He had received instructions that there was to be nobody on the pitch at the end of the game.

"That was the rule and he interpreted it literally – no players, no reporters, nobody. That wasn't really the intention. It was meant for fans or anybody hanging around, but I only got a few words out before being removed.

"The incident wasn't actually transmitted at the time, but after we were swept off the pitch, we stepped onto the cinder track where the interview was completed. The successful take was then transmitted.

"The footage of me and Andy being swept off the pitch was then distributed to one of the 'blooper' programmes and has been shown many times."

So, too, has that Andy King Exocet – a feat he repeated when Everton snatched a 1-1 draw at Anfield later in the season.

Andy became an enduring thorn in Liverpool's side, scoring again in a 2-2 draw at Anfield the following season – but that 1978 volley which scratched a seven year itch is the one for which he became most closely identified.

"And it's going to fall for Andy King..."

DIXIE'S FAREWELL

————⋗⋗⋌⋀⋋⋖⋖————

SATURDAY, MARCH 1, 1980

MARCH 1, 1980, WAS THE DAY the music died.

It was the date William Ralph Dean, AKA Dixie – the greatest goal-scorer in the history of English football – took his last breath on this earth.

And he drew that breath at Goodison Park, at a derby match, watching his beloved Everton play their fiercest rivals. Earlier in the day he had listened to a stirring eulogy delivered by Liverpool's greatest ever manager – a tribute which ultimately became his obituary.

His daughter Barbara, who drove her dad to his last match, says: "I think he stage managed the whole thing."

Maybe. Because everything about March 1, 1980 was unusual.

Everton were playing Liverpool in the 136th Merseyside derby and while Dixie had played in 17 of these tribal conflicts and had scored 19 times in them, he had never visited one as a spectator.

Not one – until that fateful Saturday afternoon.

But on March 1, 1980, Dixie agreed to attend a launch of that year's Everton and Liverpool club annuals at the now demolished Holiday Inn on Paradise Street, enjoy a lunch with his good friend Bill Shankly

187

– and then go on to the match. In preparation his daughter Barbara, who lived with and cared for her dad, had polished the one shoe he then wore, after having his leg amputated in 1976.

"I got him all spruced up, polished his one shoe and drove him to the hotel. But as we got him into his wheelchair I noticed he still had his slipper on!" she recalled.

"He said not to worry, but it had drops of tea and bits of biscuit on it and I always liked him to look his best. So I ran to the toilet and wiped it with some tissue. It was a leather slipper and he probably felt more comfortable in it.

"I was due to start work at Clatterbridge, where I was nursing, and as I left he shouted me, I turned around and he said 'Don't worry about me, I'm going to be alright.'

"Then he gave me a thumbs up.

"He didn't usually do that. I think he knew."

But that was only the start of the day's unusual events.

If Dixie knew, Bill Shankly, who passed away himself the following year, certainly didn't.

Yet he delivered the most eloquent and moving eulogy to his pal sat alongside him during that Holiday Inn lunch.

He got to his feet and in that resonant brogue declared: "We have in our midst today, ladies and gentlemen, a man who was the greatest at what he did. You can't say that about many people in history, whatever branch of life you're talking about. But you can say that about Dixie Dean.

"Oh yes. His record of goalscoring is the most amazing thing under the sun. Nobody will ever come near to equalling his fantastic feat of scoring 60 League goals in a season.

"I played against him a few times when I was with Preston. He was a big, cocky, confident man, arrogant in his approach to the game. That is the hallmark of a great player and Dixie was the greatest centre-forward there will ever be.

"Nobody who's ever been born could head a ball into the net like him. When he connected it frightened people. You couldn't stop him scoring. He belongs in the company of the supremely great... like Beethoven, Shakespeare and Rembrandt."

John Keith, the former Daily Express journalist who penned a Dixie Dean biography and who had invited him to that Moat House book launch, recalled: "As Shankly was spellbinding his audience, a tear fell down Dixie's cheek. It was a moving, cameo moment which, for me, remains frozen in time."

Dixie Dean, the footballing-warrior never booked nor sent-off and who once lost a testicle in a match without demur, shedding a tear?

It truly was a strange day.

Then there was Doctor Ian Irving, Everton's respected long-serving physician who retired in June 2017 after almost 40 years sterling service, who was on matchday duty for the first time at Goodison Park.

One of his first duties in a long and storied career with the Blues was to attend to the club's greatest ever player after he had taken ill in the Main Stand towards the end of the match.

Dr Irving recalled that he tended to the stricken star after he had been taken into the club's boardroom, but that nothing could be done.

And he was bitterly upset that that some members of the media had become aware of what had happened. He desperately wanted to protect the family from discovering the dreadful news second hand.

Dixie's beloved grand-daughter Melanie, Barbara's daughter who had lived with her granddad all of her life, was a 13-year-old watching the match from the Gwladys Street End with family friends.

She was aware that something had happened, because she could see her granddad being taken into the Main Stand before the match had finished, but didn't know what.

She was driven back to the friends' house in Claughton Village and while she was aware of a subdued atmosphere in the house – and the knowledge that something strange had happened because she was served her tea there – she was spared the fate of discovering the sad news over the airwaves.

Barbara was not so fortunate.

On duty at Clatterbridge Hospital, Everton's club chairman Bill Scott had immediately set off in his plush car to deliver the sad news in person. But as he arrived at the hospital the news was already being broadcast on the television.

"It was a terrible shock," recalled Barbara. "But Mr Scott couldn't have done more. He drove me to pick up Melanie, then he drove us home. And because my car was still at Clatterbridge he arranged for us to be taken back there on the Sunday to collect it.

"Then on Monday I had to go to the mortuary at Walton Hospital to identify my dad."

So William Ralph Dean, the footballer who illuminated Goodison Park so many times during his stellar playing career, saw his life's light extinguished there.

And he has remained there ever since.

Following his funeral service on Friday March 7, at St James' Church in Birkenhead, the church where he had been baptised and married, Barbara insisted on scattering his ashes along the halfway line at Goodison Park.

The very next day, in an uplifting epitaph, Everton won a famous FA Cup quarter-final there.

The derby match at which Dixie had died was a grim ugly affair, a game which saw Everton defender Geoff Nulty's career ended by a crude tackle.

But seven days later, against a wonderfully gifted and attractive Ipswich Town team which had won 4-0 at Goodison Park just a month earlier, Everton triumphed. They won with a goal from their then celebrated centre-forward Bob Latchford, a proud Dixie successor, and another man who had worn the number nine shirt for the Blues, Brian Kidd.

Several years later Liverpool songwriter Gerry Murphy penned the moving Ballad of Dixie Dean.

It's a stirring, evocative anthem and opens with the words: "On the banks of the River Mersey, it is morning in the street. There's a boy in a football jersey... playing music with his feet."

Dean created an orchestral symphony with those feet – and that anointed head – creating a goalscoring record which still stands 97years after it was set, and which will surely never be broken.

Dixie Dean scored 60 goals in a single league season, scored 383 goals in an incredible Everton career, scored 18 goals in 16 England appearances – and made supporters' spirits sing everywhere he played.

And if March 1st, 1980, was the day that music died, that night's Match of the Day, for the first time in the programme's history, also silenced its famous theme tune at the end of the show.

A black and white image of the great man filled the screen instead – accompanied by a powerful, poignant silence.

It really was the day the music died.

But Dixie's legacy lives on to this day.

"WE DID IT
FOR DIXIE"

SATURDAY, MARCH 8, 1980

IF A WEEK IS A LONG time in politics, in football a month can be an eternity.

As Gordon Lee's Everton underlined in the spring of 1980.

The Ipswich Town team managed by Bobby Robson in the 70s and 80s were both enterprising and effective.

And on the afternoon of February 9 they were both, when they shocked Goodison Park with a sparklingly inventive 4-0 rout, a one-sided stroll the margin of which could and should have been even greater.

Gordon Lee declared: "They were brilliant. We were disgracefully pathetic – a shambles."

The People's Norman Wynne advised his readers: "Get on Ipswich for the Cup! And grab the 6-1 odds quick – because they are sure to change before Saturday's fifth-round tie with Chester.

"Bobby Robson's men, who won the Cup two years ago, look good value for Wembley again after stretching their unbeaten run to a dozen games by outclassing Everton. The gulf between the teams was obvious."

With Dutch artists Arnold Muhren and Frans Thijssen weaving elaborate patterns in midfield, Terry Butcher, Kevin Beattie and Russell Osman part of an often impenetrable defence and Alan Brazil, Eric Gates and Paul Mariner a mesmerizingly mobile strike trio, Ipswich were a terrifically talented side. And in Cup competitions they proved particularly effective.

FA Cup winners in 1978, UEFA Cup winners three years later, they also twice finished runners up in the league.

Ipswich duly defeated Chester City in the fifth round, but Everton manager Lee's response to beating Second Division Wrexham at Goodison Park was unexpected.

"Now we want Ipswich at home in the quarter finals," he declared. "We showed the critics today that last week's 4-0 defeat was something of a fluke."

Astonished Evertonians thought Lee had lost the plot.

The 5-2 win over Wrexham was the only match his side won in the four which followed that Ipswich debacle.

But the Blues boss saw his wish granted – and just one month after exasperated Evertonians had rained cushions down on the Goodison pitch they witnessed one of the stadium's great Cup afternoons.

More than 45,000 Evertonians crammed into the stadium bouncing with eager anticipation.

And they saw their under-pressure manager pull off a tactical masterstroke.

George Wood was back in goal for Martin Hodge. Brian Kidd replaced Eamonn O'Keefe up front, Andy King was in for Asa Hartford – but the biggest switch of all was a tactical switch by Lee.

Eric Gates' ability to drop deep and play as a number 10 was ahead of its time in the days of rigid 4-3-3 systems, and the towering centre-backs teams usually employed were torn between holding their lines or breaking ranks to combat the little striker.

Lee innovatively lined up with a three-man defence and detailed his right-back, John Gidman, to track Gates' marauding runs.

MIGHTY BLUES TURN TABLES ON IPSWICH trumpeted that night's Football Echo.

And Lee crowed: "We out thought them tactically."

The People reported: "Lee's master stroke was a defence of three, with a man-to-man marking system that left Gidman loose in midfield.

"And it worked from the start. Gidman, a darting hero, popped up in the outside-left position to throw the Ipswich defence completely out of gear. His long centre was measured perfectly to clear the giant Butcher and plop invitingly on to Latchford's head."

The centre-forward guided his header precisely beyond Paul Cooper's despairing dive – and then deep into the second half Brian Kidd crashed a wickedly swerving free-kick past another helpless Cooper plunge.

Goodison celebrated wildly.

Gary Megson spurned an outstanding chance to make it 3-0 before Kevin Beattie leaped prodigiously to head what turned out to be a consolation.

Monday's Echo triumphantly reported: "Bobby Robson's talented Ipswich team found their feet swept from under them by a resurgent Everton display at Goodison.

"Nothing in logic suggested that Everton had the capability to beat an Ipswich side which was bidding for a club record of 17 matches without defeat. But football, and most of all Cup football, has little time for logic, and so the unbelievable unfolded before our very eyes.

"Everton, so dull and unresponsive in so many games this season – notably in that 4-0 home pasting by Ipswich in the league last month – found the speed, purpose, ambition and character to clinch their 2-1 victory on merit."

The Echo described Lee as a gambler who had hit the jackpot.

"With their midfield resources stretched to the limit Everton played a gambler's card and struck this jackpot," wrote Charles Lambert.

"Manager Gordon Lee decided to push Gidman into midfield

and the move was an outstanding success. Snuffing out the Ipswich dangermen at one end and moving forward to create openings at the other.

"He started as an orthodox right-side midfielder, then had a spell shadowing Eric Gates, and ended up plugging the inevitable gaps that cropped up in his usual right-back position as Everton protected the two-goal lead won thanks to Brian Kidd's strike for goal number two."

There was also an emotional subplot to Everton's victory.

Just one week earlier Goodison had seen the final breath drawn of the club's most celebrated star – the legendary Dixie Dean.

Skipper Mick Lyons, the bluest of blue bloods, said: "The lads wanted to do it so much for the fans and the boss. And in a way we wanted to do it for Dixie Dean too. The minute's silence before the start helped to lift us."

It did that inspired afternoon, but sadly that was as good as it got for Gordon Lee.

Having avoided Arsenal and Liverpool in the semi-final draw, Everton landing second division West Ham United, Lee saw quarter-final hero Kidd sent off in a Villa Park semi when they were leading 1-0, his side concede an equaliser and then cruelly lose an Elland Road replay in the last minute of extra-time.

But that quarter-final triumph memorably exorcised some Suffolk demons.

A ROYLE SALUTE

———— ⨯⨉⁄⁄⌃⁄⨉⨯ ————

SATURDAY, APRIL 11, 1981

ON APRIL 11, 1981, JOE ROYLE scored the 152nd and final league goal of his storied playing career, at the same stadium he had fired his first 14 years earlier.

The Gwladys Street saluted and celebrated the strike, just as they had the first, but this time there was a significant difference.

Royle was wearing the yellow of Norwich City not Royal Blue.

The crowd reaction was an indication of the love the Goodison faithful had for a footballer who had made 276 appearances for his beloved Blues, celebrated 119 goals and been top scorer in a famous title winning season.

Royle would have even more memorable afternoons to cherish as an Everton manager in the seasons to come, but in 1981 Evertonians were looking back, not forward.

The following day's People newspaper reported: "The sight of Joe Royle bearing down on goal was enough to stir the nostalgia in any Goodison fan.

"The fact that only 'keeper Jim McDonagh stood between him and an Everton disaster did not to matter.

"Royle, still part of modern-day Everton folklore despite his departure from Goodison seven years ago, calmly accepted the chance to stroke in Norwich's first goal.

"Big Joe hugely enjoyed it as the crowd warmed to him. They were even on his side when he had a little run in with a linesman minutes later."

Despite having worn the Sky Blue of Manchester City, the red of Bristol City and then the Canary Yellow of Norwich since being sold on Christmas Eve in 1974, Royle remained one of Everton's most favourite sons.

In 1981 Blues fans also had little to cheer.

The visit of soon to be relegated Norwich against their own relegation threatened team attracted just 16,254 fans, the lowest League crowd at Goodison for 20 years.

But they genuinely applauded Royle guiding the ball past McDonagh after Billy Wright had misjudged Greg Downs' punt downfield.

Royle had even more glorious afternoons to come as an Everton manager, but his goal helped seal the fate of the then Everton boss, Gordon Lee.

A statement issued by Everton chairman Philip Carter to the press shortly after the game said the position of the manager and coaching staff were under review.

A month later Lee was gone.

But Royle still had many more chapters to add to his Goodison story.

HOWARD'S
WAY BACK

THE 1981/82 SEASON WAS A HISTORIC one in English football.

For the first time in 93 years of league football clubs were playing for three points for a victory, not two.

It was the latest kick-off to a campaign – August 29 – since the very first post-war season in 1946.

And at Goodison Park Everton fans were welcoming the return of a conquering hero. Howard Kendall had formed one third of the immortalised title-winning midfield trinity in 1969/70.

Still only 35, he was back at Goodison Park, this time as manager – and he was unveiled against the club Everton had sold him to seven years earlier, Birmingham City.

Evertonian excitement was palpable.

Just 15,352 had listlessly watched the final home match of the Gordon Lee era, a 1-0 defeat by Stoke City.

More than double that number, 33,045, eagerly flocked to see the return of a player they had idolised.

Kendall strode out onto the Goodison pitch pre-match to take the acclaim of those supporters – then settled down into a seat in the front row of the Directors' Box, alongside former chairman and long term benefactor Sir John Moores.

It was a new look Everton. Kendall had famously made seven new signings in the summer – all featured on the cover of the new-look gatefold sleeve matchday programme. Six were included in the 12 selected for duty, the only absentee being the man who would go on to be the most inspired purchase of them all, the peerless Neville Southall.

But the signing who captured the imagination of the supporters that August afternoon was an instantly identifiable striker.

The Daily Post's Nick Hilton reported: "The Gwladys Street choir has already found new favourite in Alan Biley, a character of flamboyant looks with a Rod Stewart hairstyle and nickname of 'Spike'.

"More endearing to them still is Biley's impressive ability in tight situations. He looked most dangerous when time and space were at a premium, got up well in the air for a shortish player, rather like Kevin Keegan, and most strikingly showed a cunning range to his delivery of passes and crosses into the penalty-area.

"Biley's 88th-minute goal cutely lofted over advancing keeper Wealands after Asa Hartford's through pass had exposed the offside trap put the flourish on Everton's afternoon."

It had been an eventful afternoon's football. Tony Van Mierlo punctured the early euphoria by heading a third minute opener.

One of Kendall's new boys, midfielder Alan Ainscow, quickly levelled, then after 33 minutes Everton had the opportunity to take the lead from the penalty spot.

The new manager had instructed Alan Biley to take spot-kicks, the usually reliable Trevor Ross was also on the pitch, but something had been lost in communication and Asa Hartford stepped up – twice.

His first effort was saved by Wealands, diving to his left, then after referee George Courtney ordered a retake Hartford aimed for the same corner, Wealands dived the same way again and this time made a save which counted.

Evertonians had to wait until three minutes after the half-time break before their new look side finally edged ahead, Peter Eastoe diving bravely to head into the Gwladys Street goal.

And it was two minutes from time when Biley ended the afternoon with an extravagant flourish, lifting the ball over the advancing Wealands.

The Post's Nick Hilton produced a report which was of its time, but also captured perfectly the excitement – and the guarded optimism of the Blues fans.

"The wives of Evertonians hardly got a word in during their Saturday night out," he wrote. "It was men's talk in the pubs and clubs of Howard Kendall the new team and the new hope at Goodison. Typically the conversations were guarded. Eleven seasons of deepening disappointment and frustration have hardened the true blue into a doubter of fairy-tales. He cuts through his own euphoria before a neutral can do it for him.

"The fans' welcome for the new manager was thunderous and emotional and there were enough of the right ingredients in the 90 minutes that followed to earn an even greater accolade at the finish.

"But for all the entertainment and encouragement this victory over Birmingham provided it was only first episode of a saga yet to unfold and neither Everton nor the fans judge it as anything other than that."

Hilton was right to be guarded.

There would be ups and downs, false dawns and performances of rich promise in the three years which followed – before Kendall supervised the most successful period in the club's long history.

It all started that August afternoon – when coincidentally two managers who brought so much success to Merseyside were spotted sitting side by side in the Directors' Box, once rivals now friends, the legendary Bill Shankly and Harry Catterick.

In August 1981 Catterick was still Everton's most successful ever manager.

That was all about to change...

GOODISON HAILS A NEW SHARP-SHOOTER

———✕✕╱╱⌃╲✕✕———

SATURDAY, JANUARY 30, 1982

"I'LL PROBABLY NEVER SCORE A GOAL like that again in my career," said a young Graeme Sharp – two years and nine months before he did volley an even more memorable strike.

But the wonder goal Sharp exploded past Tottenham goalkeeper Ray Clemence on January 30, 1982 – captured by the ITV cameras – became the talking point of the football world.

Sharp was only 21 – the goal he scored against Spurs was only his fourth in an Everton shirt – but it proclaimed to the world that the Blues had a very special young talent emerging in a fast developing young team. Few anticipated anything remotely hinting at a goal when Mick Lyons hoisted a hopeful punt towards the Spurs' penalty area, where Adrian Heath gave chase.

The little forward reached the ball first, headed it up into the air and Sharp explained what happened next.

"I wasn't going to hit it," he said. "But I saw the ball drop and thought I'll take a chance. I hit it and next thing I saw was it nestling in the back of the net! I'll probably never score a goal like that again in my career."

It was a prosaic description of a spectacular goal. And Graeme certainly would score a goal as good again.

But the impact of that wonder-strike was seismic.

The ITV commentator declared: "Oh my goodness! You won't see a better one than that! From a young man who really is finding that First Division football is to his liking now after a couple of years in the reserves.

"Heath gave chase, it was a hopeful header but look what Sharp made of it!"

It was a venomous, angled volley which flew past Clemence like a missile.

Manager Howard Kendall purred afterwards: "Sharp is looking a natural. He's quick and brave, good in the air, is starting to learn and is picking up the right positions. A lot of people in the game are starting to talk about Graeme Sharp now. Wherever I go they say 'I like your number nine.' I say to them 'Yes, I do as well'! "

Spurs 'keeper Ray Clemence, making his first return to Merseyside since leaving Liverpool in the summer, said: "It was a fantastic goal. It reminded me of Terry McDermott's goal at Spurs in the Cup that became the Goal of the Season.

"As soon as he hit it I knew it was in. There was no way I could get anywhere near it."

The Liverpool Echo even dedicated an entire article to the goal, to supplement Ian Hargraves' match report.

Ann Cummings wrote: "I watched Graeme Sharpe's goal again on television yesterday after the roast beef and Yorkshire pudding and enjoyed a really tasty dessert.

"Television, though, can't capture the magic moment experienced by actually being there and which left even the Press box corps open-mouthed with wonderment."

Everton were eventually pegged back by a Ricky Villa equaliser but Sharp's goal was a hint at the promise an emerging Everton side was starting to show, promise which would be richly fulfilled two-and-a-half years later.

Kendall added after that match: "It was a difficult game for some of our lads to have played in and I think they will have grown up out there."

None more so than a young centre-forward who dramatically and spectacularly came of age.

MERCER'S MASTERCLASS

SATURDAY, OCTOBER 27, 1984

JOE MERCER PLAYED IN AN EVERTON team which won a league title featuring legends like Tommy Lawton, Ted Sagar and T.G. Jones.

He managed a Manchester City team which between 1968 and 1970 won all three domestic trophies plus the European Cup Winners' Cup.

And for seven matches he took charge of the England national team, which won the Home International Championship and lost just one of the games he oversaw.

But on one memorable autumn afternoon in 1984 he watched an Everton team produce a performance better than any he had ever seen in his life. Genial Joe was then 70. His experience of watching truly great Everton teams was unmatched.

Yet after Howard Kendall's exciting young team had demolished title pretenders Manchester United 5-0, Mercer told the assembled media: "That was the best performance by any Everton side I remember.

"Everything about them was right from the goalkeeper right through the team. It was a fabulous display."

It alerted excited Evertonians that they were on the brink of witnessing something very, very special. There had been hints through-out that autumn that a magnificent football team was emerging at Goodison Park. But it needed a definitive marker.

The Blues kicked off the 1984/85 campaign with a confidence boosting victory over reigning champions Liverpool at Wembley in the Charity Shield.

But that was followed up by a 4-1 home defeat by Tottenham and a 2-1 defeat at West Bromwich Albion.

Howard Kendall's young team recovered to scored three goals and five goals respectively in victories at Newcastle and Watford – but each time had to come from behind, conceding twice on Tyneside and four times at Vicarage Road.

If Evertonians weren't quite sure what to make of their exciting but unpredictable team they were handed a convincing argument at Anfield on October 20, when Graeme Sharp's goal for the ages secured a first win at the home of their fiercest rivals for 14 years.

Four days later the same team won 1-0 in Bratislava in the European Cup Winners' Cup. Then Manchester United came to Goodison...

What transpired has since passed into Goodison folklore.

"The scene was set in the opening seconds when United kicked off but immediately lost possession as Sharp and Reid homed in like guided missiles," wrote the Echo's Ian Hargraves – memorably articu-lating the attitude of a team which did gegenpressing decades before German coaches made it hip and fashionable.

Added to a voracious appetite for regaining possession, this Everton team could pass the ball swiftly and precisely – and they had goal-scorers sprinkled throughout their XI.

Midfielder Kevin Sheedy scored the first two goals, striker Adrian Heath added the third, while right-back Gary Stevens and centre-for-ward Graeme Sharp completed a one-sided rout.

Ron Atkinson's talented team had started the day third in the First Division table. Everton lay one place lower.

They were overhauled by the Blues that afternoon and never caught again by their Red rivals.

"Manchester United arrived at Goodison as championship favourites, fairly stuffed with internationals, and having lost only one match previously," reported Hargraves. "They were totally outclassed by opponents whose all-round speed and inventiveness made a mockery of United's title pretensions."

The Daily Post's Nick Hilton agreed.

"United were made to look a poor side in the eyes of 40,000 assembled at Goodison," he wrote. "They are not.

"It would be folly to underestimate the strength of their challenge for the championship this winter, just as it would be to underestimate Everton's.

"The bookmakers are now certain to cut the odds on Everton, galled as they may be at the prospect of the title remaining on Merseyside because this result has finally jolted the rest of the country into taking Everton seriously.

"Everton's football was never less than good and at times exhilarating. One passing movement out of defence brought forth an instinctive roar of 'Ole!' from the crowd as each pass was played. This was the stuff from which golden visions were fashioned."

Golden visions – and a glorious, famous title winning team which had announced its arrival at Goodison Park in spectacular style.

THE CATT'S
FAREWELL

------- ⋙⋰⋏⋱⋙ -------

SATURDAY, MARCH 9, 1985

AN FA CUP QUARTER-FINAL WITH IPSWICH Town contained most of the ingredients of a typically pulsating tie.

There was drama, a dismissal and a stirring comeback.

It contained an iconic Everton goal.

But ultimately the 1985 clash is perhaps remembered most poignantly for its aftermath.

Just minutes after Derek Mountfield's late equaliser had scrambled a replay for Everton, keeping hopes of an unprecedented treble alive, legendary manager Harry Catterick collapsed and died from a heart attack in his Goodison seat. Catterick was only 65.

The boss who created two title-winning teams and ended a 33-year wait without an FA Cup, was taken ill in his seat in the Directors' Box at the end of a dramatic match and, despite efforts to revive him, passed away at the scene of some his greatest triumphs.

Catterick's passing was a sombre legacy of a thrilling match.

Everton had the ball in the Ipswich net three times in the opening five minutes – but only one counted.

Andy Gray had a header disallowed for pushing, then Kevin Sheedy curled a trademark free-kick past Paul Cooper – but was told that referee Alan Robinson hadn't blown his whistle. That simply created a platform for one of Goodison's most celebrated strikes.

Having curled his first attempt into the top left-hand corner of Cooper's goal, Sheedy cheekily and brazenly curled the ball into the opposite corner!

Sheedy scored 97 goals in his Everton career, but explained: "For most Evertonians of that era, when I meet them, it's the one they always talk to me about."

Sheedy also detailed his thought processes as soon as the free-kick was awarded.

"I used to practice all the time," he said. "Because when you've got 40,000 Evertonians chanting your name at a free-kick you'd better be able to deliver!

"I used to try and get on the ball early to gain an advantage, Ipswich's wall wasn't put together correctly, so I took it quickly and bent it into Paul Cooper's left hand corner. The referee disallowed it.

"So I put the ball down and Paul Cooper had sort of edged over to the side where I'd just put the ball into the net and left a nice gap on the other side. So I managed to put the ball over to the other side."

A very matter of fact description of an extraordinary piece of expertise.

That was after five minutes but the tales of the unexpected had only just begun.

After 15 minutes Kevin Wilson tried a speculative shot from distance. The ball bounced once in front of the soon to be announced Footballer of the Year Neville Southall, squirmed under his body and crept over the goalline for an equaliser.

"Neville's the kind of bloke you would let wash and dry your best china blindfolded," the Daily Post's Roy Hayes memorably reported "but 14 minutes into Saturday's clash he almost dropped a cup."

When Romeo Zondervan volleyed an unstoppably spectacular

second goal after half-an-hour an upset looked on the cards – but this Everton team was renowned as much for its resilience and never-say-die spirit as it was its quality – and the Blues laid siege to Cooper's goal.

Andy Gray headed the clearest opening over the bar, but just when Ipswich looked to have finally weathered the storm, Steve McCall was red-carded for the latest in a long line of crunching assaults on Everton players – a brutal high and late lunge at Trevor Steven this time.

The numerical advantage also gave Everton a psychological boost and just four minutes from the end left-back Pat Van Den Hauwe, fresh from having a shot kicked off the line, popped up in the inside right position to volley a cross for centre-back Derek Mountfield to stab home his ninth goal of the season.

It earned Everton a replay – but any celebrations were swiftly muted when the news filtered through about the passing of a genuine Everton legend.

SUN-SHINE
SUPERMEN

———⋈⁄⌃⋉———

SATURDAY, APRIL 6, 1985

IT'S EVERY DOCUMENTARY-MAKER'S GO-TO GAME.

Whenever a package is needed about the 1984/85 season, a routine home win against a soon to be relegated side always makes the cut. But then the 4-1 victory over Sunderland in early April wasn't just routine.

Everton faced the relegation threatened Wearsiders just three days after a vital victory at White Hart Lane had given them a decisive edge in the title race. The Blues desperately didn't want to toss away that hard-earned advantage, just days before they faced semi-finals in two cup competitions.

And Sunderland actually scored first, in the opening minute.

Squeaky bum time? Not a bit of it. Howard Kendall's young team were as belligerent as they were brilliant and they simply rolled up their sleeves and set about dismantling Sunderland.

They did so in swashbuckling style.

There were two gloriously headed goals from Andy Gray, one into each corner of the Gwladys Street goal.

Reid crossed from the right at the end of a flowing and penetrating move and Gray bulleted a dive-header into the bottom right hand corner, then four minutes later Steven crossed from the left and the dashing daredevil Gray flashed another improbable header into the top left hand corner.

The Gwladys Street, bathed in early spring sunshine, was in raptures.

Then the whole stadium paid homage to one of the most celebrated passes in Everton history.

Paul Bracewell was on the halfway line on the Bullens Road side of the ground when the ball was headed towards him. Without seeming to look up even he volleyed a 50 yard pass across to Trevor Steven hugging the Goodison Road touchline. Steven turned on the afterburners to leave Nick Pickering in his wake and flashed another glorious effort into the roof of the Park End net.

From 1-0 down to 3-1 up with three of the most thrilling strikes Goodison had witnessed from one of its greatest ever teams.

Graeme Sharp was almost apologetic when he bundled Kevin Sheedy's cross past goalkeeper Chris Turner midway through the second half to complete the 4-1 rout. It was another majestic masterclass from a magnificent football team.

"For me, that was their finest performance that season," recalled the journalist Ian Ross, who witnessed most of those memorable successes.

"The quality of the football was something else and the stadium was just like you could see a glow coming off the punters," he added. "At it's best, that's what football is, mesmerising entertainment."

It was the fourth in another sequence of 10 straight league wins, just a few months after the same side had won 10 in a row in all competitions.

"They look more and more like champions," declared BBC commentator John Motson as he ended his commentary for that evening's Match of the Day show.

He would soon be proved right.

Rarely had Everton's motto Nil Satis Nisi Optimum – Nothing But The Best Is Good Enough – been observed so closely.

THE
GREATEST NIGHT

————⋙╱╱⌃╲⋘————

WEDNESDAY, APRIL 24, 1985

NEVILLE SOUTHALL IS EVERTON'S MOST decorated footballer.

Two league titles, two FA Cups – won 11 years apart – a European Cup Winners' Cup, The Football Writers' Footballer of the Year, more Everton appearances than any other man in history and a record 92 caps for his beloved Wales.

Yet Big Nev insists he would gladly have handed over everything he ever achieved in football for one single night.

It is regarded as Goodison's greatest ever night by every single one of the 49,476 fans who were lucky enough to be there and every player blessed to have been involved.

It is the semi-final second leg of the 1985 European Cup Winners' Cup, against two of the most in form teams in Europe.

Everton were soon to be crowned champions of England, Bayern Munich were on the brink of becoming Bundesliga champions.

Both teams reached their respective national cup finals, and Bayern boasted players of the calibre of Lothar Matthaus, a German legend, another World Cup winner in Klaus Augenthaler, a World

Cup finalist in Dieter Hoeness and the exciting Soren Lerby and Ludwig Kogl.

Southall said: "I would swap everything I ever achieved in football for that one night. Everything. Because that just said to me 'this is what Everton is about. This is what the city is about."

It truly was an electrifying evening.

Graeme Sharp said: "Talking to people who were here and had witnessed big games in Europe before, not necessarily at Everton, they thought that was the best atmosphere, the best they had ever witnessed."

While Andy Gray added: "If you talk to any Evertonian who was there that night, who actually got in that ground that night, if you told them they could take one game to the grave with them, if there were 55,000 in there I'm guessing 50,000 would choose this game.

"I'd be one."

Even impartial observers were enraptured by that incredible evening at Goodison Park.

Ian Ross was a journalist working for the Liverpool Daily Post in 1985 and soon to switch to The Times.

He recalled: "It was one of those nights where you didn't want to go home. It was the most fantastic night of sporting entertainment I had ever seen. I don't think I will ever see another sporting event to match that no matter what it would be. I've covered World Cups and European Championships but I've never witnessed anything to match that. I doubt I ever will. It was pure theatre at its best.

"I think the crowd that night turned the tide in Everton's favour because there was such a will; the fans were so noisy and the players were so desperate to do it for them. If there hadn't been that passion from the crowd, maybe they wouldn't have got through."

What happened that night has passed into Goodison folklore.

The noise and pandemonium and raucous cheering was silenced – briefly – when Ludwig Kogl sprang Everton's offside trap, raced through on goal, was denied by Southall but then saw the ball spin loose to Dieter Hoeness who prodded the visitors into the lead.

These were the days of the away goal rule in European football, meaning Everton needed to score twice to reach the club's first European final, against a German team who had beaten AS Roma, the previous year's European Cup finalists, home and away in the quarter-finals.

Howard Kendall's half-time teamtalk was memorably simple – and ended with the instruction: "Get the ball into the box to Sharpy and Andy and the Gwladys Street will suck the ball into the net."

The words were as prophetic as they were inspiring.

Graeme Sharp glanced in the first from a long Gary Stevens throw-in.

Andy Gray repeated the feat in the 75th minute, just when Bayern were starting to harbour thoughts of holding on to a draw.

Then four minutes from the end Trevor Steven added a delicious denouement to Goodison's greatest ever night.

Kevin Sheedy picked up possession from a Paul Bracewell interception, then probed and prodded at the Bayern defence, refusing to give up possession until the moment was right.

When Andy Gray made a cavalier run it was, and Sheedy threaded a perfect pass into the dashing Scot's path. Gray, in turn, swept the ball on sweetly to Steven and the magnificent midfielder clipped the ball imperiously over the advancing Pfaff to spark delirious scenes of unbridled joy.

Goodison's greatest ever night?

If it wasn't it was certainly in the top one.

TITLE-CLINCHING
LOCKOUT

———————————✕✕╱╱⌃╲╲✕✕———————————

MONDAY, MAY 6, 1985

EVERTON'S AVERAGE LEAGUE GATE throughout the sparkling, splendid, spectacular 1984/85 season was 31,984.

A few hundred more had watched a home victory over Norwich on April 27, a few hundred less had turned up for a midweek stroll over West Bromwich Albion a week-and-a half earlier.

But every single Evertonian wanted to be inside Goodison Park on May 6, 1985 – a Bank Holiday Monday – to see Everton crowned as champions for the first time in 15 years.

The official attendance was 50,514 – with the gates locked almost three hours before kick-off. Goodison was bouncing.

Football attendances in the 1980s, prior to the advent of the Premier League, suffered through a combination of poor stadia, outdated facilities and the blight of football hooliganism.

In the previous season, 1983/84, only one team enjoyed an average gate of more than 40,000 – Manchester United with 42,521. Only one other team even topped the 30,000 average gate mark, Liverpool with 32,022.

It was an era of dwindling gates, which makes that Bank Holiday crowd – and the subsequent 51,045 who watched the Goodison derby match – all the more remarkable.

Mind you they were watching a once in a generation football team.

The 1984/85 season was a campaign when so many factors fell gloriously into place at just the right time – to create the most dominant, dazzling and destructive Everton side many of their supporters had ever seen.

Neville Southall was at the peak of his powers as a world class goalkeeper.

Andy Gray was an infectious, charismatic catalyst whose force of personality was so important in allowing talented but hitherto retiring players like Trevor Steven and Graeme Sharp to grow their personalities and express themselves. And he was one hell of a centreforward, too.

But at the start of that sensational season he couldn't even get into Howard Kendall's starting line up because of the form of Adrian Heath, a whirling dervish of a forward who was enjoying the most sparkling spell of his career – 13 goals in 26 appearances – before Brian Marwood's reckless challenge cruelly ended his season on December 1 – and pitched the original Bruise Brothers together.

Gray and Sharp were just as effective as Heath and Sharp or Gray had been. Even serious injury worked in Everton's favour that campaign.

Steven, Reid, Bracewell and Sheedy formed the best balanced midfield since Ball-Harvey-Kendall were weaving mesmerising patterns around the Goodison playing surface.

Kevin Ratcliffe and Derek Mountfield were a defensive partnership which had pace, power and authority, Gary Stevens was the very epitomy of a modern raiding full-back, while Pat van den Hauwe oozed steely ruthlessness.

Despite the quality of those players individually, as a team they were even greater than the sum of their parts.

They were swashbuckling, stylish, fiercely competitive and enormously entertaining.

And there was little doubt that they were going to be crowned champions on that Bank Holiday Monday afternoon.

Derek Mountfield crashed a 24th minute volley off the Park End crossbar, against the back of QPR keeper Peter Hucker to open the scoring.

Gary Bannister tried to poop the party with a header which crashed off the inside of the post early in the second half, but it was a rare foray into Everton territory.

Everton dominated, as they had so many matches that season, and eight minutes from time the title party started in earnest when Pat van den Hauwe crossed accurately into the Street End penalty area for his second assist of the afternoon – and Graeme Sharp rose to loop a header past Hucker and confirm the coronation.

The celebrations were long and hard … for most.

Captain Kevin Ratcliffe knew exactly what he was doing two hours after celebrating Everton's first league title for 15 years in front of 50,000 fans.

"I went home and cut the grass," he explained. "I honestly don't know why. It was a nice day and it needed cutting!"

And besides, Everton had another match barely 48 hours later, the visit of West Ham. Of course they won that, too.

THE GLASS
COLLECTORS

———⟡⟋⟍⟡———

SATURDAY, MAY 9, 1987

WHEN EVERTON WON THEIR FIRST LEAGUE title for 15 years in 1985, skipper Kevin Ratcliffe didn't have a trophy to hoist aloft.

The Football League preferred not to have the trophy present at a stadium until success was mathematically confirmed, so Rats had to wait a few days later – when Everton had already been confirmed as champions – to receive the golden Canon League trophy.

Two years later, however, when Everton were crowned champions again, he made up for it.

After beating Luton Town at Goodison Park, five days after clinching the title at Norwich, Everton were presented with TWO trophies to show to their fans.

One was the traditional old League Championship trophy, created in 1891 and the very first winners of which were Everton. The other was a glass hexagonal memento created by the new Football League sponsors Today (a daily newspaper published between 1986 and 1995).

One trophy proved more popular than the other!

After a feisty 3-1 win skipper Ratcliffe led out the victory parade from the players' tunnel to a small trestle table erected in the centre circle.

England boss Bobby Robson handed over the brand new Today trophy to the Everton skipper, whose reaction was telling. He turned and passed the glasswork straight to a non-plussed Graeme Sharp, then headed to the near century-old silver league championship trophy, handed to him by Everton chairman and President of the Football League Philip Carter – and immediately hoisted the silverware aloft to rousing roars.

Each player then took it in turns to raise the old trophy aloft as it was passed down the line, while Gary Stevens was left holding the unwanted baby.

The odd award did make it onto the lap of honour, held aloft by Trevor Steven down the Bullens Road, but the battery of photographers only wanted images of players holding the more recognisable trophy during the celebrations.

Luton Town's players had long since slunk back into the Goodison dressing rooms after an unsuccessful attempt to gatecrash the title party.

Everton and Luton had become unlikely enemies in the 1980s, sparked by two feisty FA Cup ties in 1985 and 1986 – a semi-final and a quarter-final each eventually edged by Everton after the Hatters had led in each tie.

The visitors were desperate to spoil Everton's celebrations – by fair means or foul.

Mark Stein gave the visitors a fourth minute lead, then they started to rack up yellow cards.

Mike Newell was booked. So was Peter Nicholas. However this Everton side were far from shrinking violets and Luton goalkeeper Les Sealey then needed treatment for a full five minutes following a collision with Graeme Sharp. Fears for the goalkeeper's safety grew as a doctor was called for but he was finally able to continue after treatment.

Sealey might have wished he'd been substituted.

Mounting Everton pressure after half-time finally resulted in referee George Tyson pointing to the penalty spot after a Peter Reid shot had struck the crossbar and defender Rob Johnson handled in the resulting melee.

Sealey led vehement Luton protests and when it became clear that Mr Tyson was not for changing, booted the ball petulantly into the stand in disgust. He joined the players receiving yellow cards.

Trevor Steven then added insult to injury by sending Sealey the wrong way from the penalty spot.

Things went from bad to worse for the mad Hatters three minutes later when centre-half Stacey North bundled Steven to the ground allowing that season's top scorer to repeat his inch-perfect penalty performance.

Peter Nicholas – who played throughout like someone who had an urgent appointment to fulfil before the end of the game – finally got his wish for an early departure after 57 minutes. Having been booked for elbowing Reid he was sent off for a ridiculous lunge on the Blues midfielder.

Everton's day of delight was complete on the hour when Graeme Sharp diverted Gary Stevens' shot past Sealey.

It was a performance which summed up the secret of Everton's success that season. Despite the fact the title was already safe, they still displayed untold reserves of determination and a will to win that proved just too much for Luton.

And they had two trophies to polish and place in the Goodison trophy cabinet.

A DEBUT TO REMEMBER

———— ✕✕⁄\‿✕✕ ————

SATURDAY, AUGUST 27, 1988

IN THE FIRST 96 YEARS OF football at Goodison Park, only two Everton players had marked their debut with a hat-trick. A scarcely remembered striker called Frank Oliver did it against Notts County in October 1905 – then curiously only played three more league matches for the Blues.

Almost sixty years later, in 1964, Fred Pickering celebrated his British record-breaking transfer from Blackburn to Everton with a hat-trick against Nottingham Forest. On the opening day of the 1988/89 season FOUR Everton players made their debuts against Newcastle United.

Defender Neil McDonald, midfielder Stuart McCall and winger Pat Nevin all made impressive introductions to life in Royal Blue. But for Tony Cottee it was an unforgettable afternoon. Cottee was the most sought after striker in the country during the summer of 1988.

Everton smashed the British transfer record to land the little forward from West Ham, beating off the attentions of Arsenal.

And Cottee took just 34 seconds to start repaying the huge £2.2m investment in his services.

Newcastle, themselves fielding a newly reshaped side with a £2.2m transfer fee they had received from Spurs for Paul Gascoigne – goalkeeper Dave Beasant, defender Andy Thorn and midfielders John Hendrie and John Robertson all making their debuts – failed to deal with a long high ball from Neil McDonald.

With the Goodison crowd still bubbling from the kick-off Graeme Sharp chested the ball down and saw his shot parried by Beasant. Cottee latched onto it with all the predatory instincts of a born goalscorer and lashed the rebound in left-footed.

"I could spend the rest of this book trying to explain my feelings as I turned away in triumph, but I can't explain it," he wrote in his 1995 autobiography Claret and Blues. "I'd scored 118 league and cup goals for West Ham but my first at Goodison on that glorious day gave me the biggest thrill since I scored on my debut for the Hammers five-and-a-half years earlier.

"It's one of the oldest cliches in football but it really was a dream start for me ... and it got even better."

After half-an-hour Peter Reid rolled back the years with a mesmerising, penetrating run and pass which Cottee swept past Beasant right-footed.

"By the time half-time came I really fancied my chances of a hat-trick," Cottee wrote. And just past the hour he did exactly that, with the sharpest, most clinical finish of the three.

"I just couldn't believe it as I ran with both arms raised in triumphant salute towards the fans at the Gwladys Street End," he added. "It was a wonderful feeling of elation."

The press reaction was just as excitable.

"Potty for Cottee!" screamed the headline in the next day's Sunday Mirror, with the new striker offering an excited interview.

"The whole day was a fairytale and it has taken a lot of pressure off me," he declared. "To play alongside Graeme Sharp is a dream. He is one of the main reasons why I came to Everton I reckon we can forge a great partnership."

LFC THANKS
EFC... WE NEVER
WALKED ALONE

————✕✕╱╱⌃⌄✕✕————

WEDNESDAY, MAY 3, 1989

THE 140TH LEAGUE DERBY MATCH PLAYED out at Goodison Park on May 3, 1989 was low on incident.

But its symbolism and poignancy was immense.

Liverpool's players had not kicked a ball since the appalling tragedy at Hillsborough 18 days earlier – and a trip to their neighbours and closest rivals was seen as the most appropriate occasion on which to make a return to competitive action again.

Everton had not stepped out at Goodison Park since the disaster.

The fences, so culpable in one of British football's worst disasters, had been removed and the atmosphere at Goodison was surreal.

Liverpool were resuming a title battle with Arsenal. Mid-table Everton were preparing for an FA Cup final against their neighbours.

But thoughts were on far more than football.

A giant banner, draped from the Stanley Park stand, carried a simple, but moving message from the Liverpool supporters: 'The Kop Thanks You All. We Never Walked Alone.'

Respective club chairmen John Smith and Philip Carter, followed by managers Kenny Dalglish and Colin Harvey, led their teams out onto the pitch to a huge roar, immediately followed by an all-enveloping silence when an Everton stadium announcer declared: "Your loss is our loss too. We will observe a minute's silence."

Then at half-time a group of fans paraded a chain of 95 red and blue scarves, the number of victims of the tragedy at that time and a number which would sadly grow, around the perimeter track also holding a banner which read "LFC fans thank EFC fans."

The match was televised live and the eyes of the footballing world were on the occasion.

Visiting manager of the West German national team, Franz Beckenbauer, said: "There would never be an atmosphere like this at any game in Germany."

While Leeds United legend Johnny Giles wrote an emotive description of the night for the Dublin Evening Herald.

"Sport is a great healer, particularly in a soccer mad city," he wrote. "Yet there is no denying the feeling last night that the result of the Liverpool derby counted for less than the occasion itself.

"Even if Liverpool fail to win the League on account of dropping two points at Goodison Park, they know that the ghost of Hillsborough was exorcised and that footballing life will go on.

"That is much more important than any frenetic race for this season's title with Arsenal. It was a night of reflective sadness, yet the defiance of the city to take the horrific punch on the chin and still keep their heads held high was a great tribute to the character of her people.

"The beauty of Liverpool people is their lack of pretence. The night could have been contrived to shroud the occasion with recrimination, sorrow and bitterness which would only have opened the wounds again.

"Everton personified the dignity of the city too. On the terraces their fans stood side by side with their greatest sporting rivals; on the field the Blues paid the Anfield side the tribute of playing the game to win as if the result to them was crucial.

"They could so easily have taken it the other way because they have no worries themselves about the points in their mid-table position. But that would not be the city's way.

"Last night was the beginning of the thawing process from a city under emotional siege. The euphoria of a point gained or lost in the Liverpool derby games didn't come into it. Merseyside was as one last night.

"Truly, in that area, no person, no family or no football team ever walks alone."

The action on the pitch was as frenetic as ever.

Neville Southall made a double save from first Peter Beardsley and then John Aldridge described in the next day's Times newspaper as "astonishing."

While referee Neil Midgeley waved away Everton appeals for a penalty after Gary Ablett upended Pat Nevin.

But it was the dignity, the compassion and the togetherness displayed on the night which was more significant.

The Daily Mirror reported: "This was a day when English football showed the world it has compassion. It has a heart and a soul.

"English football is not all about mindless hooligans. It is about passionate football, fervent fans, high class, top speed soccer – and caring.

"The memories will linger on – and they include some of the most touching moments ever witnessed inside a football stadium in this country.

"When the memories of Steve McMahon's biting tackles, the goalmouth scrambles at both ends and the arguments over a possible Everton penalty have faded, the occasion itself will live long in the mind of those who were there.

"I'll remember the Liverpool fans thanking the nation as a 30 feet by five feet red and white banner was draped over the stand behind the goal. It read: 'The LFC fans thank you all. We never walked alone.'"

BIG NEV'S POSTAL DISPUTE

——×✕／︿＼✕×——

SATURDAY, AUGUST 25, 1990

THE GREAT NEVILLE SOUTHALL PRODUCED COUNTLESS moments of spellbinding brilliance and imperious majesty during his 751 match Everton playing career.

But none earned more headlines or generated more comment than the moment when he was sat on his backside in front of 34,412 fans at Goodison Park – doing precisely nothing.

It was the opening day of the 1990/91 season – and the Blues found themselves 2-0 down at half-time to newly promoted Leeds United.

Neither of the goals had been Southall's fault, but the goalkeeper had already endured a turbulent summer, submitting a series of transfer requests – all rejected – and the first half mood in the stadium had been one of frustration as a team which had won the league title just three years earlier struggled to recapture those highs.

One frantic fan, unable to stand the sight of his side struggling, ran onto the pitch screaming at the Everton players to take more pride in wearing a blue shirt and had to be escorted off by Leeds striker Lee Chapman.

But it was Southall's emergence onto the pitch – during the half-time interval – which became the big talking point.

A full five minutes before his team-mates returned, Southall walked out onto the pitch alone, briefly applauded the Leeds United fans in the Park End of the stadium, then headed down to that goalmouth and sat against a goalpost gathering his thoughts.

Most of the fans inside the stadium were bemused. Some booed and jeered.

Almost all of the watching media described the incident as a sit-down protest.

The Liverpool Daily Post reported: "Neville Southall, a man clearly determined to leave Goodison Park, staged a pitch protest of his own. The Welsh international keeper emerged from the half-time interval a full four minutes before his teammates and awaited their arrival to the jeers of many home supporters by sitting dejectedly against a goalpost."

The Sunday Mirror suggested Southall was clearly heading for an Everton exit, writing: "Neville Southall's days at Everton look numbered following an amazing act of defiance during the 3-2 defeat by Leeds at Goodison Park yesterday.

"Southall, who has repeatedly been refused a transfer this summer, staged a remarkable demonstration after his defence had leaked two first-half goals. He emerged from the dressing room at half-time five minutes before his team-mates and sat, head between his knees, propped against a post.

"Everton fans responded to his display with a hail of derision, although manager Colin Harvey amazingly claimed he was unaware of the incident."

Plenty of pundits passed comment on the incident.

Liverpool legend Tommy Smith, in his Liverpool Echo column, said: "I don't honestly know what's behind Southall's discontent. We read the newspaper speculation, but we never seem to get a satisfactory explanation from the man himself."

That's because Southall himself couldn't offer any explanation.

With the benefit of 22 years' hindsight, Southall gave his own interpretation of the events that day in his 2012 autobiography The Binman Chronicles.

"At half-time I needed to get out of the dressing room and get my head together, so I left and went and sat down in the goalmouth. People went on about it and said it was a protest, but it wasn't at all.

"At worst it was badly timed coming around the same time as my transfer request. I certainly wasn't protesting against Colin, who didn't even know about it until that evening. I'd actually done the same before at Wimbledon a year earlier and nobody had said a word about it then. It cleared my head and allowed me to focus on the second half. But coming when it did propelled me to the back pages."

Southall was in a very confused state of mind at the time.

He added: "Things came to a head before the start of the 1990/91 season, on the eve of which I asked for a transfer. It was my third transfer request in a year, all of which were rejected. I don't know why I asked to move: I didn't really want to leave Everton and was sure I wouldn't be as happy elsewhere. I liked Colin Harvey and my team-mates but I couldn't see things getting any better at Goodison. In truth, I didn't know what I wanted.

"Knowing what I know now it was the right thing for me to stay at Everton. I could have gone to (Manchester) United or Liverpool and won the title again. But it wouldn't have ever been my club. I don't think I would have felt at home.

"Everton, by contrast, were my club; we were meant to be. When I walked in every day at Bellefield I felt at home. It was my club and I could do whatever I wanted to do within it. They used to give me a free rein. I was very happy there; it was just the fact we weren't winning things that meant I got more and more frustrated."

And that frustration proved costly.

Following talks with his manager, Colin Harvey, he was fined a week's wages and left the club's Bellefield training ground "angrily refusing to say anything printable to waiting Pressmen."

Harvey later explained: "Neville Southall has been disciplined according to club rules and basically that is it.

"There was no bust-up between Neville and myself as I pointed out earlier I think he regrets going out on to the field.

"It was something he did in the heat of the moment in frustration at things that had happened in the first half.

"No slight was intended to myself, the management or the fans of Everton Football Club."

Southall was back in goal for the trip to Coventry the following Wednesday and was still a fixture between the Everton goalposts for the next SEVEN seasons – collecting an FA Cup winner's medal in 1995 to add to the one he had won 11 years earlier.

He famously drove straight home after that Wembley triumph preferring to avoid any publicity – but for one afternoon in 1990 he was very much the centre of attention.

DERBY WHICH HAD EVERYTHING EXCEPT A WINNER!

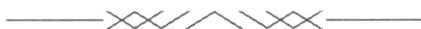

WEDNESDAY, FEBRUARY 20, 1991

EIGHT GOALS, TWO GOAL OF THE Season contenders, near-misses, world class saves and no winners. On the pitch, anyway.

Off it, the clear winners of the 1991 FA Cup fifth round replay were 37,766 fans lucky enough to be inside Goodison Park to witness a match described as "the greatest in the competition's history."

Ironically the match may never have taken place at all.

Liverpool were drawn at home to face Everton and at the peak of an impressive first half performance from the Toffees, referee Neil Midgeley waved away a stonewall penalty claim when Gary Ablett sliced Pat Nevin's legs from under him.

Midgeley later joked with Howard Kendall that his non-decision had led to a replay still talked about today. But before the teams went again the match official had to endure an uncomfortable moment.

"I couldn't believe it when I was asked to come out half an hour before kick-off and receive the matchball from the sponsors," he said.

"I agreed and next thing a supporter had rushed over and draped a red scarf around my shoulders!"

Fortunately the most controversial question posed after an FA Cup classic was whether a frantic, thrilling 4-4 draw was the greatest Merseyside derby of all time?

Most agreed that it was.

Everton boss Howard Kendall declared: "It was one of the greatest cup-ties that has ever been seen on Merseyside, if not in football."

His Reds' counterpart, Kenny Dalglish, added: "If there have been any better cup ties than that I wish somebody would send me a video."

Graeme Sharp, scorer of the first two Everton goals, agreed: "It was just different class, the greatest game I have ever played in. I don't think you will ever see a game like that again."

While John Barnes, who scored the goal of the game, said: "It was an outstanding match." And his team-mate Gary Ablett added: "I haven't been involved in a game like that since I left school."

So what was all the fuss about?

Words can only give a skeletal sketch of two hours' worth of absorbing, electrifying entertainment.

If Everton had been the better side at Anfield, Liverpool impressed at Goodison – but they simply couldn't shake off their belligerent neighbours.

After a thrilling back and forth for half-an-hour Everton committed too many numbers forward and were caught on a lightning counter – which Kevin Ratcliffe was well positioned to cover.

But on a night full of tales of the unexpected the most successful skipper in the club's history dropped a rare clanger – and his friend and international team-mate Ian Rush raced clear on Neville Southall's goal.

Rush clipped the ball over his advancing compatriot but Andy Hinchcliffe had raced back to clear acrobatically off the line. Everton's relief turned to anguish when the ball dropped to Peter Beardsley who drove the ball into the Gwladys Street net.

It nearly got worse, but Southall made a truly miraculous point blank block from Barnes.

The first half had been positively tame compared to what happened after the interval.

Just a minute after the restart Hinchcliffe crossed, Sharp met the ball with his head and Liverpool keeper Bruce Grobbelaar could only help the effort into his own net.

Then Pat Nevin raced clean through, tried to effect his trademark flip and lifted the ball over Grobbelaar – and the crossbar.

Beardsley then scored his second goal with a jinking run and strike that was touched by genius. Only for Grobbelaar and Nicol to get involved in a tragic mix up which Sharp slid in to touch over the line. 2-2.

Perhaps fittingly it was Sharp's last goal in a Royal Blue shirt (he did score one more at Goodison, wearing an Oldham Athletic jersey).

It wouldn't have been a derby of that era without an Ian Rush goal, and he obliged with a jack knife header.

But four minutes from time Tony Cottee replaced Nevin – and 40 seconds from the end Stuart McCall pushed the ball into the Liverpool penalty area where more uncertain defending was met by some decisive Cottee finishing.

That meant extra-time – and if Beardsley's second goal had been touched by genius, the curling effort from John Barnes 12 minutes into the extra period was from the Gods. 3-4.

But still Everton's spirit was unbroken and six minutes from time Glenn Hysen allowed a Jan Molby backpass to trickle through his legs, thinking it would reach goalkeeper Grobbelaar. It didn't, it reached Cottee who fired it through the goalkeeper's legs to spark celebratory mayhem.

Four times Liverpool had led. Four times they had been pegged back.

And the gentlemen of the press somehow had to make sense of it all – quickly – to meet their morning paper deadlines.

The Daily Mirror's Harry Harris offered a personal view.

"Goodison Park last night staged one of the greatest Merseyside derbies of all time, with every single person in the 37,766 crowd rising at the end of this pulsating cup tie to give both sets of players a four-minute standing ovation," he wrote.

"It was a privilege to have been present at a game that lifts British football apart from any of the fancy versions on the continent.

"There was passion, commitment, technical skills of the highest level, individual brilliance, world class goalkeeping from Neville Southall and marvellous goals."

The Times' report was more prosaic, but just as praiseworthy.

"Last night's extended Merseyside derby at Goodison Park, the 172nd to be staged between the city neighbours, is justifiably being hailed as the finest in memory.

"For unremitting quality and dramatic twists, the FA Cup fifth round replay touched heights which stretched credibility, especially towards the end of a breathtaking two hours."

The Daily Telegraph kept it straight.

"Never in the previous 172 matches between the two Merseyside giants has there been a game filled with such incident and excitement as this 4-4 draw, after extra-time."

While the Echo's Ken Rogers had the benefit of a few extra hours to gather his thoughts before delivering his verdict for the following night's edition.

"I have often wondered what it must have been like to have been in the crowd the night Muhammad Ali and Joe Frazier took each other to the brink of human endurance, exchanging punch for punch, blow for blow in the legendary thriller in Manila," he mused. "Now I know.

"I was one of 38,000 mesmerised football fans who marvelled, gaped and marvelled again at a sporting spectacle of similar heavy-weight proportions last night.

"Everton 4 Liverpool 4 was one of those FA Cup occasions we will all look back on in years to come and proudly recall: I was there!

"We used to do a lap of honour when one goal settled a derby because they were always so tight. But EIGHT! And still no result. It was absolutely unbelievable."

There were contrasting legacies to the most remarkable of derbies.

Two-goal Everton saviour Tony Cottee was back in for extra training at Bellefield the next morning while his knackered team-mates enjoyed a lie in!

"I didn't mind. Don't forget the other lads played the full 120 minutes," he said. "I've got to build up my fitness to help me find consistency."

Everton won the toss to stage the second replay and that proved decisive with Dave Watson lashing in the winning goal.

But Liverpool didn't have a manager in their dugout.

Such had been the emotional intensity of the Cup tie that Reds boss Kenny Dalglish caused a football bombshell by resigning.

"After we took the lead for the final time, I knew I had to make a change to shore things up at the back," he explained.

"I could see what had to be done, and what would happen if I didn't, but I did not act on it. That was the moment I knew. I was shattered.

"I needed to get out and away from the pressure."

Even the aftermath of the most eventful derby match of all-time was dramatic.

BLUE MONDAY

---XX/⌒\XX---

MONDAY, DECEMBER 7, 1992

EVERTON'S FIRST APPEARANCE IN FRONT OF the BSkyB television cameras, in the first season of the Premier League, wasn't exactly the "whole new ball game" the fledgling satellite company had promised.

On a chilly Sunday afternoon in October Howard Kendall's side lost 1-0 at Oldham's Boundary Park, to a far post Richard Jobson header from a flicked on corner.

More Blooper Sunday than Super Sunday.

Their next appearance in front of the cameras was much more like it – the 147th Merseyside derby at Goodison Park, and the Blues' first appearance in the soon to be established Monday Night Football.

It would be a historic night for one vastly experienced Everton player – and a poignant one for a rookie midfielder.

The teams entered the fray to a 'guard of honour' from the Sky Striker Cheerleaders, while commentator Ian Darke prophetically started his night's work by saying: "Peter Beardsley ... bidding to become only the second man in history to score for both clubs in Merseyside derbies. The other was David Johnson."

But while Darke talked of "a couple of shocks" in the Everton starting line-up, 19-year-old Billy Kenny, making only his fourth league appearance, wasn't even mentioned.

He certainly was after the match.

Everton kicked off hovering one place above the relegation zone.

Following four league wins in a row Liverpool were an upwardly mobile ninth.

Reds' shirt sponsors, Carlsberg, were so confident they took out a tongue-in-cheek advert in the Liverpool Echo, with a special form for writing down the match goalscorers. The side-splitting gag was that Blues had just one line, the Reds five.

It proved to be probably the biggest advertising own goal ever conceded.

When Reds skipper Mark Wright rose to bullet a header into the Gwladys Street net after an hour the Liverpool supporters inside Anfield instantly broke into a gleeful rendition of "Going down!"

The chant stuck in their throats when seconds later Mo Johnston wheeled onto a penetrating pass forward from Ian Snodin and clipped an equaliser in off goalkeeper Mike Hooper's right hand post.

Then Beardsley claimed his slice of Mersey football folklore.

With six minutes remaining the ingenious little forward chipped a pass over Rob Jones' head to Gary Ablett on the Bullens Road touchline. Ablett fired the ball back into him and Beardsley took one sure touch before drilling a low, right-footed drive past the helpless Hooper.

It sealed Everton's first win over their neighbours for four years.

Afterwards manager Howard Kendall revealed the psychological stroke of genius he had employed before kick-off.

Young midfielder Kenny was named the sponsors' man of the match after an assured engine room performance and Kendall revealed he had asked the teenager to sign a new two-and-a-half year contract just hours before the match.

"I thought the lad was absolutely tremendous," said Kendall afterwards. "The victory was cause for celebration in itself but the best news for me was before the game when Billy signed that contract.

"He had earned it and he fully justified it on the night, passing the ball superbly and looking a top class prospect."

What happened next in the Billy Kenny story wasn't such a feel good story, but his match-winning display in Everton's first Monday Night Football appearance certainly was and was something which could never be taken away from him.

In true Sky TV tradition fireworks exploded into the night sky as Land of Hope and Glory blasted out over the tannoy system and excited Evertonians exited the stadium.

THE GREAT ESCAPE

———✕✕⁄ ⌃ ⁄✕✕———

SATURDAY, MAY 7, 1994

IT IS EVERTON'S JFK MOMENT.

Every Evertonian old enough to recall May 7, 1994 knows exactly where they were on the day of 'the Wimbledon match'.

Whether that was inside Goodison Park, huddled on Goodison Road with a transistor radio pressed to their ear, or hanging from a tree in Stanley Park. Yes, really.

Everton may have faced The Dons on 36 occasions, in five different competitions – one League Cup tie even ended 8-0 – but there is only one fixture which springs instantly to mind whenever 'the Wimbledon match' is mentioned.

It was the day Everton found themselves 2-0 down in the last match of a Premier League season, a match they had to win to even stand a chance of escaping relegation for the first time in 43 years.

The 1993/94 season had been a turbulent one at Goodison Park.

Two factions were vying to buy control of the club from the Moores family, while manager Howard Kendall resigned his position on December 4 after a 1-0 victory over Southampton.

He left with the club Everton 11th in the table.

Under caretaker boss Jimmy Gabriel Everton then failed to score for six matches, losing five of them and when they did finally score, at Chelsea, they still folded 4-2.

Mike Walker was finally appointed as successor to Kendall and new manager bounce saw his side win three of his first six league matches.

Then a slump set in.

The Blues recorded 1-2, 0-3, 0-1, 0-0, 1-5 and 0-3 results before a desperately needed 1-0 win at West Ham.

But that wasn't the prelude to an upturn in fortunes.

Everton lost to an 87th minute goal at QPR, were held 0-0 at home to Coventry and collapsed 3-0 at Leeds United.

That meant Everton kicked off the final match of the season in the relegation zone.

Swindon had long since been relegated, but Oldham, Sheffield United, Ipswich Town, Southampton and ourselves all went into their final fixtures needing results to survive.

The Blues began the match in the bottom three, a point behind Southampton, Sheffield United and Ipswich Town, and one ahead of Joe Royle's Oldham Athletic.

The permutations were endless, but there was one certainty, Mike Walker's team simply had to win.

Wimbledon were flying high in sixth position, were looking for a win to cement their highest ever Premier League finish and their players had been promised a holiday to Las Vegas by owner Sam Hamman if they could finish the season unbeaten.

Oldham's hopes of escaping were extinguished when, needing a win at Norwich, they could only draw 1-1.

But that left one place still to be filled.

Blues fans had pinned most of their hopes on runners up and soon to be champions Blackburn making Ipswich that team by beating the Tractor Boys.

They didn't. A goalless draw saved Ipswich's skins.

Southampton stayed up with a 3-3 draw at West Ham.

And in the only other fixture which might have helped save Everton, Sheffield United led Chelsea 2-1 after an hour.

But the Everton players who took to the pitch that afternoon were unaware of the events and permutations elsewhere.

They simply knew they had to win – and then hope for the best.

Only 31,297 were physically inside Goodison Park, because a new Park End stand was being built. That end of the stadium was a building site.

That added to the surreal atmosphere around the ground, with scores of supporters hanging from trees in nearby Stanley Park trying to gain a view of the action through the framework of the new stand.

The tension around the stadium was suffocating – and it got to the players.

After just four minutes Anders Limpar, a winger never usually to be found anywhere near his own penalty area, inexplicably and bizarrely threw up his arm and batted away an innocuous cross with no Wimbledon player near him.

"Crazy! Absolutely crazy!" bellowed BBC commentator Barry Davies.

Dean Holdsworth stepped up to crash the penalty low to Neville Southall's right. Initially there were cheers when the legendary goalkeeper got a hand to the forward's firmly struck shot – but those cheers stuck in throats when the shot carried too much power and squeezed in.

Sixteen minutes later a calamity looked like becoming a full blown catastrophe. Warren Barton hoisted a hopeful free-kick into the Everton box, but so frantic and so panic stricken were the Blues defenders that after Andy Clarke had headed the ball on, Dave Watson and David Unsworth both challenged for the same ball, which dropped conveniently for Clarke. Even then his sliced shot was drifting wide of the Street End goal until Gary Ablett, another defender acting on nerve-shredded instinct, tried to hook the ball clear and deflected it into his own goal.

One plaintive, ear-piercing scream from a female supporter before the ball trickled into the net underlined the severity of the situation.

Everton were drowning – and needed a lifeline.

They got one when Anders Limpar used his feet rather than his hands, skinned Dons defender Peter Fear and then tumbled theatrically.

The incident would not have survived VAR scrutiny in the 21st century, but this was when referees acted with impunity – and Robbie Hart pointed to the spot.

Wimbledon had kicked the ball down the pitch in disgust and it appeared at one stage like Neville Southall was going to take the kick.

He strode down the pitch with the ball held out, as if he was offering to take it but waiting to see if anybody else fancied the responsibility of keeping 40 years of top flight football intact.

Somebody did.

"I was thinking what everybody else was thinking," recalled Graham Stuart, the man who had been designated to take his first penalty kick for Everton a couple of weeks earlier.

"This mad man is walking up and if ever there was a goalkeeper crazy enough to take a penalty it was Nev. I genuinely thought to myself 'I'm not having this'. There's no way on the planet you can allow your goalkeeper to take such an important penalty."

So the man nicknamed 'Diamond' strode purposefully back to the halfway line, took the ball from his goalkeeper and headed back to the Park End penalty area.

There was a smattering of applause as some supporters recognised the courage of a player putting his balls on the line, then there was a tense, nerve-shredding silence heavy with anxiety.

Segers dived to his left, Diamond's penalty arrowed sweetly, decisively and perfectly into the other corner.

And the roar was primeval.

Everton were back in it.

Dean Holdsworth headed a glorious chance over the Street End bar, Dons keeper Hans Segers parried a Stuart shot at the start of the second half then Stuart's eventful afternoon saw him block a goalbound, point-blank header from Holdsworth on the line with his chest.

But Everton weren't creating chances – and they still needed two goals.

Then Barry Horne happened.

The combative midfielder had scored on his Everton debut almost two years earlier – and hadn't looked like ever adding to that tally.

The match was drifting when he picked up possession midway into the Wimbledon half, nudged the ball forward on his thigh and then unleashed a venomous, swerving, dipping shot of a lifetime.

Segers never stood an earthly. The ball sizzled into the top corner off the inside of the post.

What possessed a man who ended his Everton career with just three goals in 151 appearances to shoot?

"I was having a good season, I was playing well and in good form leading up to the game and I was having a good game," he explained years later.

"When you're confident you just do things.

"If that ball had bounced up to me some 12-15 months previously, I'd have taken another touch and then another touch and would have fallen over it or passed it sideways.

"But as things stood it sat up and before I knew it, the ball had left my foot and it was on its way.

"Earlier on I'd have thought about doing it and decided against doing it but on that occasion, I was in such good form, I was doing things instinctively, as you do when you're confident. It never occurred to me to shoot or not to shoot – I just did it."

And that decision set up the great escape.

A few minutes later he tried again, from closer in, and this time the ball skimmed over the crossbar.

Only eight minutes remained when finally a Wimbledon player was overcome by the tension of the occasion.

Graham Stuart played a one-two with Tony Cottee, lunged in on the edge of the penalty area with a half-shot, half block tackle and the ball span crazily towards goal where Segers hopelessly misjudged its flight.

The ball nestled in the corner of the Street End net and the scenes of celebration were riotous. Stuart gleefully charged down the Goodison Road touchline and was finally apprehended by team-mates, supporters and stewards.

Everton led 3-2, while seven minutes earlier across the Pennines, Mark Stein had equalised for Chelsea at Sheffield United.

A draw would still have saved the Blades and sent Ipswich down, but Stein's second goal in time added on ensured the Yorkshire club suffered the fate which had seemed earmarked for Everton just an hour earlier.

The scenes inside and outside Goodison Park at the final whistle were astonishing.

Inside the stadium fans invaded the pitch.

Inside Stanley Park one fan recalled: "A guy fell out of the tree in front of me and when I turned around there were hundreds if not thousands of people running out of the bushes.

"Most were crying, including us, and laughing and hugging everyone and everything in sight."

Not one single Evertonian wanted to experience an afternoon like that – but those that did will never forget it.

THE DAY Z-CARS
DIDN'T PLAY

———×××/︿＼×××———

SATURDAY, AUGUST 20, 1994

IT HAS BEEN 60 YEARS SINCE the rousing drum beat and pipes of the Z-Cars theme tune first accompanied Everton onto a football pitch.

And it seems Fritz Spiegel's evocative arrangement of an old Liverpool folk song was fated to become the club's anthem.

The circumstances are peculiar – and poignant.

Z-Cars was a new police drama first screened by the BBC on January 2, 1962.

Based in a fictitious district just outside Liverpool called 'Newtown' – it was widely assumed that Kirkby was the inspiration – and the actual overspill town created to re-house people was used as a location for many of the scenes.

Z-Cars quickly became wildly popular – and during the first seven or eight home matches of the 1962/63 championship winning season the theme tune was played over the tannoy at Goodison Park before matches.

The sequence was broken and the theme was not played when

Blackpool visited Goodison Park on November 10 – and that's where fate stepped in.

Leonard Williams, the Liverpool-born actor, who played PC Percy Twentyman in the show, had been invited by the club directors to the match.

It was such a big deal that despite Everton putting five past the Tangerines, the front page headline in that night's Football Echo was: "Z-Car Man Sees Everton 'Gerrit in (Goal) Book' " referring to the character's catchphrase when booking criminals.

Tragically, just five days later, Leonard Williams died of a heart attack.

The Echo's renowned reporter Leslie Edwards wrote in his 'Looking At Sport' column: "Two followers of Everton from Childwall add their wonderment to mine that Everton's Z-cars theme has not sounded before the last two home games.

"Ironically, after it had been played for the first seven or eight home matches, it was left out on the very day when the late Mr. Leonard Williams of Twentyman fame was a guest of the club, only three or four days before he died.

"The club say there was no official adoption of the tune and that it has not been stopped for any special reason.

"As one who counted Twentyman and his Liverpudlian cracks as the most authoritative mirror of football fans in this city it mightn't be a bad idea to adopt the Z-cars drums and fifes and commemorate one of the city's notable sons. What do you think?"

The suggestion appears to have been taken up.

A feature on June 25 1963, reported: "Everton's Z-Cars signature is becoming well known."

And in the report of the 1963 Charity Shield, staged at Goodison Park between champions Everton and FA Cup winners Manchester United, Leslie Edwards wrote: "When Everton came out to their Z-Cars theme tune they got a tremendous reception."

Marianne Williams, daughter of the late Leonard Williams, wrote to the Echo in 2014 and explained: "My father was Leonard Williams (Sergeant Twentyman) and he was indeed a guest at Goodison in November 1962 – shortly before his untimely death some days later.

"My mother always told us that because of the huge success of Z-Cars and the fact that my dad was the only genuine Scouser in the cast, he was invited to the match and it was because of that, that Everton decided to play the Z-Cars theme as a tribute to him after his death.

"I don't think any of us could have envisaged that the theme would still be played all these years later, but it is a lovely memory for me and all of his family."

It has been played – almost – ever since.

In 1994, with a new owner, a new Park End Stand and a new manager in place at Goodison, the Everton hierarchy decided other changes may be welcomed.

In the pre-internet era the club contacted the Liverpool Echo to ask them to conduct a poll amongst their readers to decide which piece of music should be used to welcome the players onto the pitch for the 1994/95 season.

More than a thousand Blues fans responded – and the verdict was overwhelming.

Retain the Z -Cars theme.

A whopping 54.2% of traditionalists far outweighed those who suggested Simply The Best (15.2%), Forever Everton (13.1%), Here We Go (7.2%), We Shall Not Be Moved (5.2%) and Chariots of Fire (5.1%).

So what accompanied the players onto the pitch for the visit of Aston Villa on the opening match of the new campaign?

The theme tune to 2001: A Space Odyssey.

There was no announcement. No explanation in the matchday programme.

Just a series of baffled looks amongst supporters followed by angry letters to the Echo the following week!

The backlash was ignored.

A month later, when QPR were the visitors and the new Park End Stand was officially opened by MP David Hunt, the Echo reported: "Everton don't just want the fans to listen to the pre-match entertainment, but join in themselves. The club is still in the process of experimenting with a view to finding a new club song.

"An Echo poll indicated that many supporters wanted the club to retain Z-Cars as the official theme, but the Blues would prefer a song that can inspire fan participation. Two new offerings were being set before the supporters today.

"The first is an adaptation of the Creedence Clearwater Revival classic 'Bad Moon Rising.'

"The Swedish branch of the Everton Supporters Club impressed club officials during a pre-season tour by writing special words to the song and singing them on the terraces prior to the games.

"This song has now been recorded by a group called Lemon Tree and is being played at Goodison today with the words flashed up onto the main scoreboard. Will it be a hit with the Goodison faithful? Time will tell."

Time did tell.

Z-Cars was quickly reinstated and has been played ever since.

Almost.

It was silenced on September 18, 2022 as mark of respect to the passing of Queen Elizabeth II. But it returned the following home match against Manchester United and has been ever present ever since.

SLAM DUNC!

MONDAY, NOVEMBER 21, 1994

IT WAS THE NIGHT DUNCAN FERGUSON became a legend, before he became a player.

And it was the occasion when another legendary Everton centre-forward lit the blue touchpaper on an unlikely escape from relegation.

Everton's start to the 1994/95 season had been the worst in the club's 106-year league history.

The squad which had escaped relegation just nine minutes from the end of the previous campaign had been boosted by new signings Vinny Samways and Daniel Amokachi, and loan deals for Iain Durrant and Duncan Ferguson – but still started horrendously.

Just one streaky win, five draws and eight defeats from 14 matches had left the club rock bottom of the Premier League, marooned on eight points – and resulted in manager Mike Walker being relieved of his duties.

Ferguson had started the last five league matches of Walker's ill-fated tenure, without troubling the scoresheet.

But the man appointed to replace Walker was a centre-forward of 24-carat Royal Blue heritage – Oldham boss Joe Royle.

"We hoped a big old English centre-forward would be able to

motivate a big young Scottish centre-forward," said Blues chairman Peter Johnson.

He did just that – with a little bit of help from a rival from across the park.

Royle's first match in charge was against Liverpool in a Merseyside derby – with the Reds riding high fourth in the table. It was a night when Ferguson's legendary status was born.

"I meant it nicely," Royle said, when asked about his 'legend before the player' comment.

"He'd hardly kicked a ball for the club before I arrived. Until about 50 minutes in against Liverpool on my debut game, I have to confess I was wondering what all the fuss was about."

Then Liverpool centre-back Neil "Razor" Ruddock made an ill-advised decision to kick Ferguson from behind. The Scot's reaction was predictable.

"He got angry and he became unplayable," recalls Royle. "He went to war."

Ferguson soared higher than the Gwladys Street crossbar to direct a firm header past David James to open his goal account for the club – a centre-forward wearing number nine, opening his account in a Merseyside derby, down at the Gwladys Street End.

It got even better. A minute from the end Ferguson challenged James for another cross, the spooked Reds keeper punched the ball against Ferguson and it broke kindly for Paul Rideout to slide in a match-clinching second.

Ferguson left the pitch to the adulation of Goodison Park, pitch-invading children hanging off him like some modern day Pied Piper.

Three months later his loan deal was made permanent – and a lifelong love affair between Big Dunc and the Blues had begun.

"That very first night he scored, he changed the match, and probably Everton's season," recalls the chairman who sanctioned his signing, Peter Johnson.

Director Bill Kenwright, who would later lure Ferguson back to

Goodison Park after he had been sold to Newcastle, added: "Commitment, aggression, goals, leadership and, yes, maybe a bit of devilment. And even the ability to intimidate. Evertonians loved him for that.

"The Gwladys Street would have followed the big man everywhere. He was a talisman who terrified opponents and was adored by Blues. There was just nothing other than a total bond between him and the fans at that moment. Football rarely gets more emotional or passionate."

Duncan would have many more emotional moments to share with his devoted fanbase.

He scored in his next match in front of the home fans too, another header from another Andy Hinchcliffe corner, down at the Street End obviously.

An enduring love affair which shows no sign of cooling had begun.

FRIENDS
REUNITED

———————⋈⌣⌢⋉———————

TUESDAY, JUNE 6, 1995

WHEN WORLD CHAMPIONS BRAZIL CAME TO Goodison
Park in 1966, Evertonians were excited at the prospect of watching
the world's most exciting and charismatic international team in the
flesh.

But the party was cut short when Pele was brutally kicked out of the
tournament and Brazil were beaten by Hungary and Portugal to exit
the competition in the group stages.

Thirty years later Brazil were back – and this time an appreciative
Goodison audience were treated to the full range of Brazilian party-
pieces.

The occasion was the Umbro Cup – a rehearsal for the Euro 96 tournament – and with Goodison not selected for the summer showpiece
Everton were selected to host Brazil against Japan.

Brazil had already opened with a win over Sweden at Villa Park, 24
hours after England had edged past Japan at Wembley.

But Brazil's performance at Goodison Park brought the tournament
to life.

With soon to be superstars like Roberto Carlos, Cafu and an 18-year-old called Ronaldo in their ranks, Brazil sparkled.

They triumphed 3-0, Roberto Carlos showing his remarkable shooting power and precision with the opening goal and Zinho supplying a goal straight from the book of Brazilian blockbusters, a soaring, swerving, dipping volley from 25 yards which zipped into the Park End net.

The Liverpool Echo's Hyder Jawad was in raptures in the Goodison press box.

"Brazil went back to the future last night, treating the near-30,000 crowd to flashes of sheer brilliance, creating triangles in midfield that defied logic, holding possession as if the ball was a priceless diamond, and striking long-range shots with the speed and accuracy of a revolver," he purred.

"Japan, lively against England on Sunday, were way behind Brazil in thought and action. Conceding only three goals was perhaps an achievement.

"The Brazilian players seemed to have hands where their feet should have been, so breathtaking was their skill.

"They have, in Jorginho, one of the best right backs in the world and in Dunga, a midfielder with experience and inspirational qualities. Throw in the talent of 18-year-old striker Ronaldo, World Cup heroes Aldair and Marcio Santos, and you begin to see why nearly everyone is a Brazilian fan."

The only disappointment of a spellbinding night was 3,000 local fans locked out, with the official attendance figure just 29,327.

A national newspaper reported: "The South Americans could have reached double figures, so complete was their control of the game, and some of their football was breathtaking.

"The remarkable pulling power of the current world champions was evident, with 3,000 fans being locked out. The police advised that gates be closed for safety reasons after delaying the kick-off by 15 minutes."

SHEAR GENIUS

———✕✕╱╱⋀╲✕✕———

SATURDAY, AUGUST 17, 1996

IN THE SUMMER OF 1996 NEWCASTLE UNITED broke the world transfer record to land the most prolific centre-forward of the era.

Alan Shearer cost £15million and made his Toon debut alongside another world class striker Les Ferdinand.

But both were upstaged by a number nine wearing Royal Blue.

Duncan Ferguson wanted to make a point on the opening day of the 1996/97 season – and he did so spectacularly.

"Honestly it was one of the best individual performances I've ever had pleasure to witness," raved the correspondent of the Glasgow based Daily Record newspaper, who had sent Keith Jackson south to witness the clash of the titans.

"He has the ability to be the world's best player of his type," declared Neville Southall, who had watched in admiration from the opposite end of the pitch.

Duncan's club boss Joe Royle, who knew a thing or two himself about the art of centre-forward play, added: "The big fella was terrific. He didn't need any motivation with all the hype involved with the other two strikers on the pitch."

While Wales national team boss Bobby Gould more colourfully claimed: "Duncan is just like a super-charged gazelle – with his giant spring and timing you can only wonder what he might have done for Scotland at Euro 96."

Ferguson had missed the tournament following surgery on a recurring hernia problem.

But interest in his exploits 'down south' was intense north of the border – and the Daily Record's report of his performance on that opening day of the 1996/97 season was typical of the hype, excitability – and stereotypical local racism – of the time.

But it also underlined just how good Duncan Ferguson was.

"Friends, countrymen, I bring forth news most wondrous from the land of Satan," wrote Jackson, hopefully with tongue firmly in his cheek.

"News of a mighty Scottish warrior who is set to be crowned the King of England. A laird who lives in a strange town where the men folk have dodgy perms impressive moustaches and earn their rent monies by trading in cheap car stereos.

"A town where the women folk marry their loved ones dressed in white shell suits. A town where everyone knows his name – and half of them have it written across their own backs.

"His name is Duncan Ferguson – the man they think is God – AND BY GOD HE'S GOOD!

"Yep, whisper it but it looks like Big Dunc has grown up at last.

"Now we've always known this boy has a very special talent. No question. But believe me this was something different. This was awesome.

"The world and its aunty had turned up at Goodison to see £15million man Alan Shearer make his Premiership debut for Newcastle. But from the moment Big Dunc strutted out the tunnel it was HIS day.

"He didn't lose a ball in the air, every header was inch perfect and his flicks and feints on the deck were just sublime.

"And it was all topped off by a gallous swagger and an attitude so mean you could almost taste from your seat in the stand.

"In those magical first 45 minutes he had reduced Kevin Keegan's Toon Army – and England stopper Steve Howey in particular – to a shaken wreck.

"Honestly it was one of the best individual performances I've ever had pleasure to witness. And the best bit is the local lads tell me he's been playing this way all summer – after spending every single day of his break in training.

"Ferguson finally looks ready to conquer the soccer world."

There was a buzz of expectation when Ferguson darted away from Philippe Albert as early as the third minute, a buzz which grew to a roar when he rose to head an Andrei Kanchelskis free-kick towards the roof of the net only to be denied by Shaka Hislop's fingertips.

He cleverly created an opening for strike partner Graham Stuart, crashed in a shot of his own which was saved again by Hislop, had another header saved a minute later – then was brought crashing down by a combination of Hislop and Steve Watson as Newcastle struggled to contain him.

David Unsworth calmly rolled in the resulting penalty.

Before half-time he rose magnificently to direct another header into the path of Gary Speed who rapped in a debut goal – so that by half-time everyone was talking not about Shearer but about his opposite number.

Fergie ran out for the second half with his right hand bandaged and then later took a kick in the face from Albert which left him needing stitches above his eye.

But he still wreaked havoc for another 20 minutes before finally tiring.

Newcastle boss Kevin Keegan said afterwards: "In Duncan Ferguson Everton have a player who will give a lot of defenders a lot of problems this season.

"He just about won everything against our guys.

"We managed to handle him better in the second half but by then he'd probably just got tired of heading the ball so often."

Shearer did get off the mark three days later against Wimbledon, but on the opening day of the 1996/97 season Duncan Ferguson was the centre-forward who was centre-stage.

CAPTAIN MARVEL

————✕✕╱╱⌃╲╲✕✕————

SUNDAY, DECEMBER 28, 1997

DUNCAN FERGUSON WAS AN UNLIKELY SELECTION to lead Everton out as captain when Bolton Wanderers visited Goodison Park in December 1997.

The Scottish striker had never worn the armband before as a professional. He had missed the previous three matches through suspension – the fourth of his short Blues career – and it was the day after his 26th birthday.

But Howard Kendall's unexpected decision proved a master-stroke of psychology, and it inspired the most productive performance of Big Dunc's Everton career.

Gary Speed, who had worn the armband since the opening day, was sidelined by an ankle injury; the man Speed had succeeded, Dave Watson, was missing with a knee problem,

So Kendall needed a new leader.

But even Ferguson's old team-mate, Neville Southall, was surprised by his former manager's choice. Big Nev had recently left the club to join Southend but still penned a column for the Liverpool Echo. After the match he wrote: "I was very interested to see Duncan Ferguson get the captaincy. He would have to lead by example because there is no way in the world anyone would understand his instructions! But you don't have to be a shouter to be a captain."

Duncan didn't shout. He led by example.

Everton desperately needed a result. Just one win in 10 matches had seen the side sink to second bottom of the Premiership.

Bolton were better off, but not by much – three places and four points further up the table – and the pre-match omens were not promising.

Everton had 11 players missing through injury or suspension, named four teenagers in their line up – and hadn't scored a goal from open play in more than 11 hours of football.

"The stage was set for a Ferguson virtuoso performance," reported the next day's Mirror "and he didn't disappoint.

"He was unstoppable in the air, a handful on the deck and inspirational as a skipper."

And even more significantly he scored his first senior hat-trick – all headers. He is still one of only two men to achieve that feat in the Premier League. (Salomon Rondon was the other, for West Bromwich Albion, 19 years later).

Ferguson had already seen one soaring header headed off the line before he started the move which led to his opener, sweeping the ball out to advancing full-back Tony Thomas.

The big Scot raced into the penalty area, leaped over Chris Fairclough and timed his run to perfection to bullet in the first.

That was after 16 minutes. His second, four minutes before half-time, was a classic near-post diving header, lunging to flash Nick Barmby's cross past the helpless Gavin Ward.

But astonishingly Ferguson did not go in at half-time with his side ahead.

Bolton hit back twice in as many minutes, a Gudni Bergsson header and a fierce Scott Sellars shot levelling the scores.

Everton desperately needed a hero – and Big Dunc was just that man. Twenty-three minutes remained when Thomas once again lofted an inviting cross into the box from the right touchline.

Ferguson's leap was monumental, butting the ball down into the turf with such force it bounced high into top corner of the Gwladys Street net with Ward well beaten.

Howard Kendall said later: "He was a bit special out there, and I felt the rest of the players responded to him.

"It was a last minute decision to make him captain. We had so many kids and young players in the side that only Nicky Barmby and Andy Hinchcliffe had played enough Premier League games each to be considered.

"In the end I felt I would get a better response from him in this situation after being out for three games through suspension and being all fired up.

"He has had to sit and watch, the frustration building up inside him, and he was really up for it.

"I told him he didn't have to do anything more than normal to be a skipper – but he decided he'd knock in a hat-trick for good measure!"

Bemused Bolton boss Colin Todd said afterwards: "He's probably the best header of the ball in the Premiership."

He could have dispensed with the word 'probably.'

GREAT ESCAPE
– THE SEQUEL

———————⋙/⋀\⋘———————

SUNDAY, MAY 10, 1998

JUST FOUR SHORT YEARS AFTER NEWSPAPER headlines had pleaded "Never Again", following Everton's last gasp relegation escape against Wimbledon, Evertonians were put through the gut wrenching turmoil of another relegation nerve-shredder.

And this time the atmosphere inside Goodison was even more tense, just as electrically charged – and ultimately just as euphoric – as that remarkable afternoon in 1994.

Richard Dunne was in the Everton dug-out for the visit of Coventry on May 10, 1998, having paraded the FA Youth Cup around the pitch pre-match with his victorious team-mates.

Still qualified to play for the youth team, he had also made a handful of senior appearances during a dreadful campaign which had seen an end of season collapse leave the Blues in the last remaining relegation place, a point behind Bolton Wanderers. Barnsley and Crystal Palace were already down.

The mathematics were simple. Howard Kendall's side had to better Bolton's result on the last day, a Bolton team who were playing at

Stamford Bridge, against a Chelsea team contesting a European Cup Winners' Cup final three days later.

Chelsea boss Gianluca Vialli resisted the temptation to rest his Cup finalists, making just four changes.

But Everton, entertaining Coventry, had the power of Goodison behind them.

Young Richard Dunne was in his tracksuit in the home dug-out and recalled: "I remember the atmosphere in the place, it was absolutely electric.

"There was no way – and I know it was close in the end – but there was no way Everton were going to lose that match, because of the passion of the fans in the stadium.

"When I think of Everton, I think of that. I think of the fans in moments like that. They were like an extra player for the team.

"It was a hard season because it was all ups and downs. There were a lot of changes at the Club... but it is experiences like that which build a club.

"It gets the fans around you, they develop their love for the club through moments like that."

Coventry defender Richard Shaw was on the receiving end of the atmosphere.

He said: "As a player, you don't often see the match from the fans' perspective. As a fan, you might turn up half an hour before kick-off but as players you're there much earlier.

"When we turned up on that day, the streets were lined with Evertonians and it was clear what a massive day it was for them.

"You could feel the tension and scale of the occasion just through the atmosphere around the stadium when we made that journey on the coach.

"I love Everton, anyway, and playing at Goodison Park with the crowd right on top of you. It is not like a lot of the modern stadiums.

"But on that day, it was incredible, such an atmosphere."

Don Hutchison revealed some of the psychology employed by

the man who had brought him to Goodison, to try and defuse the pre-match tension.

"The night before the game, Howard took us to a hotel over the water in New Brighton, just to get us away," he recalled.

"It was too big. You couldn't stay in your house and drive to the game. There was just too much uncertainty in terms of the lads being late because the streets would be packed with fans.

"Howard took us for a walk in the morning – and, typical Howard, he took us into a little deli, we all had a cup of coffee and a scone.

"Then we got on the coach and that was when the nerves hit. We started seeing a few Evertonians walking the streets. Ten or 20 of them, then a few more, and more, and by the time we got to Goodison Park, there were thousands on the streets.

"From the traffic lights nearby to the players' entrance should be a 30-second drive. It took half an hour.

"The fans were banging on the windows and sides of the coach. It could have been intimidating but I loved it. It got my juices going and my adrenaline flowing."

Gareth Farrelly's juices were flowing.

The midfielder had tried shot after shot after shot throughout the season, but only had one breakaway League Cup strike at Scunthorpe to show for his efforts.

Just like Barry Horne four years earlier, he chose the most important stage of all to become an unlikely goal hero.

Duncan Ferguson leaped like a salmon in the Coventry penalty area to direct a header into the midfielder's path – and the persistent midfielder slashed a swerving 20 yard shot in off Magnus Hedman's left hand post.

Goodison erupted.

Hedman hadn't stood an earthly, and by all rights he shouldn't have got near a Dave Watson shot deflected off Mikael Madar's heel a few minutes later. But he did, instinctively flashing out a left hand to deflect the ball wide.

One-nil up at the break, with Bolton still drawing 0-0 in London, Everton's destiny was in their own hands – and when Vialli scored after 73 minutes to give Chelsea the lead the roar around Goodison as the message was passed around the fans was almost as if the Blues had scored a second.

The opportunity to do just that came six minutes from time when Paul Williams was harshly adjudged to have fouled Danny Cadamarteri.

Nick Barmby had the chance to ease the nerves and ensure a less tense last few minutes – but he fired his penalty kick far too close to Hedman who dived to his right to save.

Then the afternoon became surreal.

The second half had been played in a downpour, and two minutes from time Everton goalkeeper Thomas Myhre tried to catch a speculative Dion Dublin header, and the greasy ball squirmed through his hands and in off the same post that Farrelly's shot had struck an hour-and-a-half earlier.

Everton were ahead of Bolton on goal difference – but knowing that just one Bolton goal in West London could condemn them.

In the capital the visitors were pressing – and some home supporters in the Stamford Bridge crowd, hearing the news from Goodison and with nothing at stake themselves, were willing their opponents to score.

When Jody Morris made it 2-0 to Chelsea in the last minute, some actually booed!

Everton were safe, provided Coventry didn't score a second, and the mood for the final few minutes of added time at Goodison was of terrified, nerve-filled tension.

Coventry's enormously experienced Swedish international defender Roland Nilsson said: "You could feel the stress in the ground and the crowd was so up when they scored. I can remember the cheers when Chelsea got their first goal against Bolton, too.

"Then as soon as we equalised, everything went quiet. You could feel how tense it was. Every single decision – throw-in or free-kick, everything – they were desperate for it to go to Everton.

"And really late on, they were screaming for the referee to blow his whistle.

"We tried to keep going and went close to a winner a couple of times."

But Everton hung on and the scenes at the final whistle were rapturous.

Kendall hugged assistant Viv Busby and the substituted Madar, dancing an impromptu jig of delight on the touchline – while supporters invaded the pitch in ecstatic relief.

But it wasn't long after that the enormity of how close Everton had come to suffering a first relegation for almost half-a-century dawned on the most successful manager the club has ever had.

Don Hutchison, who had been brought to Everton by Kendall, revealed: "All the lads were celebrating, having a drink and a bit of champagne. It was a party atmosphere and it didn't sit right with me, celebrating staying up.

"But you do, you get on with it because it is part of the team spirit. You don't want to be a loner or an outcast.

"I looked around the dressing room, the lads celebrating and the music on and I could see Adrian Heath and Viv Busby. But not Howard.

"I asked kit manager Jimmy Martin where he was. He told me he was in the boot room.

"I knocked on the door and opened it slightly – wanting to be polite.

"The lights were off but I fully opened the door and saw Howard, sat with a glass of champagne in his hand, crying.

"It makes me hugely emotional when I think of the emotion on his face. I sat in a darkened room with Howard for 10-15 minutes, just hugging him, basically.

"I was chatting to him, trying to distract him from crying. We were both in tears.

"He said to me, 'Listen, I just did not want to be the man who took Everton down'. He loved the club so much.

"With that, we got ourselves together, wiped the eyes, went back into the dressing room and got on with having a good time.

"But it was very emotional."

Emotional, but ultimately successful.

SUPER KEVIN CAMPBELL

————⋙⟋⋀⟍⋘————

SATURDAY, MAY 8, 1999

KEVIN CAMPBELL ENDED THE 1998/99 SEASON as Everton's top scorer – by some distance.

Which was some achievement given he only made his debut on April 3 – and played just seven league matches on loan from Turkish side Trabzonspor.

But Everton fans had been yearning for a new striking hero to wear their number nine shirt after the controversial sale of Duncan Ferguson six months earlier.

And the man who had made his League debut for Arsenal at Goodison Park more than a decade earlier became that man.

Campbell's debut was in a 3-2 derby defeat at Anfield. His home debut saw Sheffield Wednesday win 2-1 at Goodison, to plunge Everton deep into the relegation zone.

Four weeks and a one-man goal blitz later, Walter Smith's side were safe from relegation with a match to spare and up into the relative comfort of 14th place in the table.

And the man quickly christened Super Kev was largely responsible.

He scored both goals in a vital victory over Coventry, scored two more in a 3-1 win at Newcastle, added another two in a 4-1 demolition of Charlton – then his purple patch reached its zenith with a hat-trick against West Ham.

Campbell had already received his Carling Player of the Month award for April before kick-off, and celebrated by scrambling in the opening goal against the Hammers after just 14 minutes.

If his opener was scruffy, his second was classy, a delightful dink over Shaka Hislop after being sent clear – while his hat-trick strike was a flashing left-footed shot from a defence-splitting Don Hutchison pass.

It was an afternoon when the Goodison crowd, who had sat through SEVEN goalless draws earlier in the season, was in party mood.

Michael Ball flashed a penalty high into the net, Don Hutchison scored a screamer – and Francis Jeffers confirmed his burgeoning promise with the seventh goal of his brief Everton career.

"Stand up if you love the Blues!" was a new crowd anthem which reverberated around the stadium – and centre-stage was the new crowd hero.

It was the start of an enduring love affair.

"I fell in love with the club," Kevin later said. "I was doing my job of trying to score goals for the team, but the fans were great to me.

"The people there are so passionate about their football club and they know to support the players. It is quite a unique experience being an Everton player with the fans supporting you, and that love I have for the club has not waned."

The love the supporters had for Super Kev never waned either. It was still very much in evidence a quarter of a century later, with the outpouring of love shown when Campbell tragically passed away at the far-too-early age of just 54.

THE WRIGHT
STUFF

———— ⟩⟩⟩⟩⟩⟨⟨⟩⟩⟨⟨ ————

SUNDAY, DECEMBER 26, 1999

AS ONE OF THE UK'S LEADING theatre producers, Bill Kenwright knew more than most about the art of theatrical timing.

And the day he bought the Blues from Peter Johnson in the winter of 1999 he delivered a fitting plot twist.

Following weeks and weeks of intense negotiations Kenwright's True Blue Holdings had finally completed the paperwork to prise the club away from the previous owner, Peter Johnson.

It was an enormously popular switch – and the deal had been concluded the day Everton were due to entertain an upwardly mobile Sunderland at Goodison Park.

It was Boxing Day, the visitors were managed by Goodison legend Peter Reid, lay third in the Premier League table and were seeking to establish a club record run of unbeaten away games.

Two hours later those statistics lay in ruins.

Sunderland were annihilated 5-0 – and Don Hutchison waited until the 15th minute before clipping in the opening goal, seconds after Kenwright had taken his front row seat in the Goodison Main Stand!

Everton's new owner elect had missed the kick-off as a result of several impromptu motorway service station stops – a direct result of a stomach bug.

"I must admit, I felt rough. But I just had to be there," he later explained.

"A journey that normally takes three hours stretched out to five and a half. The motorway was manic. The cars were bumper to bumper. but that was only the half of it. I had to keep making emergency stops at every service station. My stomach was churning and I can only think that it was a direct result of intense negotiations over the past week."

He had just taken his place when Hutchison opened the scoring. Four further goals followed – the club's biggest win of the season.

Kenwright had enjoyed many ecstatic afternoons during his lifelong allegiance to Everton, but few will have compared to this one.

And with his producer's hat firmly on, he delivered a rousing encore.

Blue Bill announced that he had persuaded Everton's manager Walter Smith, a man who had threatened to quit the club during the previous chairman's tenure, to pledge his future to the club.

The 5-0 victory elevated Everton to eighth in the table – and following neighbours Liverpool's draw at Newcastle the same day ensured that the Blues started the new millennium at the summit of the all-time League table.

On the morning of January 1, 2000, Everton had collected five more points than their near neighbours in top flight football – 4,326 points to 4,321.

"That's the most pressure I've been under since I became a manager," joked Smith afterwards, joining in the celebratory theme. "At least now I can say I've managed the Team of the Millennium!"

RETURN OF THE PRODIGAL SON

———— ✕✕/∧\✕✕ ————

WEDNESDAY, AUGUST 23, 2000

"SOME THINGS ARE SIMPLY MEANT TO BE."

That was a national newspaper's response to the night Big Dunc came home, in August 2000.

Duncan Ferguson's Everton exit, in November 1998, had been mourned, berated and ultimately led to a change of ownership at Everton Football Club.

His return, after a 21-month exile on Tyneside, was cause for wild celebration.

Fans flocked to Goodison Park and blocked the Stanley Park End car park just to witness him, wearing a grey suit, walking back into the stadium for a press conference.

Days later they returned, hoping to see their hero in a Royal Blue jersey once again.

Sixty-seven minutes into the opening home game of the 2000/01 season, against Charlton Athletic, they got their wish.

And, of course, Big Dunc delivered.

The next day's Times reported: "Some things are simply meant to be.

In keeping with the opening words of the match programme, which talked of his 'Roy of the Rovers relationship with Everton Football Club', Duncan Ferguson announced his return to Goodison Park in comic-book style, scoring two goals in the most glittering of cameo appearances."

Ferguson celebrated each one by flexing his left bicep and revealing his famous Number 9 tattoo, an image which had remained steadfastly hidden throughout his spell at Newcastle United.

Every one of the 12 goals he had scored for Newcastle was celebrated with a baggy, long-sleeved black-and-white striped shirt hanging off his frame.

For the visit of Charlton on August 23rd 2000 Fergie opted for a short-sleeved number.

The decision was pre-meditated.

His two late goals, following an earlier Francis Jeffers opener, sealed a handsome 3-0 win.

Ian Ross, writing for the next day's Guardian newspaper, declared: "As a purveyor of theatrical dreams Bill Kenwright probably expected nothing less.

"When Everton's new owner opted to bring the talismanic if inconsistent Duncan Ferguson back to the club, he was taking the sort of gamble he normally reserves for either the West End or Broadway.

"But Kenwright was wearing the smile of a vindicated man last night at the final whistle: Ferguson had returned not merely as decorative icon but as a conquering hero.

"The big man, the big enigma, came off the bench with 23 minutes remaining to squeeze the life out of Charlton with two late goals. The place went crazy, of course."

It wasn't just Big Dunc who was being unveiled that night.

English football icon Paul Gascoigne was also wearing royal blue.

If Kenwright had gambled with Big Dunc, so too had manager Walter Smith with Gazza.

And it was the English football legend's pass which had given

Francis Jeffers the opportunity to open the scoring nine minutes after half-time.

Oliver Kay of The Times added: "Walter Smith, never one to get carried away, resisted the temptation to gloat after seeing Ferguson and Paul Gascoigne, whose arrivals at Goodison Park were condemned as insanity on his part, justify his decision to give them the opportunity to relaunch their respective careers."

Gascoigne's Everton career was brief, but had its colourful cameo moments.

Duncan Ferguson's was still going strong more than two decades later – and on his left bicep remains a permanent reminder of the bond which is also engraved upon his heart.

Big Dunc was back home.

HAIL THE
MOYESIAH

―――――― ✕✕╱╱‿‿✕✕ ――――――

SATURDAY, MARCH 16, 2002

THESE DAYS, THE LYRICS WOULD PROBABLY be deemed inappropriate.

But on March 16th 2002 the Gwladys Street wantonly boomed to a new anthem … "He's got red hair but we don't care, Davey, Davey Moyes!"

A 38-year-old flame-haired firebrand had just been appointed Blues boss in succession to the sacked Walter Smith.

And at his introductory press conference the former Preston manager pulled off a PR master-stroke.

In understated fashion the Glaswegian said: "This is the people's club in Liverpool. The people on the street support Everton and I hope to give them something they can be proud of over the next few years."

The slogan quickly caught on but it wasn't all that Moyes did differently.

With Everton hovering dangerously close to the Premier League's relegation zone and Jean Tigana's attractive Fulham team the visitors to Goodison Park, Everton defender David Unsworth explained: "I have never had a manager join in with us in the warm-up out on the pitch before the match, but I have a few pals who are Preston season ticket holders and they told me that's what he likes to do.

"It was great and we produced a great reaction."

After 32 seconds!

Evertonians hadn't witnessed a league win for two months. Goodison hadn't celebrated a goal for six weeks – but when Unsworth made a sugar-sweet connection with his left foot to drive the ball past Edwin van de Sar the old stadium erupted.

The cheers and the chants had barely subsided when Duncan Ferguson made it two. The talismanic striker hadn't featured because of injury for six weeks and hadn't scored a goal from open play all season, but he eagerly charged down a dallying van der Sar to pinch possession and slide in a second goal from a narrow angle.

The Daily Post's always colourful columnist Len Capeling opined: "After the prison rations of recent times, this was expense account dining at the Savoy Grill. With the only danger being the onset of indigestion. A goal after 32 seconds? Was it possible? Yes...it was. It was even possible for the Goodison tannoy to announce the time as 27 seconds, thus inviting a spot of pushing and shoving at the Golden Goal payout window."

After the euphoria came a 'they shall not pass' attitude – especially after midfielder Thomas Gravesen's 28th minute red card left the Blues to battle on with 10 men for more than an hour.

Steed Malbranque pulled one goal back, but with players putting their bodies on the line for the fans and the new boss, the People's Club saw the job through to claim three vital points and start a whole new era.

Andy Gray, a 24 carat Goodison legend then working for Sky TV and not short of a snappy catchphrase himself, said: "The People's Club was fantastic. It's almost like you'd have paid a marketing company a million pounds or something like that to come up with a slogan that the others from across Stanley Park would be very, very jealous of.

"In fairness they haven't been jealous of much that we've done over the years but that I bet they'd wished they'd captured that for themselves."

REMEMBER
THE NAME

ON SATURDAY, OCTOBER 19, 2002… AT round about ten to five, Clive Tyldesley hollered one of the most iconic pieces of commentary of the Premier League era.

The nation's pre-eminent TV commentator declared: "Remember the name… Wayne Rooney!"

The nation heard it later that night, on ITV's The Premiership show, which replaced Match of the Day for three seasons. But for Evertonians the advice was largely unnecessary.

Clive had cut his broadcasting teeth on Merseyside a couple of decades before, and his words were presumably aimed at a national audience … because every Evertonian had already been hearing the name Wayne Rooney for months.

Two years earlier, when the youngster had scored his first goal for Everton's Academy Under-19 team – at the age of 14 – a handful took note.

Just 18 months later, three months after his 16th birthday, 30,736 supporters saw him sign his first professional contract at Goodison

Park – on the pitch at half-time of a Premier League match against Sunderland.

It wouldn't be long before they'd be seeing the youngster in action on the same pitch with a ball at his feet rather than a pen in his hand.

Before then Sky TV cameras screened a Youth Cup semi-final second leg at White Hart Lane – when the teenage tyro unleashed a thrilling 30-yard blockbuster described by former Spurs boss David Pleat as the best goal he'd seen at the stadium all season.

Walter Smith named him on a first team substitutes bench at Southampton in April, but with Everton hanging on to a narrow 1-0 lead he never got the opportunity to become the youngest player in the club's history.

There were still two games left of that season when he might have achieved that feat – but England Under-17s took him to the European Championships instead.

An early exit would have seen Rooney heading back to Merseyside still with a chance of making appearance history. But he scored five goals in five games in Denmark to earn England a bronze medal, before finally coming back to score in the first leg of a Youth Cup final at Goodison in front of 15,000 fans.

David Moyes vainly tried to douse down the hype – even when Rooney became the youngest goalscorer in Everton's history with two clinical strikes in a Worthington Cup tie against Wrexham.

He was fighting a losing battle... and the point of no return came with the visit of champions Arsenal, a team unbeaten for a record-breaking 30 Premiership games.

It was Rooney's last chance to score a league goal as a 16-year-old, he came on after 80 minutes with the scores locked at 1-1 – and in the 89th minute he did something truly memorable.

Thomas Gravesen hoisted a long ball forwards from the halfway line. Rooney instantly plucked it from the sky with one sure touch of his right instep. Such was the quality of that first touch he was able to turn immediately inside, glance upwards at the distant target then explode a wickedly curving shot – from 25 yards – over England goal-keeper David Seaman and off the underside of the Park End crossbar.

It was a reverberating moment – the likes of which Goodison had not witnessed for years.

Monday's Liverpool Echo reported: "Saturday witnessed a phenomenon, a pivotal point maybe in Everton's developing fortunes. No-one wanted to go home. More than 30,000 stayed behind after the players had left the pitch, for quarter-of-an-hour. They joined in with yet another rendition of 'It's a grand old team...;' they waited for an encore, they beamed inanely at each other. Maybe they were waiting for the enormity of what they'd just witnessed to sink in."

They got the opportunity to relive it again when the Saturday night highlights were screened on TV and Tyldesley screamed: "Gravesen forward. Rooney. Instant control. And he curls it... Oh a brilliant goal! Brilliant goal! Remember the name! Wayne Rooney."

Many years later Clive revealed the inspiration for that iconic commentary.

"The 'remember the name' line actually came from a fan who I had known for a number of years up there," he said.

"He came up to me at the wrong end of a sportsman's dinner when we'd both had a glass or two and he whispered in my ear, 'Remember the name: Wayne Rooney'.

"I can picture him now. He was over six feet tall, with a really striking beard, moustache and glasses.

"He actually said the words 'Remember the name'. Of course I was aware of Wayne – we all were – but he was the man who said those words."

The genie was out of the bottle.

When Rooney scored another wonder goal at Elland Road a week later – to end a 51-year league hoodoo there, it was never going back in.

NATURAL VAUGHAN HERO

————×××⁄∧⌣×××————

SUNDAY, APRIL 10, 2005

IN THE SPACE OF A WEEK James Vaughan leapt from Everton unknown to a triple record breaker – and Goodison rejoiced.

Evertonians were holding out for a hero as the club's unlikely quest for a fourth place finish – and the prize of a Champions League qualifier – started to falter at the business end of the 2004/05 season.

But they didn't expect that hero to be 16 years 271 days young!

David Moyes' team had lost three in a row for the first time in an unexpectedly upbeat campaign – and seen centre-forward and record signing James Beattie ruled out for a month with a knee injury.

That saw the visit of Crystal Palace to Goodison Park unusually labelled by the Blues boss as must-win. "This match takes on extra significance for us now," he declared "we have to win it."

A veteran Duncan Ferguson was drafted in for just his second start of the season – and Vaughan was named as a first team substitute for just the third time.

The teenager's previous two spells in the dugout had been as an unused sub, but that all changed on Sunday, April 10 2005.

Neighbours Liverpool, Everton's closest rivals in the chase for fourth, had been beaten at Manchester City the day before, giving Moyes' team the opportunity to open up daylight between themselves and the Reds.

And they decisively did just that.

Goalkeeper Gabor Kiraly carried the ball outside his penalty area to give an on loan Mikel Arteta the opportunity to beautifully fire in his first Everton goal from a 20-yard set piece.

Tim Cahill, playing alongside the Spaniard in midfield, took advantage of the opportunity to arrive late in the box behind Ferguson and Marcus Bent and crashed and headed in two goals of his own.

But the moment Goodison craved came three minutes from the end.

With Everton cruising manager Moyes took the opportunity to introduce Vaughan 17 minutes from time.

That saw Joe Royle's 37-year record as Everton's youngest ever player eclipsed by 11 days.

But that wasn't enough for Vaughan. With three minutes remaining the young striker bullishly darted into the Gwladys Street six yard box to lunge onto the end of Kevin Kilbane's cross and become the youngest goalscorer in Everton's history – removing Wayne Rooney's name from the club record books.

At 16 years 271 days young Vaughan also became the youngest marksman in the Premier League, overtaking Leeds United's James Milner. It is a record he still holds.

"There wasn't a dry eye in the house," reported the next day's Echo. "The youngster was submerged in a derby-day style celebration piley-on. 'You can stick your Wayne Rooney ...' chanted both ends of the ground. Well you can guess the rest. Suffice to say the sun doesn't shine there, which cannot be said about Goodison Park yesterday."

Comparisons were inevitable, but assistant manager Alan Irvine moved quickly to douse them.

"He is a different type of player to Wayne," he warned. "There will be comparisons because of their age but James is a different type of player altogether.

"James likes to play right up there whereas Wayne likes to go deeper. It is unfair to call him the new Wayne Rooney. He is James Vaughan."

And he is still Everton's – and the Premier League's – youngest ever goalscorer.

THE NIGHT BIG DUNC SAW RED

———⚔/⁄\⁄⚔———

WEDNESDAY, APRIL 20, 2005

THROUGHOUT HIS DECADE LONG EVERTON PLAYING career Duncan Ferguson was the footballing equivalent of a Raging Bull – and everyone knows how bulls respond to a red rag.

The sight of a Manchester United or a Liverpool jersey was usually enough to inspire feats of derring do from Everton's braveheart.

Six times in his Everton career Big Dunc put Manchester United to the sword. Four times he celebrated strikes in Merseyside derbies.

But arguably his most significant goal against a team wearing red – certainly since his first in November 1994 – came more than a decade after that towering header and was another hammer blow to our fiercest rivals and neighbours. It was another header, this time diving, against Manchester United that was instrumental in Everton finishing above Liverpool for the first time in the Premier League and claiming a fourth place finish.

It was the only goal of a never-to-be-forgotten April evening when Goodison shook to its very foundations and a 33-year-old Ferguson spectacularly turned back the clock.

David Moyes had used Ferguson as a highly effective impact sub throughout his penultimate season as a player.

But for the visit of United on April 20 Big Dunc made only his third league start of the season – and made it count.

The Echo's Scott McLeod summed up a special night.

"Superlatives cannot do last night justice," he wrote for Thursday evening's edition. "Even before you take into consideration the wider context, it equates to one of the most thrilling nights Goodison has witnessed for many years. Bayern Munich, 1985, anyone?

"As with that famous night, the mix was perfect. The crowd were rocking, the players were outstanding and the outcome was ridiculously satisfying. All across the city, ears are still ringing and minds are still buzzing. Victory has rarely tasted so sweet."

The denouement of a dramatic night came 10 minutes after half-time.

Despite his lack of match fitness Ferguson decided to chase shadows in the United defence. He hunted down Rio Ferdinand, until he passed sharply to Wes Brown, so Duncan turned and sprinted after him. Brown shuttled the ball nervously again, so Ferguson wheeled and chased down the ball again . . . and forced United into giving up possession.

The roar from the home crowd was riotously appreciative – and it was not entirely coincidental that the Blues took the lead 60 seconds later. United couldn't escape the periphery of their own penalty area, conceded a needless free-kick and Mikel Arteta rammed a rapier thrust into the heart of the United defence. The man on the end of the free-kick with a stooping, diving header? Need you ask?

"When he plays like that, Dunc has got the edge on anybody," said his team-mate Steve Watson afterwards. "He is virtually unmarkable, no matter who he is playing against. He was up against Rio Ferdinand, a player I regard as one of the best defenders in the world, but when Dunc plays like he did last night he is virtually untouchable.

"I don't think he lost a header all night, but it wasn't just about what he can do in the air. His hold-up play was great, he was charging down defenders, he was getting back to defend, he was winning defensive headers at corners. It was a hell of a shift from him.

"He gave a complete centre-forward's performance and set the tone for everybody. He was awesome."

On a night when the atmosphere was incendiary, Gary Neville saw red for United after kicking a ball at a young Everton fan in the crowd.

Paul Scholes followed in time added on as United finished with nine men and Evertonians celebrated a win which left them in the driving seat for fourth place and a play-off shot at Champions League qualification.

David Moyes said afterwards: "The crowd were awesome tonight. The supporters played their part, but I think that they realised what the players were doing as well. They responded to how the players were going about the job. We needed the three points, and it was maybe three points that people hadn't got us down for. Nevertheless, it was a proper game."

It ended with Moyes and his managerial compatriot Alex Ferguson locking horns on the touchline.

"We were having some Scottish banter," offered Moyes as an explanation. "That's what we do in Scotland. But that comes close to being our best result of the season. It was a big win psychologically. I don't think people thought we'd do that tonight, particularly after the way United beat Newcastle on Sunday, but we bridged the gap in quality. The togetherness, the spirit, it was all there.

"Another couple of wins and the clubs around us will have run out of games. But for the moment our advantage has been maintained in fourth place and we've kicked on again. Duncan Ferguson was terrific from the opening minutes but that was a magnificent team performance."

A magnificent team performance and a memorable Goodison evening.

FAREWELL...
FOR NOW

SUNDAY, MAY 7, 2006

TWELVE YEARS AFTER HE FIRST STRODE purposefully onto a Goodison Park pitch, Duncan Ferguson trudged wearily off it – with a tear in his eye and adulation from Everton fans ringing in his ears.

If Carlsberg did Goodison goodbyes they might have scripted the afternoon Big Dunc brought the curtain down on his colourful playing career.

It had been more than a year since the 34-year-old had last celebrated a goal. It had been four months since he'd even started a match – but he was given the opportunity to lead out his beloved Blues against already relegated West Bromwich Albion and with the last match of the season entering time added on Everton were trailing 2-1.

Then Everton were awarded a penalty, at the Gwladys Street End. Captain for the day Ferguson was initially thinking more about his team-mates' salvaging a draw than a poignant farewell goal.

"He had to be talked into taking it!" explained manager David Moyes afterwards.

"Duncan was the penalty taker here before James Beattie but he wasn't going to take it because he had cramp in both calves.

"He felt he wouldn't be right to take it."

Mikel Arteta was initially ready to grab his first Goodison goal of the season, before the Scottish mafia stepped in!

"We got the penalty and Faddy (James McFadden) came running over," said Arteta. "He said 'Micky, Micky what are you doing? It's his last game!' I said 'Fine, here, have it!' That's the way it was. I understand that he wanted to score and I'm very happy for him."

Ferguson duly stepped forward – and even West Brom goalkeeper Tomasz Kuszczak couldn't spoil the moment. The Baggies' keeper saved Ferguson's first kick, but the ball rebounded back to the striker's right-foot and he squeezed it under the keeper before patting his heart in mock relief.

"The reception he got was unbelievable," added Arteta. "It was really nice to have a team-mate like him.

"It was his last day and everyone was terrific with him. Everybody would love to have a last day like he has done. He has been someone special at the club, a special character."

In keeping with the way he had conducted his entire career, there was no post-match interview from Ferguson, but it was clear from his demeanour what the farewell meant to him.

He led his team-mates onto the pitch wearing the captain's armband, and left it to a guard of honour from them.

As he walked around Goodison Park with the rest of the squad on the post-season lap of appreciation, Ferguson carried a banner which read 'Once a Blue, Always a Blue, thanks for the memories' – and could be seen telling the crowd: "Every one of you is quality."

"What Ferguson brought to the party was something mystical and magical," wrote Dominic King in the following day's Echo. "He might have been born in Scotland but his love for the club made it seem as if he was brought up on Scotland Road. This is one Blue who will stay Blue."

Little did he realise how prophetic those last words would be.

The match had begun with an ovation for Everton legend Brian Labone, who had passed away a fortnight earlier.

The last word on a special day lay with Ferguson's former team-mate, Steve Watson, who received an ovation of his own from the Goodison gallery when he was substituted in the second half, despite having been wearing West Brom colours!

"He is a talisman for Everton," he said of his former team-mate. "He wears his heart on his sleeve. He is an Evertonian and has done fantastic over the years. He will be a big miss.

"Duncan is a big, old-fashioned type of centre-forward and people found it very difficult to play against him. On a day when we said goodbye to one legend, Everton have said goodbye to a second.

"It was bad news for us that he scored at the end but from an Everton point of view, it was fitting."

Entirely.

THREESY DOES IT!

───×××/\×××───

SATURDAY, SEPTEMBER 9, 2006

DERBY CELEBRATIONS HAD BEEN IN SHORT supply at Goodison Park throughout the 90s and noughties.

But the 204th Merseyside derby provided something very special.

Everton hadn't scored three goals in a league derby since August 1966. It had been 11 years since an Everton player had scored twice in a match against Liverpool. And the Toffees hadn't enjoyed a three-goal margin of victory over their fiercest rivals since a 4-0 win at Anfield, 42 years earlier! All three statistics were blitzed as Everton trounced their fiercest rivals in an afternoon to remember.

"It is hard to recall a team so happy in victory," reported the following day's Observer. "David Moyes, who cares passionately about this club, could not stop punching the air, slapping backs, waving to the crowd and generally looking like a 10-year-old who had just seen his first whale."

The anthem of the afternoon was the chant directed towards the club's new record signing, an £8.6m summer capture from Crystal Palace.

Andy Johnson had already scored on his home debut against Watford, then clinched a rare away win at White Hart Lane.

But scoring two goals on his derby debut, in a 3-0 rout, ensured that the words: "Der, der, der der! Andy Johnson!" roared around Goodison Park and the surrounding area for hours after the lunchtime kick-off.

Tim Cahill had sparked the demolition job with his third goal in as many derbies – but the first as a winner.

Johnson ruthlessly rifled in a second – but Blues fans had to wait until virtually the last touch of the game for the third goal which finally gave Everton's dominance the scoreline it deserved.

Liverpool goalkeeper Pepe Reina tried to explain it away afterwards.

"It all started when Lee Carsley had a shot from outside the area in the 94th minute," he said. "I parried it away, but as the ball went into the air, it headed back towards the goal. I turned to get it but in a split second opted to try and catch it, realising too late that I would carry it over the line. I tried to push it over the bar but could only direct it into the path of Johnson, who had an easy task to head it into the roof of the net."

That spawned a gleeful new chant from some inventive members of the Everton fanbase: "Reina drops keep falling on my head!"

It was Liverpool's first defeat of the season – in a match in which the bookmakers had made them pre-match favourites!

But Everton tore their defence apart in a memorable first half.

Monday's Echo declared: "Everton delivered the kind of performance many have spent years fantasizing about. But how many fans will have leapt out of bed yesterday morning with sore heads to buy every paper and watch repeats of Match of the Day, Football First and Jimmy Hill's Sunday Supplement to make sure it wasn't a dream?

"Fear not. There was nothing imaginary about the way Everton systemically dismantled and tormented a side that has visions of challenging Chelsea for the Premiership. On this evidence, such claims seem fanciful.

"Conjuring up a breathless performance that oozed calm and class, the 11 men David Moyes selected for duty secured a result which will be talked about for many, many years to come."

It was. For some, it still is.

THE DAY ROCKY
CAME TO TOWN

—✕✕╱╲╲✕✕—

SUNDAY, JANUARY 14, 2007

SYLVESTER STALLONE WAS NOT A COMPLETE stranger to the sport of association football – he once broke a finger attempting to save a penalty from Pele in the movie Escape to Victory – but 'soccer' was still a largely unfamiliar concept to the man who became a Hollywood superstar on the back of his portrayal of an underdog heavyweight boxer.

But when 'Rocky' came to town in January 2007, Evertonian excitement was tangible.

It was a PR coup by the club, brought about by the presence on the Blues board at the time of Sylvester's pal and business associate Robert Earl, the man who launched the Planet Hollywood franchise with Stallone, Arnold Schwarzenegger and Bruce Willis.

Stallone was due in England for the British premiere of the sixth instalment in the film franchise, 'Rocky Balboa', but took a break from his schedule to attend Everton's Premier League fixture against Reading.

And he took the invitation as seriously as any of his movie roles.

Striding out to the centre circle wearing an Everton branded jacket, he enthusiastically waved a blue and white scarf to all four sides of the stadium while the strains of the iconic Rocky theme tune blared out over the stadium's public address system.

The Goodison crowd responded, "Rocky, Rocky" chanted all around the ground.

Then Stallone took his place on the front row of the Directors' Box, leaning forward on his elbows and gesticulating furiously for Everton to sweep forward every time they gained possession.

The match itself was disappointing, Everton relying on an 81st minute Andy Johnson header to scramble a 1-1 draw.

But Sly was so taken by Goodison's atmosphere he came back to use the stadium as a setting in his first Creed movie several years later.

On a Monday night in 2015, during a dull goalless draw with West Bromwich Albion, Stallone appeared on the stadium screen at half-time asking the 34,000 Everton fans inside the ground to become film extras.

Wearing an Everton shirt and his trademark pork pie hat, Sly asked Blues fans to cheer loudly, as if they were watching live action – and his film cameras, set up to capture a 360 degree view of the stadium, would record the reaction.

He was satisfied enough to use the footage – and Goodison Park – as a backdrop to the movie's climactic fight scene between Adonis Creed and Pretty Ricky Conlan – and he even persuaded the soon to be cruiserweight champion of the world and lifelong Evertonian, Tony Bellew, to play the role of Creed's nemesis, Conlan.

The setting of Goodison gave the movie a gritty, realistic feel with Creed flown into England to face a formidable English opponent.

Barely four months later life would imitate art when Bellew faced Ilunga Makabu at Goodison for the WBC world cruiserweight title.

It was the culmination of a chain of events sparked way back in 2007, by the day Rocky visited Goodison Park.

MAGNIFICENT
SEVEN

———✕✕╱⋏╲✕✕———

SATURDAY, NOVEMBER 24, 2007

THE VISIT OF ROY KEANE'S SUNDERLAND in November 2007 started with a scare.

Adored Everton icon Dave Hickson, on duty at Goodison Park as a club ambassador, was rushed to hospital after suffering a heart attack in the foyer of the stadium.

The Cannonball Kid got the greatest possible pick me up when Everton recorded a scoreline which went out of fashion when the swashbuckling centre-forward was in his prime.

Aiyegbeni Yakubu was the Blues centre-forward in 2007, and he struck twice as Everton triumphed 7-1.

Exultant Everton boss David Moyes described the display as "the best performance in my time here" – and he'd already clocked up more than five years in the Goodison dugout by November 2007.

Moyes' Everton – with Yakubu spearheading a flexible attacking formation ahead of Tim Cahill, Steven Pienaar, Leon Osman and Mikel Arteta – were really starting to click.

The victory over Sunderland was their sixth in seven matches. The following six matches saw another five wins in a campaign in which the Blues finished fifth, reached the semi-final of the League Cup and enjoyed a run to the last 16 of the UEFA Cup.

The quality of football served up was as impressive as the run of results.

After this 7-1 success The Liverpool Echo opined: "Everton have produced, in flashes, some of the finest football their fans have seen for years.

"Last season saw sporadic flashbacks to School of Science stuff... the 10 men at Tottenham, the Luton Town demolition, an hour against Chelsea.

"This season it has been more sustained.

"Leon Osman is involved in a contest with himself to stage his own personal Goal of the Season competition.

"Saturday's elegant and incisive run from the halfway line – Trevor Stevenesque in its construction and execution – went straight in at number two.

"The outstanding move and finish which sealed Larissa's fate is still top of the charts, but there's plenty of competition bubbling under.

"Steven Pienaar is an under-rated and accomplished performer and his succession of one-twos with Nuno Valente which opened up Sunderland for the third time on Saturday was a joy to behold."

While a colourful BBC radio commentry enthused: "I'm oft accused of exuberant hyperbole, but the School of Science revelled in this superb display of quality.

"Classic, inspirational football that demolished Sunderland, reduced Mr Keane to impotence and apoplexy and brought priapic joy unconfined... Sunderland were simply overwhelmed by the beautiful game. Arteta, the artful dodger, several sublime sleight of foot. Cahill the assassin, lethal, incisive. Pienaar flitting like a dragonfly, linking play. Yakubu the bludgeon. Keats – ex School of Science – once said 'A thing of beauty is a joy forever.' This was his day."

Yakubu opened the scoring with a right-footed drive, the second was sumptuously crafted.

Steven Pienaar picked out Phil Neville, who in turn found Yakubu. His first time ball sent Mikel Arteta racing clear. He laid a pass onto Neville, whose neat cross found Cahill. The Australian did the rest with a cool right foot finish.

Pienaar finished crisply to make it three, Joseph Yobo launched an inch perfect 60-yard pass to Cahill for the fourth then Yakubu made it five.

Substitute Andrew Johnson joined in the fun with the sixth and the coup de grace was added by Leon Osman, a nonchalant drop of the shoulder carrying him past Higginbotham and McShane and his left-footed drive completing the rout.

"That was probably the best performance in my time here," declared Moyes. "Some of our football was fantastic and our passing and movement was just outstanding.

"It is how I have been hoping to get an Everton team playing and I hope we see them playing that way more often – hopefully it's the first of many."

The final word on an excellent afternoon, however, lay with the legendary Dave Hickson.

His best pal John Kearney, reported back from Liverpool's Royal Hospital.

"Typically Dave was more worried about getting autographed shirts and balls to people he'd promised them to, than himself," he said.

"He was only disappointed to have missed all those goals going in."

THE ITALIAN JOB

————— ✕✕╱╱⌒╲✕✕ —————

WEDNESDAY, MARCH 12, 2008

NOT ALL GREAT GOODISON NIGHTS END in celebration.

In March 2008 David Moyes' Everton produced one of the finest performances of his whole tenure as Blues boss; the atmosphere inside Goodison Park was compared – favourably – with the night Bayern were sent packing; and the players were given a rousing ovation at half-time, at full-time and after extra-time.

But the cruellest of penalty shoot-outs meant that an outplayed Fiorentina side progressed to the UEFA Cup quarter-finals rather than Everton.

The damage had been done in an uncharacteristically flat first leg performance on a rain drenched night in Florence a week earlier.

Unbeaten in seven and on the back of five straight wins in league and cup, the Blues were beaten 2-0 at the Stadio Artemio Franchi – but the post-match response was defiant.

"We have got it all to do now but football is crazy," said goalkeeper Tim Howard. "When you watch enough of it, you know that anything can happen.

"We are two goals down but we are certainly not out of it. When they come to us next week, it is not going to be a walk for them. We can definitely turn it around and if we play like everyone knows that we can do, there's no question that we can do it.

"There will be a reaction at Sunderland. We'll be like hungry wolves."

Howard was true to his word.

The Blues won 1-0 on Wearside, but their performance three days later was even more fired up, even more driven – a magnificent display of controlled passion.

The early goal Everton craved came after 15 minutes, Steven Pienaar's cross squirting up off goalkeeper Sebastien Frey for Andy Johnson to bundle over the line.

That intensified an already cacophonic atmosphere as Everton lay siege to the Italians' goal.

Shots were blocked, parried and saved, efforts fizzed narrowly wide and last ditch tackles were launched – until a close range strike from Yakubu almost saw the roof come off the stadium. The noise was quickly abated by a linesman's flag, Mikel Arteta, who had crossed the ball, ruled offside.

Everton were undaunted and in the second half continued where they had left off. The moment of lift off came after 65 minutes.

Arteta picked up the ball near the halfway line and drove forward on an angled run. The Fiorentina defenders backed off, judging the distance and the angle to be prohibitive – but the best little Spaniard we knew unleashed a drive of laser guided ferocity which flashed inside Frey's right hand post and sent the Gwladys Street into raptures.

Rarely has a Goodison goal been greeted by such noise.

That gave the Blues the impetus to pile forward with even more fervour in the 25 minutes which remained – but Fiorentina survived. Just.

In the penalty shoot-out Yakubu sent Frey the wrong way from his spot kick, but saw the ball strike a post, then Phil Jagielka was denied by the inspired keeper and the Blues were out. But they were far from dismayed.

"The word which springs to mind after that is proud – I'm proud to play with this set of players," said skipper Phil Neville. "I thought we were fantastic. We should have won the game by four or five goals.

"There's a lot of fighting qualities in our dressing room, but more importantly there's a lot of quality. We took on the fourth best team in Italy tonight; I've watched videos of them and I've never seen them have that many chances created against them in four videos, never mind one.

"We can be proud of the way we've played tonight."

David Moyes was more succinct. "We battered them. The players played really well but they have not been rewarded for it and I have to admit that is hard to take."

But the fans who were so influential on the night were unbowed.

Writing in the following night's Echo, Mike Williamson of Chester declared: "Leaving Goodison Park last night, I cannot remember feeling so proud and disappointed at the same time. Every player in a Blue shirt was simply magnificent.

"Indeed, it is genuinely difficult to think of a better team performance since the great days of Reid and Gray and those of us who were lucky enough to be present at the legendary Bayern Munich game in April 1985 will have felt the same tingle go down their spine when Arteta sweetly hit home the second goal. It really was that good."

THE RIOT ACT

WE CAN'T SAY WE WEREN'T WARNED!

For the second half of Tony Hibbert's 329 match Everton career – when it became clear that even goalkeeper Tim Howard was more of a goal threat than the shot-shy full-back – the Blues fans had playfully teased: "Hibbo scores, we riot!"

And they proved true to their word when Hibbert broke his duck on the evening of his own testimonial match against Greek visitors AEK Athens.

Eleven years earlier, on his senior debut at West Ham United, Hibbert was fouled by Stuart Pearce to earn his side a penalty kick – but it was an isolated foray into an opposition penalty box.

As his career progressed it became clear that defending was his priority – and his failure to trouble the scoresheet led to cult hero status.

In the 2009 FA Cup semi-final against Manchester United a banner was displayed bearing the legend: "If Hibbert scores, we riot!" He didn't – but the gag caught on.

And when AEK Athens were invited to Goodison in August 2012 to supply the opposition for Hibbert's testimonial – he had equalled

298

a club record by making his 18th European appearance for the club against the Greek side in the 2009 Europa League – 17,508 Evertonians turned up in party mood.

Steven Naismith's first half-hat-trick was almost overlooked in the wake of what happened in the 53rd minute.

There was a rumble of expectation around the ground when the right back strolled purposefully across the field to take a 20-yard free kick.

Steven Pienaar teed up a shot and Hibbert rifled the ball through the wall and past Dimitrios Konstantopoulos in the Gwladys Street goal.

"Tony Hibbert... he scores when he wants," sang the jubilant supporters as almost 1,000 fans poured onto the pitch to enjoy a good-natured and long predicted riot.

Athens players retreated to the sidelines to watch in bemusement as Hibbert's team-mates laughed and celebrated.

Hibbert's Everton career ran for a further FOUR seasons – but injuries meant that his high point had already been celebrated – by everyone fortunate enough to have been inside Goodison Park to riotously enjoy it!

THE GREATEST DERBY EVER?

SATURDAY, NOVEMBER 23, 2013

FOOTBALL FANS HATE DERBIES – TOO much tension, anger, intensity and uncontrolled aggression.

They are games to be enjoyed only when the final whistle has blown – and only if you've finished on the winning side.

Neither side was victorious after the November 23, 2013 classic – but both sets of fans were left smiling, and shaking their heads in disbelief, following a rollercoaster ride of a derby completely out of keeping with traditional derby match fare.

"A modern classic," declared Monday's Echo, adding: "The Mersey press box is made up of plenty of former fans who cut their teeth on the terraces of Anfield and Goodison before making their way in front of a keyboard. And the dazed, exhilarated, head-shaking expressions post-match spoke volumes. They'd just witnessed a modern classic."

The scoreline finished 3-3 but that was only half the story.

After 90 minutes of spellbinding action referee Phil Dowd allocated four minutes of added time – and even in that brief spell both teams had two glorious chances to win, while Liverpool's Daniel Sturridge had a goal disallowed.

The match had goals, howling misses, great goalkeeping, one moment of controversy and an unyielding devotion to attacking football borne of the principles of the two respective managers.

Brendan Rodgers' Liverpool ran Manchester City agonisingly close to the title in 2013/14, slipping up in the penultimate match of the campaign against Chelsea with the trophy in their grasp.

Everton finished fifth and had to settle for the Europa rather than the Champions League – despite having gathered a club record Premier League total of 72 points – but everything about Roberto Martinez's first season as Everton manager oozed positivity.

That mindset was never outlined more clearly than in his first derby match.

The previous clash between the two historic rivals had ended 0-0 at Anfield in May.

This one produced three goals – and as many missed chances – in the opening 18 minutes.

Philippe Coutinho scored after just five minutes, Kevin Mirallas replied three minutes later.

Romelu Lukaku sprinted clear of the Reds rearguard two minutes after that but was denied by the outrushing Simon Mignolet. That particular duel became a recurring theme of the match.

Luis Suarez bent in a free-kick after 18 minutes to restore Liverpool's lead, then Kevin Mirallas flashed a shot just wide at the other end.

The one moment of controversy came after 34 minutes, when Mirallas clattered Suarez with a challenge which was high, late – and in the days of VAR would almost certainly have led to a red card.

In the previous season's corresponding fixture Suarez had raked his studs down Mirallas' calf, and also escaped censure, an injury which led to the Belgian being sidelined for months. But Mirallas insisted afterwards he was not seeking retribution. "I said to Suarez soon after the kick-off, when we were standing close to each other, 'do you remember last season, you kicked me?' He laughed and said 'yes, fair enough', but that tackle today was nothing to do with a year ago.

"The first thing I thought was that it was going to be a red card but I was genuinely going for the ball. I know I caught him on the knee and I said sorry straight away."

But this was not a derby where controversy would be the residual memory.

Left-back Leighton Baines limped off injured five minutes into the second half and Martinez's response underlined his philosophy. With defenders on his substitutes bench he introduced a winger, the pacy Gerard Deulofeu.

"We had to take risks," explained the Blues boss. "We had to gamble and we had to open the game. We wanted the game to be really open, to be box-to-box."

It was a bold strategy – and it oh so nearly brought a deserved reward of only Everton's second come-from-behind derby victory since the war.

Within seconds of his introduction Deulofeu raced clear from the halfway line but as Mignolet advanced the forward placed his shot too close to the keeper's left foot.

The box to box match Martinez wanted had arrived – and on the hour Liverpool midfielder Joe Allen entered the derby hall of infamy with one of the worst misses seen in the fixture, sidefooting carefully, methodically and precisely wide of the Stanley Park goal from 12 yards.

Lukaku ran clear again – and Mignolet saved again. The irrepressible Belgian made another angled run, got off another shot, and Mignolet made another save.

But the equaliser he and Everton deserved came after 72 minutes, and 10 minutes later he headed the Blues in front. But that was only after Suarez had missed a close range chance – his manager Rodgers actually celebrated on the touchline until he realised Tim Howard had clawed the effort out.

Mignolet's feet denied Deulofeu twice in as many minutes, then in the 89th minute Daniel Sturridge strained his head to flick on a free-kick from the Goodison Road touchline and steer in an equaliser.

Three goals apiece – and still no-one wanted to close the match out. In time added on Victor Moses and Suarez both went close, as did Lukaku and then James McCarthy with neither team willing to settle for a point.

It was fitting that the final act of the game was a McCarthy shot deflected behind for a corner which couldn't be taken. Even referee Phil Dowd decided he couldn't take any more of such a pulsating affair.

Such bewilderment extended to the stands as supporters paused briefly to catch breath after a remarkable, ridiculous, roller-coaster 90 minutes. And then it came, the applause thundering down from all four corners of the famous old ground, Everton and Liverpool fans united in their appreciation of an instant classic.

"Wow!" was Brendan Rodgers immediate reaction in his post-match press conference.

While in a local newspaper column, published on Monday morning, Ian Snodin declared: "Like everybody else privileged enough to be at Goodison Park on Saturday, I don't think I've ever seen a better derby match."

No-one was arguing.

GOOD LUK CHARM

---×××／＼×××---

SATURDAY, MARCH 12, 2016

FARHAD MOSHIRI'S FIRST EXPERIENCE OF GOODISON under the lights was an unforgettable one.

The Iranian billionaire had just completed his 49.9% investment in the club off the pitch, and on it Wembley was the prize for the winners of an FA Cup quarter-final tie between Everton and Chelsea.

As convincing as chairman Bill Kenwright's sales pitch had been, nothing could have sold the Everton dream to Moshiri as well as what unfolded at Goodison Park on an atmospheric Saturday tea-time showdown.

It had been a tense, tight clash and even a roaring performance by Everton's fans couldn't inspire their heroes to break the deadlock – until 13 minutes from the end.

Romelu Lukaku went into the tie having scored 59 goals for the Blues – but not one of those had been against his former club Chelsea.

That changed spectacularly in a dramatic five-minute spell.

Ross Barkley's penetrating pass from the halfway line gave Lukaku the opportunity to run with the ball, but the big striker was tight to the Goodison touchline, closer to the Gwladys Street corner flag than the goal.

But with a moment of world-class forward play Lukaku twisted and barged his way past Cesar Azpilicueta and Branislav Ivanovic, he body-swerved past John Obi Mikel and then sent Gary Cahill's head spinning before firing a low precise drive past Thibaut Courtois.

It was a Ricky Villa strike for the millennium.

Goodison exploded into a cacophony of noise and Lukaku dropped to his knees and pushed his face into the turf, such was the emotion of the moment.

The Belgian hadn't finished. The celebrations had barely subsided when Lukaku latched onto another Barkley throughball and this time fired through Courtois' legs.

Cue pandemonium.

The stadium rocked and reverberated with noise. Even late red cards for first Diego Costa, and then Everton midfielder Gareth Barry failed to dim the atmosphere.

At the final whistle Moshiri left his seat in the Directors' Box with a beaming smile, shaking hands with jubilant supporters as Goodison celebrated long and loud.

The fans stayed behind afterwards to soak up an intoxicating atmosphere.

"It was very satisfying," said a delighted Roberto Martinez. "It got up to a moment that needed a bit of magic and Romelu's goal is going to be one of the best goals scored in the FA Cup; well worth it to take us to Wembley. It's a great memory for every Evertonian."

BELL TOLLS

SUNDAY, MAY 29, 2016

GOODISON PARK HAD STAGED FOOTBALL MATCHES, royal visits, baseball, international football and even paraded a Hollywood icon on its turf in its 124 years of existence – but on a glorious Bank Holiday weekend in 2016 the Grand Old Lady hosted a famous first.

On Sunday May 29 lifelong Evertonian Tony 'Bomber' Bellew strode out of the Goodison dressing rooms aiming to be crowned world boxing champion.

Staging an outdoor boxing bill at a football stadium was an ambitious plan brought to life by the affinity between Bellew and Blues' chairman Bill Kenwright – no stranger to hosting challenging shows.

A boxing ring was erected on the pitch in front of the Gwladys Street End, seats were constructed around the ring – and the Gwladys Street and sections of the Goodison Road and Bullens Road stands repurposed for fight fans.

And the weather played ball, too.

It was a glorious, sunny Bank Holiday weekend for a stacked 14-fight card – topped by Tony Bellew v Ilunga Makabu for the WBC cruiserweight championship of the world.

Darkness had fallen when the time for the top of the bill had arrived – and the atmosphere was crackling.

Bellew emerged from the home team dressing room to the familiar sound of the Z-Cars theme – but only after Bellew's traditional air raid siren had preceded it. The combination proved so intoxicating the first team adopted it two seasons later.

Bellew paused midway through his ringwalk, gestured for his security detail to also halt – and visibly mouthed: 'This is unbelievable.'

It was.

In his autobiography 'Everyone Has A Plan Until They Get Punched In The Face' Bellew described his emotions during that walk.

"For a moment my aggression is interrupted by a brief surge of sadness, because I know that if I lose tonight, I won't ever come back here. It's an idea that's been going round and round my head for weeks. I love Everton Football Club. After my wife and kids, it's the most important thing in my life. I've been going to Goodison Park every other Saturday since I was ten. But if I'm defeated, there's just no way I'll be able to face coming here again. It would hurt too much."

He needn't have worried.

Bellew boxed like a man inspired.

Dropped at the end of the first round … "He catches me with his left hand. Just seconds ago I'd been looking forward to victory, now I've just been hit by one of the hardest punches I've ever experienced. Four, maybe five times throughout my career I've been hurt really badly by punches. This is one of them."

But he recovered his composure, came roaring back and midway through the third round unleashed a furious fusillade of punches, culminating in a vicious left hook which floored Makubu and sparked emotional celebrations.

Bellew collapsed onto the canvas and wept, while the Gwladys Street Enders jumped for joy.

"They were so loud – they got me up off that floor," said Bellew afterwards. "They dragged me off the floor. I'm so happy. This place has been my life since I was a kid. This is the place where I come and feel so happy. I love it here."

Bellew was mobbed by family and friends in the ring afterwards before embracing with his friend, Blues chairman Bill Kenwright.

Evertonians had been here before yet, on an historic night, never seen anything like it.

Neither had Goodison.

WEDNESDAY, NOVEMBER 29, 2017

FIFTEEN YEARS, ONE MONTH AND 10 days after firing his first, rapturously received, Goodison goal, Wayne Rooney scored his penultimate home goal. According to the man himself, it was his very best.

Wayne was 32 in November 2017 and nearing the end of his second spell at Everton. The legs may not have moved across the turf as quickly as they once did but his football brain was still as razor sharp as it had ever been – and his amazing technique remained intact.

He utilised both to score a goal he described as: "It might be the best goal I have ever scored. I hit it as well as I have ever kicked a football."

The goal capped an iconic Everton evening.

West Ham were the visitors to Goodison in the final match of David Unsworth's eight match spell as caretaker-manager – and with the Blues kicking off the match just one place outside the bottom three it was a crucial fixture.

Soon to be first team boss Sam Allardyce was sat in the Main Stand watching – and he witnessed a masterclass from a Grand Master.

After a first half penalty was parried by Joe Hart the ball rebounded for Rooney to nod in the opening goal.

Later in the half he timed a run to perfection to arrive at the far post and clip in his second.

But the piece de resistance came midway through the second half.

Hammers keeper Hart got to a long ball Dominic Calvert-Lewin was chasing first and hacked the ball to apparent safety. The ball reached the Everton half – which in ordinary football terms would mean the threat to his goal had been extinguished.

Unless it fell at the feet of an extraordinary footballer.

Without even hesitating to consider his options, Rooney instantly clipped a delicious and clinically executed shot which flew barely a couple of feet above head height as it arrowed past the stranded Hart and a covering defender and into the Gwladys Street net.

It completed Rooney's first Everton hat-trick, the distance was calculated as 59-yards – and it ensured that Unsworth, a team-mate of Rooney's when he scored his first Goodison goal 15 years earlier, celebrated the second league win of his second spell as caretaker boss as Everton jumped to the relative comfort of 13th place in the table.

Ashley Williams added a fourth as a triumphant evening ended in style.

There were still a couple more additions to the Rooney goalscoring roster before he crossed the Atlantic to join DC United six months later, a penalty at Anfield, a matchwinner against Newcastle and another spot kick against Swansea, but that 59-yard stunner against West Ham remained the highlight of his second spell.

Rooney scored 208 Premier League goals in his long and storied career, but by his own admission that November Hammer blow was one of the very, very best.

THE SILENT DERBY

————— ⋈⁄⌒⌣⋈ —————

GOODISON PARK WAS AT ITS MOST raucous in the closing stages of a 1-1 draw with Manchester United in March 2020. The noise reached an indignant crescendo when manager Carlo Ancelotti was red-carded for disputing a controversially disallowed winning goal.

Everton's next home match was a Merseyside derby – but this time Goodison lay eerily silent, before, during and after.

Sixteen weeks had elapsed in between the fixtures – a period in which the country had been placed into lockdown by the Covid-19 pandemic.

When football restarted again in mid-June the national landscape was surreal.

All sports stadia were closed to supporters up and down the country and the 236th Merseyside derby – usually the most vibrant atmosphere of the season – was played out to the shouts of players and the plaintive sound of a lone saxophonist playing outside the stadium near St Luke's Church.

It was a Sunday evening, June 21, and Liverpool city centre was deserted, as were the streets around L4, while four mounted policemen patrolled an empty Stanley Park.

When the players arrived for the showdown – Everton in their cars, Liverpool on team buses – only a handful of youngsters were there to greet them.

The UK's national football police chief, Mark Roberts, had actually requested that the fixture be switched to a neutral venue in case some fans tried to defy the ban and turn up to watch their heroes arrive.

Both clubs resisted the move and after the match passed off, uneventfully, the police tweeted thanks to both sets of supporters for keeping away. "A credit to both your clubs and our city," read the message.

The teams had to enter the fray from opposite ends of the pitch – and the only observers inside the stadium were a handful of club officials and a limited number of journalists, spaced apart according to the government's social distancing guidelines, in the main stand.

Those fans forced to stay away missed a match which understandably lacked its usual intensity, with players showing obvious signs of rustiness after the long lay-off.

Liverpool were on the brink of clinching the league title, but Everton became only the third team to take Premier League points off them – and might even have won.

Dominic Calvert-Lewin's inventive backheel was parried away by Liverpool goalkeeper Alisson, and Tom Davies' follow up shot struck the inside of the post and bounced back out.

That was in the 80th minute and the Blues created a flurry of other late chances which couldn't be taken.

Ultimately the match ended goalless, which seemed appropriate for a strangely soulless experience.

GREATEST CUP
TIE *NEVER* SEEN

———————— ✕✕╱⌃╲✕✕ ————————

WEDNESDAY, FEBRUARY 10, 2021

EVERTON AND TOTTENHAM SHARED A REMARKABLE nine goals on a chilly February evening in a magnificent FA Cup contest.

But for a match with no fans allowed in to experience it, the most popular post-match image was of Everton manager Carlo Ancelotti's reaction to what turned out to be his side's fifth – and winning – goal from Brazilian forward Bernard. While his backroom staff cavorted wildly on the touchline, the ice-cool Italian simply blew into the cup of hot coffee he was holding!

It was a reaction in keeping with the surreal world of lockdown football.

A fifth round FA Cup tie against Tottenham Hotspur would usually see an insatiable demand for tickets.

But with the country in the midst of a third national lockdown once again, the official attendance at Goodison Park was zero.

The BT Sport cameras did televise the match, though, and screened a classic.

Robin Olsen had already clawed out one goalbound shot before

Davinson Sanchez headed in from a corner after just three minutes – but showing enormous reserves of resolve and character Everton rattled three goals in an eight-minute burst before half-time.

Dominic Calvert-Lewin, Richarlison and Gylfi Sigurdsson, clinically from the penalty spot, gave Everton what looked like a commanding lead until Erik Lamela struck seconds before the interval.

Sanchez levelled on the hour, again from a corner, before brilliant work by Richarlison restored the Blues lead.

But despite the goal rush Harry Kane still hadn't scored. That changed seven minutes from the end of normal time, predictably enough from a Son Heung-Min assist.

Suggestions that Spurs had now grabbed the momentum were rubbished when Sigurdsson clipped a left-footed pass over the Spurs' defensive line and Bernard darted clear to lash a left-footed volley beyond Hugo Lloris.

That goal yielded Ancelotti's coffee-cooling gesture – the calmest man in the stadium amidst all the mayhem.

And afterwards he declared: "At 3-1 you're thinking 'get to half-time at 3-1' and then they score to put us on the back foot. But exciting game, fantastic."

Spurs' counterpart Jose Mourinho was less enamoured.

"If you say it was fantastic, it was fantastic. I'm not a neutral," he snapped, before begrudgingly conceding: "Okay, I take positives. Amazing to watch."

It certainly was.

GOODISON CALLS
THE TOON

———— ⋈⁄⌃⟍⋈ ————

THURSDAY, MARCH 17, 2022

A RED CARD, A DRAMATIC AND important victory by 10 men, the latest winning goal Goodison had ever celebrated – and a pitch invader tying himself to the Gwladys Street goal frame, by his neck … the night Newcastle visited Goodison Park in March 2022 provided one of the most unexpected evenings of Premier League football the old stadium had ever witnessed.

It was the sixth time manager Frank Lampard had taken his place in the home dugout at Goodison Park – and came just four days after Wolves had won 1-0 at Goodison. The stakes were critical.

Everton kicked off the match just one point above the bottom three – with a difficult clutch of fixtures to come.

Such was the enormity of the fixture that chairman Bill Kenwright visited the first team's Finch Farm training headquarters the day before the clash to deliver a heartfelt message to the players.

Lampard said: "The chairman came to the training ground yesterday of his own accord and delivered a talk to the lads for half-an-hour – and that's not normal.

"A lot of chairmen are corporate, but our chairman grew up an Everton fan. He takes the stick, but he and Denise Barrett-Baxendale and Graeme Sharp were there.

"I speak to the players all the time, and it's not an easy audience, 25 young men, but the chairman showed his passion for the club. It was a big deal for me and us."

It also had the desired effect.

After the drama had subsided on a dramatic 1-0 victory, match-winner Alex Iwobi said: "Bill Kenwright gave an emotional speech. He's definitely someone who loves the club. Me and all the players were thinking 'If the owners love the club and puts his all into the club, we have to at least give 100%, the same way he does for the club.' "

Manager Lampard added: "I thought the start of the game was a bit special. I know I'm new to this, an evening game at Goodison, but you could feel the crowd. Maybe they had a couple of pints of Guinness for St Patrick's Day. Fair play, we need that. We need them behind us. If we get out of this it's together."

That togetherness was evident on a night when so many things conspired to work against Everton.

Unable to break down a stubborn Toon defence, the second half took a bizarre twist when a protestor tied himself to a goalpost at the Gwladys Street End, around the neck, leading to an eight-minute delay while stewards attempted to safely free him.

Then seven minutes from time the home side appealed for a penalty after Seamus Coleman was floored in the Park End penalty area. Referee Craig Pawson ignored the appeals, Newcastle instantly broke away on a counter-attack and midfielder Allan was yellow carded for tripping Newcastle forward Allan Saint-Maximin. That was only the beginning of the drama. The match official was asked by his VAR to consult the pitch side monitor – which saw Mr Pawson overturn his initial decision and show a red card.

It looked a harsh call and Lampard said afterwards: "We now lose

Allan for three games. Let's hope the Referees' Association can say they got that wrong."

With 14 minutes of time still to play, hanging on for a draw looked like the best Frank Lampard's side could now achieve.

But Everton's spirit was indomitable – and in the ninth minute of additional time, Coleman won a brave tackle on the halfway line. The challenge gave Alex Iwobi possession and he raced forward before pinging a pass into substitute Dominic Calvert-Lewin. The centre-forward cleverly slipped the ball back into Iwobi's overlapping run and he drilled a clinical finish past Martin Dubravka.

The celebrations were wild – and in one instance painful!

Everton boss Lampard broke his hand celebrating – but admitted he would suffer injury every week if it meant similar results.

"I did it in celebration for the goal," Lampard said. "I just connected with something. I didn't punch anything, but I realised two minutes later my hand was shaking and aching.

"I will take it for the three points, though!"

THE SMOKE ALARM

SUNDAY, MAY 1, 2022

IT HAD BEEN MORE THAN TWO decades since David Moyes uttered his memorable 'People's Club' phrase – but the message was as relevant in May 2022 as it had been in March 2002, maybe even more so.

Everton were in trouble as the 2021/22 season neared a gut churning climax.

With Watford and Norwich's relegation to the Championship almost confirmed, Everton filled the final relegation place, five points behind Leeds United and Burnley.

Crucially the Blues had two matches in hand – but had to win them both in order to scramble out of the drop zone.

And the first came on a sunny May Day against third-placed Chelsea at Goodison Park, a Chelsea team which had just won 3-2 against soon to be European champions Real Madrid in the Bernabeu Stadium and 6-0 at Southampton.

Desperate times called for desperate measures – and the Blues fanbase galvanised like never before.

Word went out amongst the supporters clubs and fan groups to welcome the team coach to Goodison, to inspire the players and reinforce the enormity of the match.

And they responded in their thousands.

In the hours before kick-off supporters lined the streets surrounding Goodison Park, blue smoke from flares filled the air – and as the team coach approached the stadium just after midday the scenes were extraordinary.

The streets were jammed with a seething blue and white mass as the supporters welcomed the players.

It was an inspiring sight – but the turnout also caused a problem or two for some local residents, and turned one into an unlikely superstar!

Walton residents Jasmine Priest and Reece Van-Aston-Kerrigan had taken their Belgian Malinois dog, Myra, for a lunchtime walk.

As they headed out to Stanley Park the trio found their route busier than usual, with a couple of hundred fans milling around the streets. But as they headed back home after their regular 45 minute walk in the park, a very different scene confronted them.

"We walked through thinking it might be the same as it had been in the morning," Van-Aston-Kerrigan said later. "But we only made it about 100 yards and the dog was struggling to get through all the crowds, as were we.

"I decided to pick her up and that got us a little further, but then I ended up saying to Jasmine 'get her front legs'.

"When we picked her up and got her above our heads, it was like a parting of the Red Sea. Everyone was clapping and cheering, we've never seen anything like it before."

The images of Myra being carried shoulder high became a social media sensation.

Just a couple of hours later an image of a different kind was also trending. Brazilian forward Richarlison harried Chelsea captain Cesar Azpilicueta into giving up possession on the edge of his own penalty area, Demarai Gray rolled the ball back into the striker's path and Richarlison clipped a priceless winner into the Gwladys Street net.

The celebrations were manic. A blue flare was launched onto the pitch in the tumult and the image of Richarlison tossing the missile out of the ground towards safety became an iconic image. Despite the Brazilian's motivation being well intended it also cost him a £25,000 fine and a one match ban.

Just as iconic was the second half performance of goalkeeper Jordan Pickford.

The England No.1 was monumental making four incredible stops – including one which was later voted the winner of the Premier League's inaugural save of the season.

Mason Mount's shot had crashed against the inside of Pickford's right hand post, with the keeper sprawling to get a touch onto it. The ball rebounded to strike Pickford's other post, with the keeper recovering his footing to scramble back across his goalline and somehow claw out Azpilicueta's follow up close range drive.

Yerry Mina and Seamus Coleman both congratulated the keeper on a contribution which was as good as a goal.

But there was more to come.

Pickford then denied Antonio Rudiger from point blank range – with his face – and then swooped low to his right to parry another close range Mateo Kovacic strike.

"It's what I'm there for, to make saves for the team," Pickford told the Sky Sports cameras post-match. "At the end of the day it's about getting three points for the players, the club and the fans."

The combination of all three did just that on a huge day for the football club.

A spokesperson for the Everton Fans Forum said: "Nobody is happy with the position we are in – but one thing that unites every Evertonian is that we all want the best for the Blues.

"Right now, what is best is everyone pulling together, being united and doing all we can to help get the points we need on the board. All we can do is try everything in our power to make a difference, to give the players confidence and to try to make Goodison the cauldron-like fortress we know gives us an advantage."

It did just that on May Day 2022.

STORMING
THE PALACE

———— ✕✕⁄⌒✕✕ ————

THURSDAY, MAY 19, 2022

FRANK LAMPARD WAS EVERTON MANAGER FOR just 51 weeks.

By contrast, one of England's finest midfield talents spent 13 years at Chelsea and a further 18 months as manager at Stamford Bridge, winning every club honour the game has to offer.

But Frank described the evening he experienced at Goodison Park on May 19, 2022 as "one of the greatest nights of my footballing life and career."

Alan Ball was clearly correct when he said: "Once Everton has touched you..."

The events of that May night were as dramatic as anything Lampard had experienced in his long career as a legendary Premier League player – and certainly as emotional.

Twenty-eight years after the Great Escape against Wimbledon, Everton found themselves in a similar position.

They were threatened with relegation, found themselves two goals down at half-time – and only victory over an ambitious Crystal

Palace side would confirm safety for a 69th consecutive top flight season.

After 36 minutes another Premier League campaign looked a forlorn hope.

Richarlison had seen one free-kick fingertipped over the Park End crossbar by Jack Butland before Palace earned another free-kick at the opposite end of the pitch – and this time Jordan Pickford was powerless to prevent Jean-Philippe Mateta's close range header from flashing past him.

Matters went from bad to worse.

Jordan Ayew was fortunate to escape the ultimate refereeing sanction following a crude lunge on Anthony Gordon right in front of the dug-outs, referee Anthony Taylor opting to show a yellow card rather than red – and three minutes later the significance of that decision was magnified.

Ayew scrambled the ball past Pickford from close range, Abdoulaye Doucoure and Vitali Mykolenko helpless to intervene as the task to survive went from difficult to monumental.

Then boss Frank Lampard made a significant switch.

At half-time he introduced Dele for Andre Gomes and the substitute made an instant impact.

Dele started to carry the ball, added some much needed composure and penetration to Everton's attacking play – and in the 54th minute was bundled over for a decisive free-kick.

Mykolenko whipped the ball high into the box, Mason Holgate athletically headed it back and Michael Keane clinically angled a sweet, left-footed drive past Butland.

Three attacking contributions by three defenders – and the roar around Goodison Park was defiant.

Then the attacking players stepped up.

Dele chested a cross down and shot goalwards but the ball was blocked – only as far as Richarlison who reacted fastest to scuff a shot past Butland.

The celebrations were intense, but the Brazilian's instinctive reaction was to run to retrieve the ball from the Gwladys Street net. He knew another goal was needed.

It came, spectacularly, five minutes from the end.

The image is etched onto every Evertonian's consciousness fortunate enough to have been inside Goodison Park that evening. Seamus Coleman was fouled to earn a free-kick out on the Bullens Road touchline; Demarai Gray arced in a sugar sweet cross and Dominic Calvert-Lewin launched himself full length to bullet a memorable diving header.

A diving header, at the Gwladys Street End, bulleted into the net by a man wearing number nine on his back to earn the club's 1,878th top flight win .... it was a victory surely written in the Everton stars.

And the celebrations on the final whistle were unprecedented.

Fans from all four corners of Goodison Park swarmed onto the pitch, turning the green turf into a surging, swaying sea of blue and white.

But that's been seen before.

What hadn't been seen was the way the manager threw himself into the celebrations.

Lampard ran up and down the touchline like a dervish, punching the air and celebrating with staff and supporters. He then dashed down the tunnel, up the Goodison staircase and emerged at the front of the Main Stand.

He hugged world title winning boxer and passionate Everton fan Tony Bellew, he squeezed chairman Bill Kenwright in an emotional embrace, then he clasped CEO Denise Barrett-Baxendale in an ecstatic bear hug. Everton legend Peter Reid lurched across several seats to grab the Blues boss, before Frank moved on to hug Kevin Thelwell and then Graeme Sharp.

Then it was the turn of the fans. The manager leaped onto the roof of the Hospitality Boxes in front of the Main Stand, cheer-leading and orchestrating the singing from the supporters on the pitch, pausing briefly for selfies with fans – until health and safety officials feared that the roof may collapse and ushered him back into the stand.

The fans remained to sing and celebrate for more than half-an-hour after the final whistle before finally trooping away.

Lampard later admitted he had been "overwhelmed" by emotion.

"It's incredible, it's one of the greatest nights of my footballing life and career," he said. "I'm very fortunate. I've had some amazing times, especially at Chelsea as a player and as a coach, but when you feel the desperation of the people from what relegation brings to the table it's something different.

"I thought I might cry, I thought I might jump out of my body. No one can question the celebrations at the end. It's an easy one to say 'oh you haven't won anything' but you know what? Come and work at this club for a few months and see how much it means to people.

"The character of this club, fans and players just dragged us through. The spirit of the club was immense, immense."

It was a night to remember.

LADIES' NIGHT

———— ✕✕╱╱⋀⋁✕✕ ————

FRIDAY, MARCH 24, 2023

WHEN EVERTON WOMEN HOSTED MANCHESTER CITY at Goodison Park on the opening day of the 2021/22 WSL season, a club record 5,998 rocked up to watch.

Eighteen months on, with interest in the women's game booming after England Lionesses' spectacular Euro 2022 triumph, that record was smashed out of sight.

Some 22,161 fans – almost FOUR TIMES the previous club record – watched a feisty Merseyside derby at a raucous Goodison Park, despite the match being screened live on TV.

And the crowd saw a fine spectacle. Everton captain Gabby George gave the home team the perfect start when she curled a cross-shot over the head of Liverpool keeper Rachael Laws to open the scoring.

But Liverpool levelled when Taylor Hinds' turned and fired a low drive just out of the reach of Blues' keeper Courtney Brosnan.

A thrilling second half saw a goal apiece chalked off by the officials – first for the Reds as Leighanne Robe's effort was ruled out for an innocuous-looking challenge by Ceri Holland on Brosnan, then Jess Park curled a stunning shot into the top corner for Everton, only for the officials to spot an accidental handball in the build-up.

Despite some superb efforts from both sides, neither could find a winner.

Nicoline Sorensen whipped in a pinpoint cross but Jess Park directed her header wide before burying her face in the turf in disappointment.

Then Toffees' defender Megan Finnigan came to her side's rescue when Shanice van de Sanden lost her marker to set up Stengel in the penalty area. The American's effort was blocked on the line.

But the evening was all about the record gate.

"We could hear the fans all the way through the game," said Danish striker Sorensen. "Women's football is growing all the time and that is being proven almost every single week in there being a lot of fans who want to come and see us.

"Hopefully there is a lot that want to come to Walton Hall Park also after this game. You can see when we play at big stadiums, a lot of fans are coming. I think it is really important and it will keep growing the game."

Sorensen's prediction was spot on. Everton Women entertained Tottenham Hotspur in their next WSL fixture – at a sold out Walton Hall Park.

THE BOURNE ULTIMATUM

————✕✕⁄⁄‿⁄‿✕✕————

SUNDAY, MAY 28, 2023

GARY NEVILLE HAS SAT IN HUNDREDS of TV gantries in his secondary career as a football analyst.

Micah Richards has witnessed thousands of matches, both as a player and a pundit.

While Adam Smith was a 32-year-old defender with experience of more than 400 first team appearances when Bournemouth came to Goodison for the last match of the 2022/23 season.

All three were in agreement about the atmosphere they encountered.

"When Abdoulaye Doucoure's goal went in, the stadium was shaking, the gantry was shaking like no gantry I've been on in my life," said Neville.

Smith added: "It just didn't quieten down. One of the best atmospheres I've played in."

While Richards said: "I was at the game and I have to say it's the loudest I've ever heard, at any stadium, I've ever been at."

The moment which generated such a seismic thunderclap came from the right boot of Abdoulaye Doucoure.

And it ensured that Everton escaped relegation on the last day of the season, just as they had 29 years earlier against Wimbledon.

It was a nerve shredding afternoon for every Evertonian.

Leicester City and Leeds United were the other clubs threatened with the drop, but with Sam Allardyce's Leeds needing a freak combination of results to survive, and then going behind at home to Tottenham in just the second minute, Leicester became the Blues' most realistic rivals – and they opened the scoring against West Ham after just half-an-hour.

As a result Everton knew that only a win would earn safety, but a supremely committed Bournemouth were hell-bent on denying them.

Goalkeeper Mark Travers had already beaten away one rising drive from Idrissa Gana Gueye and tipped over another from James Garner – but in truth, with nerves and tension gripping the stadium, Everton had struggled to create any clear openings.

When the decisive moment came in the 57th minute it was as a result of an optimistic punt forward by Gana Gueye.

Marcos Senesi's clearing header was adequate but not conclusive, and crucially it dropped into the space outside the penalty area where Doucoure was prowling.

The big midfielder eagerly took one step forward and connected sweetly with his right-foot, unleashing a volley of such power that Travers remained rooted to his line as the ball flashed past him like a bullet.

That was the moment the stadium shook.

Tears were shed, strangers were embraced, young children were launched into the air.

A battery of fireworks exploded into the sky behind the Gwladys Street End and filled the sky with colour, noise and the smell of sulphur.

"It was incredible," said Doucoure. "I thought about all the season, all my personal life, everything.

"It was a very tense situation because we only had half an hour left and Leicester were winning.

"There was so much stress in the stadium and we felt tense because we knew if we didn't score, we'd go down. I followed a second ball and gave it everything.

"I forget what I was shouting (after I scored). I spoke with Amadou Onana and he said 'I knew you were going to score' because, even at half-time, he was saying that. I knew in my head, I'd have one chance and needed to take it.

"There was a lot of emotion. Everything came through. The season. This year I also lost my Dad, so it was very tough. I said at the end of the season that I'd had some personal issues, and this was the main one.

"I was thinking about it all and the emotion came through."

But after that explosion of emotion came the dawning realisation that there was still more than half-an-hour to play!

In reality that became an agonising 40 minutes, with fully 10 minutes of time added on after an incident in which Dominic Solanke wrestled Jordan Pickford to the floor in a tussle which saw the goal-keeper dislocate his finger and require extensive treatment.

Pickford's diving save from Matias Vina in the 93rd minute was testimony to his bravery as much as his concentration.

When referee Stuart Attwell finally blew his whistle after more than 100 minutes of unbearably tense action the celebrations probably shook the foundations of Everton's new stadium two miles down the road.

Everton's admirable fans had maintained the noise, the backing, a baying barrage of sound throughout the entire afternoon – and undoubtedly played an influential role in the result.

Leicester ultimately beat West Ham 2-1, which meant that Doucoure's goal proved decisive.

Everton survived by two points – and one of the most sustained atmospheres Goodison had ever witnessed played a huge part in the outcome.

WRITTEN IN
THE STARS

—✕✕/✕✕—

WEDNESDAY, APRIL 24, 2024

IT WAS WRITTEN IN THE STARS.

On April 24, 2024, Everton entertained Liverpool in the 244th Merseyside derby.

The blue half of the city hadn't celebrated success in a derby for 14 years – their only previous triumph coming at Anfield in a lockdown derby watched by precisely zero supporters.

But April 24 wasn't just any old date.

The last time Everton had played at Goodison Park on a Wednesday night on April 24 had been 39 years earlier. The visitors? Bayern Munich on a night widely regarded as the greatest – and noisiest – in the club's history.

Almost 40 years later a crowd 11,000 fewer than that celebrated night decided to stake their own claim to supporting immortality.

As a Celtic supporting former Chelsea and Everton player, Pat Nevin knows a thing or two about crowd noise.

And after that 244th Merseyside derby he declared: "More than anything else, the crowd.

"I mean honestly. I go to a lot of Premier League games, I travel round all the time and you know where the good, the bad and the ugly are with their crowd noise.

"From before the start of the game it was mental. Off the scale. It really was.

"I've been at some big nights and I've played in some big nights. I can close my eyes right now and I can remember the 4-4 game and what it was like that night.

"This felt a bit like that. An evening game, against Liverpool, a battle, the fight, the fans … and seeing the cameras focusing on the Everton fans. You wanted to freeze it, that ecstasy.

"For all the fact that we've had a hard season, it will be one of the best memories you've had as an Evertonian. If you were a youngster watching the game you will have had absolutely one of your favourite memories and it will stay with you for the rest of your life. It's just brilliant what football can give to you."

What 14 footballers gave to Evertonians that night was truly magical.

It was a reciprocal arrangement.

Sometimes it needs footballers to inspire a crowd. Other times it needs a crowd to energise players – against a Liverpool team needing a victory to keep their charge for a Premier League title alive players and supporters fed off each other.

The noise before kick-off was deafening. During an opening 20 minutes when the intensity of Eveton's play was suffocating the decibel levels actually rose. And then when Dominic Calvert-Lewin was tripped by Liverpool goalkeeper Alisson for a penalty kick the volume reached a crescendo.

Crushingly, the Video Assistant Referee ruled – eventually – that Calvert-Lewin had been offside and so the spot-kick never happened.

Did that disappointment puncture the atmosphere? Not a bit of it. The fans continued to roar and bay and back their heroes.

And after 27 minutes they were rewarded when Jarrad Branthwaite, affectionately nicknamed the Carlisle Kaiser by the local media, squeezed a shot from 10 yards under Alisson's body and in off a post.

Once again there was a tension filled wait for a VAR check for a possible offside, but on this occasion there was no escape for the Reds.

Goodison erupted with the force of Krakatoa.

Everton's defenders and the magnificent Jordan Pickford repelled a late half rally from the Reds – then in the second half came another volcanic moment, the kind synonymous with Goodison Park.

It was a corner at the Gwladys Street End, Dwight McNeil flicked a cross in with his paintbrush of a right foot and an Everton number nine, the colossal Calvert-Lewin, rose to bury a header into the corner of the net.

Game, set and memorable match.

As well as a repeat of Goodison's greatest moment, Wednesday April 24 was also, apparently, National Scream Day – a day created to bring awareness of the benefits of screaming.

Yes really. Apparently screaming has been proven to be enormously beneficial. People so-minded can scream into a pillow, in their car, in the woods, or wherever they feel most comfortable.

They can also scream at a bouncing, reverberating football stadium.

And Goodison really did bounce that night.

Ask Gary Neville, a former Manchester United favourite who was on duty for Sky Television as an analyst that night.

"This was a night that we'll talk about at Goodison Park," he said. "I first came to this stadium, pfffft, 30 years ago? And I've seen this stadium at its best.

"I once got sent off here along with Paul Scholes in a game that we lost and the atmosphere was incredible. It was a night game and we had a good record here but when we lost here the atmosphere was special.

"This gantry is the only one left in the league that shakes when this crowd behind us jumps and goes crazy – and the fact that we're not going to be in this ground witnessing these types of atmospheres is quite sad.

"It's what I felt towards the last part of the game at this great old ground.

"Everton need to go to their new ground, we know how it works – but this is one of the last great grounds in the Premier League. It's been around such a long time, I've played here so many times and it's been at its absolute best tonight."

Well it was April 24, after all.

OVER TO YOU...

———✕✕⁄∧⁄✕✕———

THE CLOCKS WILL BE STOPPED. THE telephones silenced. One poignant day in May 2025, the Goodison turnstiles will click for the final time.

The Gwladys Street End choir will roar its songs of encouragement and support for the very last match.

And after the players and staff have driven away from the Stanley Park End car park, the Goodison gates will be locked for good.

Will that afternoon provide Goodison's 100th and final 'great moment?'

Or will there be other, more celebratory, times still to come between now and then?

We've decided to leave Goodison's 100th greatest moment for you to fill in.

Maybe you're an older Evertonian who was there when Plymouth scored four times at Goodison – and lost. Everton doubled Argyle's tally and won 8-4 in 1954, one of the greatest goalfests the stadium ever staged.

Perhaps you were thrilled by the emergence of two teenage tyros when Ronald Koeman's electrifying young team beat Pep Guardiola's Manchester City 4-0 in 2017, Tom Davies and Ademola Lookman setting the seal on a magnificent masterclass.

OVER TO YOU...

Did you delight at Duncan McKenzie's 1977 dribble from one side of the Goodison pitch to the other – feinting and dummying dumbounded Stoke City players every other step?

Or were you part of the crowd that ecstatically announced the arrival of Sean Dyche as manager with an unexpected victory over table-topping Arsenal in 2023?

'Great' moments are subjective. We all see football matches differently.

And Goodison Park has always been as much about the people on the terraces and the stands as it has been the players on the pitch.

So we've left it to the people of the People's Club to decide Goodison's final 'great' moment.

You'll all have your own great Goodison memories. It's up to you.

We merely hope our selection has stirred some of them, as we prepare to say a final farewell to a Grand Old Lady who has played a huge part in all of our lives.

Thanks for the memories...